The ethics of bankru[ptcy]

Th   solvents
ha   nise. *The
Et   tcy. The
au   rinciples,
uti   l as the
mc   ous and
cri   reforms.
Ba   he insol-
ver   atising,
yet   ects of
thi   is the
fir   hics to
ex   makes
va   recov-
er

D   ration
ar   ute of
A   ees in
Pl   e from
M

D̶n. 103   99-74

BAKER & TAYLOR

Professional Ethics

General editors:
Andrew Belsey, *University of Wales, Cardiff* and
Ruth Chadwick, *Centre for Professional Ethics, University of Central Lancashire*

Professionalism is a subject of interest to academics, the general public and would-be professional groups. Traditional ideas of professions and professional conduct have been challenged by recent social, political and technological changes. One result has been the development for almost every profession of an ethical code of conduct which attempts to formalise its values and standards. These codes of conduct raise a number of questions about the status of a 'profession' and the consequent moral implications for behaviour.

This series seeks to examine these questions both critically and constructively. Individual volumes will consider issues relevant to particular professions, including nursing, genetic counselling, journalism, business, the food industry and law. Other volumes will address issues relevant to all professional groups such as the function and value of a code of ethics and the demands of confidentiality.

Also available in this series:

Ethical Issues in Journalism and the Media
edited by Andrew Belsey and Ruth Chadwick

Genetic Counselling
edited by Angus Clarke

Ethical Issues in Nursing
edited by Geoffrey Hunt

The Ground of Professional Ethics
Daryl Koehn

Ethical Issues in Social Work
edited by Richard Hugman and David Smith

Food Ethics
edited by Ben Mepham

The ethics of bankruptcy

Jukka Kilpi

London and New York

First published 1998
by Routledge
11 New Fetter Lane, London EC4P 4EE

Simultaneously published in the USA and Canada
by Routledge
29 West 35th Street, New York, NY 10001

Typeset in Times by Routledge
Printed and bound in Great Britain by Creative Print and Design
(Wales), Ebbw Vale

British Library Cataloguing in Publication Data
A catalogue record for this book is available from the British Library

Library of Congress Cataloging in Publication Data
Kilpi, Jukka, 1954–
The ethics of bankruptcy/Jukka Kilpi.
p. cm.
Includes bibliographical references and index
1. Corporate debt–Moral and ethical aspects. 2. Bankruptcy–Moral and
ethical aspects. 3. Social responsibility of business.
I. Title.
HG4028.D3K47 1998   97–26890
174'.4–dc21 CIP

ISBN 0–415–17174–1 (hbk)
ISBN 0–415–17175–X (pbk)

A man must be perfectly crazy who, where there is tolerable security, does not employ all the stock which he commands, whether it be his own or borrowed of other people

Adam Smith, *The Wealth of Nations*

For Anu, Sohvi and Lyydia

Contents

Series Editors' foreword

Professional Ethics is now acknowledged as a field of study in its own right. Much of its recent development has resulted from rethinking traditional medical ethics in the light of new moral problems arising out of advances in medical science and technology. Applied philosophers, ethicists and lawyers have devoted considerable energy to exploring the dilemmas emerging from modern health-care practices and their effects on the practitioner–patient relationship.

But the point can be generalized. Even in health care, ethical dilemmas are not confined to medical practitioners. And beyond health care, other groups are beginning to think critically about the kind of service they offer, and about the nature of the relationship between provider and recipient. In many areas of life social, political and technological changes have challenged traditional ideas of practice.

One visible sign of these developments has been the proliferation of codes of ethics or of professional conduct. The drafting of such a code provides an opportunity for professionals to examine the nature and goals of their work, and offers information to others about what can be expected from them. If a code has a disciplinary function, it may even offer protection to members of the public.

But is the existence of such a code itself a criterion of a profession? What exactly is a profession? Can a group acquire professional status, and if so, how? Does the label 'professional' have implications, from a moral point of view, for acceptable behaviour, and if so, how far do such implications extend?

The Professional Ethics book series, edited from the Centre for Applied Ethics in Cardiff and from the Centre for Professional Ethics in Preston, seeks to examine ethical issues in the professions and related areas both critically and constructively. Individual volumes examine issues relevant to particular professions, including those which have hitherto received little attention, such as journalism, social work and genetic counselling. Other volumes address themes relevant to all professional groups, such as the nature of a profession, the function and value of codes of ethics, and the demands of confidentiality.

The subject matter of this volume, bankruptcy, raises issues common to a number of fields. The topics covered include not only bankruptcy itself, clearly of importance in business ethics, but also punishment and corporate responsibility among others. Its wider concerns include the morality of promises, contracts and debts, and the ethical theories underlying these aspects of professional and public life.

Acknowledgements

I had the privilege to carry out this study at Monash University working closely with C.L. Ten. His learnedness combines with humane appreciation of different strands of thought, and I am ever grateful for his gentle but subtle advice.

I would also like to thank Michael Smith for his help. His critical remarks guided me to a better comprehension of the metaethical position I advocate in this work. Rae Langton provided me with valuable suggestions in regard to the sections on Kant.

Jeff Goldsworthy, Heta Häyry and Matti Häyry expended their time on an early draft of the book. I am indebted to them for their commentary, criticism and encouragement, which were significant for the proceed of my research. Julian Lamont deserves thanks for the many intriguing debates we had on philosophy and philosophers.

Thanks also to Dan Vine for philosophical discussions and for checking my language, and to all the members of the Philosophy Department at Monash University for a scholarly stimulating atmosphere. I greatly appreciate the marvellous job Kate Chadwick did in proofreading the final version of the study.

My research has received economic support from Monash University, Academy of Finland, and Foundation for Economic Education. I wish to express my gratitude for their generosity. The final version of the manuscript was written when I held a fellowship in the Department of Practical Philosophy at the University of Helsinki.

Anu, Sohvi and Lyydia were the unfailing source of joy and inspiration that kept my spirits up over the years which led to the completion of this work. I dedicate this book to them.

Parts of Chapter 12 have appeared in 'Gearing up, crashing loud. Should we punish high-flyers for insolvency?', in *Journal of Business Ethics*, 15 (12), 1996, and parts of Chapter 13 will appear in *Taking the Liberal Challenge Seriously*, edited by S. Hellsten *et al.* (forthcoming 1997), Ashgate Publishing Ltd.

Prologue

Some men say they have talents and trades to get bread,
Yet they sponge on mankind to be clothed and fed,
They'll spend all they get, and turn night into day,
Now I'd have all such sots sent to Botany Bay.

There's gay powdered coxcombs and proud dressy fops,
Who with very small fortunes set up in great shops,
They'll run into debt with design ne'er to pay,
They should all be transported to Botany Bay.

Botany Bay (Traditional)[1]

This book grew out of the experiences of the late 1980s and early 1990s. The economic downturn and high interest rates scattered financial distress around the world. Many private individuals and corporations faced the grim reality of insolvency. The plague did not distinguish between race, religion or nationality.

However, the social response to the malaise did. In many countries the illness was diagnosed as terminal. Individual bankrupts may now avoid execution for excess borrowing, but it is still common not to offer them an escape from lifelong debt-bondage. As for corporations, liquidation is usually taken literally: insolvency proceedings bring the firm to an end.

There is an alternative to axing insolvents out of society, or out of existence. Some countries, most notably in the Anglo-American legal tradition, allow for the discharge of personal bankrupts' debts, and grant corporations an option to reorganise. Once the institution of bankruptcy is put into a global and historical perspective, the social response to a debtor's default covers all the extremes from capital punishment and enslavement to a quick and painless exoneration from debt.

This raises an ethicist's eyebrows. Can all clashing institutional practices be equally good or right? Most probably they cannot. If they are not, the reasons for the superiority of some practices have to lie beyond the legal technicalities. We are led to ask the ethical questions, to find the reasons which may justify some types of institutions and censure others. We are led to a moral inquiry.

This study is a moral inquiry into the ethics of bankruptcy. It examines the institutions that deal with insolvency. The aim is to establish ethical guidelines as to what kind of bankruptcy laws we ought to have. It is a task which falls under applied ethics, in particular business ethics, but the philosophical analysis of the basic social interaction that bankruptcy laws seek to control takes us into the most fundamental problems of moral philosophy – indeed, to the very philosophical foundations of the world and our relation to it. I have resisted the orthodoxy of contemporary thought which encourages us to cut the philosophical roots of an applied ethical theory. Accordingly, this study contains a section which traces the notion of human autonomy to its Kantian source, and tries to bring Kant's ideas more in tune with the modern mind and knowledge by giving them a pragmatic interpretation.

The reason for this metaethical flirtation with Kant is my conviction that in philosophical research 'can' implies 'ought'. If we can support our normative principles with further arguments, we ought to do so. The ethics of bankruptcy has a holistic element because I believe that rational arguments can support the autonomy of practical reason, and that autonomy, revitalized by those arguments, is conducive to normative conclusions.

However, the applied parts of the ethics of bankruptcy form a happy, self-supporting union on their own. The potential schisms of the metaethical affair do not pose any danger to that harmony. If my revision of Kant is dismissed, the ethics of bankruptcy loses an additive aimed at boosting its performance, but the rest of the demonstration for the practical conclusions remains valid. A reader who chooses to ignore the Kantian origins of autonomy may well close her eyes to the metaethical episode.

The study opens with material where perplexities are less immanent. Part I consists of Chapter 1 only; it asks the ethical questions underlying insolvency, charts the institutional development of bankruptcy and deals with problems specific to the creditors.

Part II starts the penetration to the ethical complexities that relate to borrowers. Before we can decide what to do with bankrupts, we should know why debts ought to be paid in the first place. The source of moral obligations in promising is the key to that knowledge. Hence, Chapter 2 presents the major philosophical theories of promising; Chapters 3 and 4 leap into metaethics and revive and revise old Kantian concepts; and Chapter 5 introduces a novel account of promises which builds on promissory autonomy. Part II establishes why we have a moral duty to pay our debts.

The task of Part III is to examine if there is a carve-out for insolvency in that duty. Chapter 6 lists a host of ethical considerations indicating that the carve-out exists. Chapter 7 attends to disputes specific to deontological ethics which, at first sight, is most prone to defend absolute duties, but which actually turns out to be firmly in favour of insolvents' release. Chapter 8 investigates what kind of discharge most appropriately serves the fresh start policy justified in the two preceding chapters.

In Part IV creditors strike back. Chapter 9 forwards arguments seeking to uphold debtors' civil liability. Chapter 10 expands the horizon to criminal liability. The conclusion of Part IV is that the counterattack stalls. It is difficult for contractual, fiduciary, or tortious considerations to shake the ethical principle that an honest insolvent deserves a discharge. The pledge to criminal liability does not do any better, because both a utilitarian and a retributivist would punish for insolvency only when a guilty mind is evident.

Part V applies the ethical principles of insolvency, substantiated in the earlier sections, to some issues of current public interest. Chapter 11 assesses the bankruptcy law reforms, either planned or already implemented, in Europe and Australia. Chapter 12 queries whether bankrupt high-flyers, whose lifestyle has been luxurious and leveraged, should be given special treatment.

Throughout Parts I to V the debate centres on natural persons who go broke. Part VI shifts the focus to corporations. In order to determine their moral liability for debt and insolvency we need to know what kind of moral entities they are. Chapter 13 attends to this problem, and suggests a new philosophy of corporate person-hood which is compatible with prevailing economic and judicial accounts of the firm as a nexus of contracts. In the light of the new philosophy of the corporation, Chapter 14 defines corporate debtors' moral obligations, and our obligations towards corporate creditors. The final chapters also contain a justification for the limited liability corporation, and thus conclude the ethics of bankruptcy.

One would expect that insolvency would not be an issue in Australia, the land of plenty, or at least would not have been in the early days when English bankrupts were deported to Sydney's Botany Bay. No way: an abundance of land, minerals, animals and climate, all in a Lockean state of nature as it was, more or less, then taken to be, did not make obsolete the fact that insolvency is a close associate of economic progress.

I was given a reminder of this during visits to two grand homesteads, now museums, in Melbourne: The Briars and The Como. The pioneer owners of both mansions had gone bankrupt at some stage of their pastoral or trading careers. This is in line with the empirical research I cite in this study: financial failures are part of building the future, they are not exclusive to sots. We cannot avoid some dreams becoming nightmares.

Over the last decade Australia may have had more than its fair share of the negatives of building the future, and perhaps of the sots too. Against this background I hope that *The Ethics of Bankruptcy* is able to contribute to the progress of this great country by helping us to put past mistakes behind us without excess stigma and reproach.

Melbourne, December 1996
Jukka Kilpi

Part I

The ethical trouble and its makers
A perennial plague

Chapter 1

The institution and the conflicts behind it

The bulk of this work will focus on the bankruptcy of natural persons. This leaves legal personalities, most notably corporations, to be dealt with in the final section. The reason for the division derives from the ethical point of view of the study: the ethical problems relating to humans differ from those relating to corporate bodies. A basic difference is that, in most cases, the existence of insolvent corporations is terminated when bankruptcy proceedings are brought to an end, while individuals are no longer executed as part of the distribution of an estate.

I shall devote the lion's share of my attention to personal bankruptcy because of the immediate and perplexing nature of the ethical controversies surrounding it: the insolvent has promised to pay the debt, nonetheless she is not able to keep her promise. What should be the consequences of this dead-end to the promisor, to the promisee and to society? Because the life of a bankrupt natural person is supposed to continue after her property is used to satisfy creditors, we have to decide what to do with her next.

An insolvent corporation breaks promises too, but I will argue that this happens in an environment where there are fewer ethical variables. A corporation is a legal fiat; it does not have the human rights that are attached to each individual by virtue of her human nature. This means that the settlement of the commitments of an insolvent corporation is more a matter of expediency than of ethics.

It should be recognized that some modern ways of handling corporate insolvency involve problems and solutions apparently similar to those seen in personal bankruptcy. Here I have in mind in particular the reorganization schemes modelled after the US Bankruptcy Code Chapter 11. But, regardless of the institutional similarities, I find the ethical dilemmas of these schemes to be in a category of their own.

Before going further, the use of concepts needs to be attended to. As legal terms, the meanings of 'bankruptcy' and 'insolvency' vary from one country to another. In the United Kingdom the statutory provisions relating both to individuals and to corporations were consolidated, in 1986, under one item of law: the Insolvency Bill. However, the Bill subjects individuals to bankruptcy proceedings while insolvent companies face winding-up. Australia follows earlier British tradition, in which natural persons and legal persons are dealt with by separate laws, and different terminology is applied in each case. In Australia the Bankruptcy Act takes care of bankrupt individuals, and Corporations Law contains provisions for insolvent companies. In the United States procedures for both natural persons and firms are included in the Bankruptcy Code, and the institution is invariably called bankruptcy. In addition to these technical differences, bankruptcy, insolvency, winding-up, liquidation, or whatever technical name a particular law has adopted for the institution, may, as a legal fiat, and depending on the jurisdiction, contain alternative ways of settling with the creditors, such as payment schemes versus straightforward distribution of property among the creditors.

If non-English legislation is placed under scrutiny, the legal terminology gets even more confusing. In the family of Latin languages alone additional notions are used. However, the basic problem the legislation addresses – an agent's financial default, and consequently the institutional response it specifies – remains much the same everywhere. This explains why, unlike the legal jargon, the ordinary language counterparts of 'bankruptcy' and 'insolvency' carry the same meaning across all borders: they denote the insufficiency of someone's means to meet her liabilities. The clarity of plain language is a good reason to follow its guidance for the conceptual definitions of this study.

When I speak without any specific legislation in mind I shall by 'insolvency' refer to a factual state of affairs: the inability to pay debts when they are due. By 'bankruptcy' I shall refer to any legal institution created to deal with insolvency. Hence, 'insolvent' stands for an agent who is unable to pay the due debts, and 'bankrupt' for an agent undergoing the institutional procedure of bankruptcy. Nevertheless, if expressed in connection to particular legislation, these concepts will carry the definition given to them in that body of law.

It should be noticed here that, in the sense given above, someone may be insolvent but not bankrupt, and the other way round. If the debtor or her creditors do not initiate legal proceedings, an insolvent never goes bankrupt, or it may well happen that after the liquidation of her assets a bankrupt turns out to be solvent. In the latter case her bankruptcy has been caused, for instance, by the illiquid nature of the assets or her unwillingness to pay. However, as these cases are not relevant to the ethical problems I wish to examine, we can have confidence in the conceptual usage adopted. After these preliminary remarks I proceed to a short summary of the institutional development of bankruptcy.

INSTITUTIONAL HISTORY

The history of credit is as long as human history. It predates the use of money. Indeed, it has been argued that money was introduced out of the need to measure and pay debts.[1] Credit represents a pattern of social behaviour. As such, it is not infallible, but subject to human weaknesses and environmental conditions. There is no causal, let alone logical, necessity ensuring that what has been given as a loan will be returned. On the contrary, default is a chance always present. Where there is credit, non-payment can occur.

Although debts are most often paid, the possibility of default can be seen as an inevitable feature of the social phenomenon called credit. Laws reflect this fact. They have attended to credit enforcement and insolvency since the beginning of recorded legal history. The early remedies for default were quite uniform: the law of Hammurab, the Twelve Tables of early Rome, and the laws of ancient Greece all placed both the property and the body of the debtor, as well as those of his kin, in the hands of the creditor.[2]

The ancient creditor had the right to enslave or even kill the insolvent. If the creditors were many, early Roman law gave them the option of cutting the debtor in pieces to be divided among themselves. According to historians, it was not only Western cultures that recognized a creditor's right to the body of the impecunious. For instance, early Hindu law permitted the killing of a defaulter and subsequent enslavement of his wife. Notable exceptions to these harsh practices were Judaic and Islamic religious teachings which proposed regular extinguishing of debts.

In Greece leveraged speculation was widespread in the seventh century BC. When the boom was over, free Greek citizens who could not service their liabilities ended up in slavery in large numbers. This was one of the evils addressed by the famous laws of Solon. They forbade slavery for debt. For the first time a legal reform was introduced limiting debt enforcement to the debtor's property only.

The reformist trend was followed in later Roman law. Through *Cessio bonorum* a penniless borrower was able to avoid the bodily liabilities by handing his property over to the creditors although no cancellation of debts was available. The judicial proceedings involved in *Cessio bonorum* were adopted in the medieval laws throughout Europe – with the notable exception of the debtor's bodily immunity. In most medieval states an insolvent was subject to imprisonment at the creditor's will even after all his property had been seized. The influence of the Roman institution is also present in the manner in which contemporary bankruptcy laws distribute a debtor's property.

In England the first bankruptcy statute was passed in 1542 by Henry VIII. The term 'bankruptcy' is present only in the title of the statute which was aimed at improving the efficiency of debt collection and at introducing justice among creditors. Debtors were seen to be absconding, and the remedy was to bring them to court and seize their property. Creditors were seen as fighting each other because the debt enforcement was on a first come first served basis. The new institution was to end the futile conflict by distributing the estate according to equitable principles.

The etymology of the word 'bankruptcy' helps us to grasp better the emphasis of the first English legislation. There are several accounts of the origins of the term, but they all agree that it was used initially around the Mediterranean to refer to traders who ran away from their debts.[3] Some authors have claimed that the French expression *banque route*, used to describe the tracks the escaping trader's cart left, was adopted by legal language, while most refer to the Spanish and Italian practice of breaking insolvent traders' benches in the market in order to prevent them from doing further business (*banca rupta*, *banca rotta*). It was hardly a wonder that in those days insolvents became fugitives. Confronted by overwhelming debts, it was their only way to avoid an indefinite jail term. Thus, etymologically, 'bankruptcy' has a criminal connotation. This is something which seems to have lingered on and which adds to the stigma experienced by present-day bankrupts.

After the 1542 bankruptcy statute the focus of English law

changed slowly but consistently.[4] The interests of debtors started to surface. The most remarkable milestone was the 1705 Act which, for the first time, made discharge part of the procedure. The possibility of being cleared of liabilities was subject to strict control and open only to traders, who were thought to be prone to unfortunate and unforeseeable accidents in the conduct of their business. Nevertheless, after the idea was introduced it was to play an important role in subsequent reforms which consolidated debtor protection as a central goal of English insolvency laws.

Accordingly, in Australia, and in other countries following British legal tradition, contemporary bankruptcy procedures end in discharge of debts. Discharge has been subject to limitations and conditions, but generally these have been made more lenient in the twentieth century. As a result, in Anglo-Saxon legislation discharge can be seen as a privilege granted to the debtor subject to her conduct being appropriate prior to and during the bankruptcy.

In the United States permanent bankruptcy law was, after a long and furious battle, enacted on Federal level in 1898. The law's emphasis was heavily on relieving the debtors' burden, and so has it been in the subsequent amendments – most notably in 1938 and in 1978. The US law allows debtors to choose between Chapter 7, straight liquidation and discharge taking only some months, and Chapter 13. The latter alternative is a payment scheme in which the debtor retains control of her property while paying off at least part of the debts over a few years. Overall, the United States' proceedings are quicker and limit a bankrupt's civil liberties to a lesser extent than has been customary in countries closely following the British legal system. The differences are so manifest that they make discharge of debts in the United States a right rather than a privilege.

This is in stark contrast to the laws in Continental Europe.[5] In most European countries discharge without creditors' consent has been unheard of. Only very recently have there been efforts to solve the vast human and social problems caused by lifelong enforcement of an overwhelming debt burden. In the late 1980s a number of Western European countries have initiated insolvency reforms,[6] mainly following the example given in Chapter 13 of the US Bankruptcy Code.

DEBTOR PROTECTION AND/OR CREDITOR PROTECTION?

Early societies applied all imaginable means of debt collection to the defaulting debtor. Creditors' rights were seen as absolute and unproblematic. Suspicions towards this attitude led some ancient legislators to question whether creditors should have access to the insolvent's body and person. Another source of concern, out of which emerged the insolvency proceedings in Roman law, was the conflict between creditors who pursued competing claims. The main purposes of a bankruptcy law are visible here. On the one hand the law should protect the debtor from unjustified hardships; on the other hand it should protect creditors by enforcing their right to receive a payment whilst preventing their individual collection efforts from damaging or unjustly distributing the debtor's assets.

From these two aims, and from their conflicting nature, arise the ethical questions. Do we have a moral duty to pay what we owe? Why should society enforce a contractual debt? If it should be enforced, why exempt debtors' bodies and persons, but not their tangible property? What are the unjustified hardships from which debtors should be saved? In particular, what is the ethical basis of discharge of debts without the creditors' consent?

These are the central ethical issues that this book seeks to answer. They affect all of the parties involved: the debtor, the creditor and society. In addition, there are questions of ethical relevance only to the creditors and, to some degree, to society. If we accept that contracts are enforceable, what justification is there for substituting individual enforcement efforts by a collective one? And what constitutes a just distribution of assets amongst creditors?

Debtor protection by means of discharge poses the biggest ethical challenge, and has caused most controversies in public debate over bankruptcy legislation. It is a complex ethical problem which has not yet been given a comprehensive explanation. As such, it forms the core of the ethics of bankruptcy and takes us directly to the fundamentals of moral philosophy. The second major objective of bankruptcy laws, creditor protection, involves ethical complications too, but to a lesser extent. So rather than trying to rush straight to the contentious points, I shall start with disputes which have better established solutions.

CREDITORS' EQUALITY AND COLLECTIVE PROCEEDINGS

Let us for a while put aside the question of whether a creditor has a moral right to collect an outstanding debt. If we assume that she generally has this right, how can we justify an institution which, in case of an insolvent debtor, terminates it at the will of the debtor or other creditors? This question has not often been asked, perhaps because for centuries bankruptcy laws – whether leading to final discharge or not – have made collective measures available to replace individual debt collection. The familiarity of the institution does not, however, amount to its ethical justification.

The need for institutional proceedings arises from the fact that an insolvent debtor who has several creditors exposes a common pool problem: there is a limited pool of assets to which each of the claimants has an equal title. Or, to be exact, we should say that within each class of creditors the titles are equal. Preferred creditors are served prior to ordinary creditors, but within each class the principle of equality applies. Since the titles are equal, no one of the creditors should be able to use her superior strength or swiftness to get more of the common pool than her just share. The substance of justice, entailed by equality, is in legislation governed by the principle of *pari passu*, which comes from Roman law and stands for a pro rata distribution in proportion to the relative size of the claim of each of the creditors.

Thus, interference in individual debt collection is justified because the target of individual seizure efforts is actually a common pool to which no sole person should have an exclusive right. Ethically it is a recognition that the debtor's insolvency has extinguished her moral right to her property and the joint right of creditors has taken over. The institution of bankruptcy, by transferring the property to the creditors' joint control, gives legal expression to this ethical idea.

This seems to be fair. It is also rational in the sense that individual debt enforcement tends to diminish the value of the pool for the creditors as a group: individual action requires more resources, sets creditors against each other, and often causes damage to them or to the debtors' property. The case for collective enforcement is so strong that it is no wonder that it has become a universally adopted practice. But we might still be prone to ask why the equality of claimants entails justice *pari passu* rather than distribution according to some other ostensibly just principle. I shall quote John Finnis for the standard answer:

> Finally, as between all the ordinary creditors, . . . 'equality is equity'. The debts they prove are paid to them *pari passu*. That is to say, each receives, from the pool remaining after payment of preferred creditors, the same percentage of the debt owed *to him* (not the same percentage of that pool); if the pool is insufficient, the claim of each abates proportionately. This is, then, another instance of the 'geometrical' equality which, as opposed to 'arithmetical' equality, is (as Aristotle said) characteristic of distributive justice.[7]

In Finnis' account equality before the law forms the basis of equal distribution. However, even if this is accepted, why would not, for instance, a Rawlsian principle of equality which would maximize the worst-off creditors' share apply?[8] Thomas Jackson has an answer: pro rata is the best apportioning rule, it mimics the value of our expected positions immediately before the bankruptcy. It does this by giving each creditor the same share of the common pool that she could grab in open competition according to the statistical odds.[9]

Jackson illustrates his case by an example where two creditors, each about to lend $10,000 to a debtor, decide prior to their lending what they would do if, at some later stage, the debtor turned to be worth only $15,000. Being rational persons, they would agree that a collective proceeding is needed, since uncoordinated competition probably would reduce the value of assets below $15,000. Jackson then concludes, that the creditors could not do anything better than agree to split the assets pro rata.

Jackson's conclusion seems a little hasty. One of his assumptions is that those creditors who have better collection skills and capacities would not take advantage of their superiority. Rather, they would be happy with the statistical odds counted from random equality of chances. However, if we assume that the rationality of lending parties is such that they would not seek profit from their individual advantages, we arrive at a similar rationality to the one Rawls employs in his original position. But then nothing would prevent us from claiming that the parties would agree upon some sort of maximin principle, a principle giving creditors with smaller claims, or creditors who are poor, a bigger proportionate share of the common pool.

Jackson pushes aside this type of criticism in another way. His fundamental point is that bankruptcy law should only recognize and enforce rights established in non-bankruptcy law:

> If nonbankruptcy law treats tort victims and the Bank of America as general unsecured creditors with similar rights and collection remedies, bankruptcy law should take that conclusion as a given if it is to implement most effectively *its* unique social and economic role of providing a collective forum to deal with common pool problems in the credit world. Whether the underlying assignment of entitlements is correct is irrelevant when the issue is one of implementing bankruptcy's collectivization policy.[10]

Jackson sees bankruptcy solely in terms of the common pool problem. I do not agree that this exhausts the function of the institution. Nevertheless, I agree that his point of view is adequate in the context of the just way of distributing the assets among creditors. For them, bankruptcy is a mere collection procedure superior to a grab system. It is hard to see what sense it could make if it purported to redistribute rights among creditors. If redistribution was desirable or justified, it would be more efficiently achieved by altering non-bankruptcy laws.

We have good reasons for the pro rata distribution of assets, and may conclude that bankruptcy is a relatively uncontroversial ethical issue from the creditors' point of view, both as a debt-collection device and as a solution to the common pool problem. Now it is time to widen the perspective and include debtors in the picture. Before assessing whether they should be cleared of their debts, we should find out why they should worry about paying back at all. For the answer we have to go to the very foundations of moral philosophy.

Part II

Philosophical fundamentals of credit
Should debts be paid?

The question of why debts should be paid cannot be answered, in the ethical sense, by saying that it is what the law requires. The law could as well be that debts should not be paid. Actually, this is the regime in the case of the bankruptcy laws recognizing discharge. In order ethically to justify debt enforcement we have to go beyond positive law. We have to give moral reasons for the obligation to honour debts.

A debt is, legally, most often a consequence of a contract. Fundamentally, a contract is a promise backed up by the enforcement powers of the state. Through a contract the parties have expressed what their future course of action shall be in regard to certain matters. A debt may also be a consequence of a tort, even of a crime, and the subsequent imposition of damages or monetary sanctions by a court. Unpaid taxes can accrue debt too. Although there are numerous liabilities which do not result from contracts, for the purposes of the ethics of bankruptcy, the most interesting problems are related to contract-based obligations.

If we can formulate a theory explaining how a debtor's voluntary obligations can be expunged against the will of other contracting parties, our theory should have no difficulty in explaining why non-contractual obligations imposed upon a debtor against her will can be expunged. If there have, in the first place, been ethical grounds for society to impose a non-contractual liability without asking the subject's consent, then, surely, it must be within society's powers to extinguish it.

So, the key to the moral obligation to pay a debt lies in the act of promising.[1] If we have a moral duty to keep our promises, it applies to our contractual debts too. The answer to the question 'What makes a promise morally binding?' will set the ethical boundaries for the public enforcement of contracts. It is logical to conclude that a society should, as a general rule, sanction only those contracts which, in some rational sense, are morally binding. There are a number of ways whereby promises can be seen to introduce moral force to contractual obligations.

Chapter 2

Natural law, consequentialism and contractualism
Theories of promising and their shortfalls

Natural law philosophy, or naturalism in its classical form, dominated early moral thinking. It assumes that there is in the world some objective entity, external to us, which imposes an absolute duty to keep our promises. This entity was thought, for instance, to be an immutable idea reached by reason (Plato), a teleological form of perfection inherent in the essence of human beings (Aristotle), or God's purpose (Thomas Aquinas). The difficulties in the way of natural law theories have turned out to be insurmountable. From the philosophical point of view they rely on ontological doctrines which are fatally vulnerable to criticism. It is impossible to grab a Platonic idea, or to distil the Aristotelian essence, and say: 'here is the duty to keep promises, don't we all have the same!' And, while it is possible to grab a book allegedly containing God's revelations, it is still a matter of faith whether the book really has the correct set of truths, and whether they are of divine origin.

A more practical criticism of classical accounts of promising arises from the absolutism they represent. The eternal, objective entities and revelations do not seem to allow any exceptions to duty. This leads to absurd consequences, which already in the seventeenth century made legal theorists reject naturalist explanations of contract.[1]

David Hume's philosophy is an eighteenth-century empiricist attack on natural law. There is a famous passage on promising in his *A Treatise of Human Nature*. To Hume the promisor's interests are the basis of obedience. The good consequences of keeping the promise maximize the satisfaction of her interests. What if the promisor later changes her mind, and no longer wants to stick to her word? There is no external naturalist basis to uphold the obligation but, Hume contends, this does not mean that promises are weakly established: 'interest is the *first* obligation to the performance of promises. Afterwards a sentiment of morals concurs with interest, and becomes a new obligation upon mankind.'[2]

This sentiment arises out of the usefulness of carrying on the deal even in apparently disadvantageous situations. It supports the institution and increases the chances that others will also comply when their compliance brings benefits to us. In addition, Hume postulates a passion inherent in human nature encouraging obedience. He thinks that we have a particular capacity to derive pleasure from keeping promises. This capacity does not amount to a duty, but helps Hume to explain why promises are seen as a duty in the instances when it clearly seems that the promisor would be better off breaking the promise.

Hume's claim is that no moral obligations can arise from promising. He defends his claim by trying to show how a moral obligation involved in promising leads to absurdities. First, he says, the act of will present in promising cannot be the willing of an action. The reason for this seems to me unconvincing: 'For a promise always regards some future time, and the will has an influence only on present actions.'[3]

This is a curious claim. It strikes directly against common sense, as well as against the basic practices of organizing our lives in a society. There is nothing which can prevent me from willing that I perform some actions in the future, or from influencing their future performance by my will. When I do something only because I have earlier promised to do it, I have refuted Hume. My past will has influenced my present action.

Nor can we, according to Hume, will an obligation instead of particular actions:

> All morality depends upon our sentiments; and when any action, or quality of the mind, pleases us *after a certain manner*, we say it is virtuous; and when the neglect, or non-performance of it, displeases us *after a like manner*, we say that we lie under an obligation to perform it. A change of the obligation supposes a change of the sentiment; and a creation of a new obligation supposes some new sentiment to arise. But 'tis certain we can naturally no more change our own sentiments, than the motions of heavens; nor by a single act of our will, that is, by a promise, render any action agreeable or disagreeable, moral or immoral; which, without that act, wou'd have produced contrary impres-

sions, or have been endowed with different qualities. It wou'd be absurd, therefore, to will any new obligation, that is, any new sentiment of pain or pleasure.[4]

Hume contends here that what we will flows from our sentiments, these sentiments determine what is moral, and that it would be absurd to assume a new act of will wanting something else and giving rise to some obligations. But Hume's "'tis certain' is not a knock-down argument. I see no reason to accept that all morality depends upon our sentiments. I may feel most willing to break a promise, yet I may end up keeping it because I think that is my obligation. Our moral judgements can go against our sentiments. This fact cannot be explained away by claiming that the obligations are just another form of sentiment. It would be a queer explanation, a distortion of our everyday motivational dispositions.

The concept of autonomy offers a much better description of the uniquely human capacity of free will, demonstrated in the respect of moral principles and obligations. And the capacity extends to promises, which are choices limiting the scope of our future choices in a binding manner. There is nothing weird in the moral obligations these choices invoke.

Hume has many followers among contemporary philosophers. They prefer to speak about promising in terms of conventional and institutional practices that establish the moral obligations. In Thomas Scanlon's words, these theories mean that

> the obligation arising from a promise is a two stage affair. First, there is the social practice, which consists in the fact that a given group of people generally behave in a certain way, have certain expectations and intentions, and accept certain principles as norms. Second, there is a moral judgement to the effect that, given these social facts, a certain form of behaviour ... is morally wrong.[5]

Scanlon tells us that one of the philosophers belonging to the conventionalist school is John Rawls, and links him to the Humean idea that fidelity to promises is an artificial virtue.

Annette Baier draws another link between Hume and contemporary thinking. Her paper 'Promises, promises, promises' points out how Hume's view has been absorbed into the analytical tradition:

> A promise, according to Hume, Austin, Searle, and Anscombe, is a speech act whereby one alters the moral situation. One does

not merely represent some possible state of affairs, one brings it about – makes it the case that, from being free in some respect, one is thereafter unfree, until the obligation taken on in the promise is discharged.[6]

The philosophers lined up by Baier take promises to be initiated by the promisor's speech act, and notice that 'change of mind is not allowed'.[7] However, they do not see that the obligation gets its moral stature from the will initiating the promise. The morality enters from outside, from community recognition and enforcement.[8]

Thus, the empiricist-analytical tradition does not detect any moral contents in the act of promising as such. This account of promising is unsatisfactory for the same reason as its Humean ancestor, the 'artificial virtue' theory, was: the absence of social pressure would make it OK to break a promise. The core of the objection to Hume and his heirs is that moral obligations are not exhausted by reference to useful community standards but imply a richer set of underlying principles.

On the other hand, modern deontological philosophers, who prefer to develop their argument within the context of hypothetical choices, have seen the promisee as the crucial agent for the emergence of moral duties. For instance, Thomas Scanlon focuses on the promisee's expectations. Scanlon sees flaws in theories taking promising to be merely one among many just and useful social practices that we have a general duty to obey. He wants to upgrade the obligation to a moral duty arising out of 'what we owe to other people when we have led them to form expectations about our future conduct'.[9]

Thus, Scanlon maintains that breaking a promise is a moral wrong independent of public enforcement or recognition of the rule that breaches are wrong. He seeks to establish the obligation on a principle of fidelity which is justified as it is in the interest of both the promisor and the promisee. The principle condones the stability of the promisee's expectations by making it a moral wrong to break a promise.[10]

Scanlon employs a contractual process in his justification as to why the promisee's expectations are morally relevant. Morality is introduced because reasonable potential promisors find the principle of fidelity to be a rational way to make promises more enduring. This is in their interest since it increases the chances that the promisee will be willing to close deals. The parties to the process choose to be bound by the principle in order to create a climate favourable to promising.[11] Here the similarity to John Rawls' position becomes obvious. The following quotation summarizes Rawls' view:

> Thus promising is an act done with the public intention of deliberately incurring an obligation the existence of which in the circumstances will further one's ends. We want this obligation to exist and to be known to exist, and we want others to know that we recognize this tie and intend to abide by it. Having, then, availed ourselves of the practice for this reason, we are under an obligation to do as we promised by the principle of fairness.[12]

Rawls' principle of fairness tells us, in short, that a person is under an obligation to do her share whenever she has involved herself in a social practice in order to advance her interests. The principle of fairness, for its part, is validated by a hypothetical choice taking place in an original position where the characteristics of the choosing parties are defined so that they reflect the fundamentally Kantian ethical notions of freedom, rationality and autonomy. The advantage of Rawls' approach is that it disentangles autonomy from Kant's dubious metaphysics and epistemology.

I feel most sympathetic to the use of hypothetical choices in establishing moral principles. It is a subtle device to introduce clarity and structure into ethical arguments. Scanlon pursues this aim by sorting out the general conditions of promising that apply for rational persons in a social context. Out of these conditions he extracts a moral principle called the principle of fidelity. According to Scanlon, his method takes him further than Rawls is able to go. At this point I disagree. The Kantian moral characteristics of Rawls' original position, first, separate him from the Humean artificial virtue tradition and, second, give his principle of fairness a firmer basis on which to explain the moral independence and permanence of promissory obligations than is established by Scanlon and his principle of fidelity.

Hence, Scanlon and Rawls seek to abstract out of social practices certain features which would make promissory obligations morally binding independent of the existence of any particular social practice. Both philosophers make an assured and inspiring penetration towards the ultimate rationality of our moral behaviour, but before the problem is exhausted they have to answer one more question: why should the hypothetical choices matter to actual promisors?

Scanlon's answer would have to be that they count because they are reasonable, because they are in the interest of both parties.[13] I do not see this as convincing enough.

Scanlon may be able to explain why moral patterns of behaviour normally pay respect to the principle of fidelity, the effect being that a breach of promise is regarded as a moral wrong. However, this does not explain why, in actual life, the rationality behind the principle of fidelity would always be ethically superior to a more egoistic rationality encouraging general conformity with promises, but with a reservation allowing for breaches whenever they bring to the breacher, all things considered, more benefits than harm. It might well be that potential promisors find a principle with an egoistic flavour more appealing, and thus worth adopting, in spite of a slight decrease in the promisees' willingness to enter into contracts.

I still think that there are circumstances when the rewards from breaking a promise are so great that it would be a rational thing not to comply, yet it would be wrong. I am not convinced that rational considerations alone can be the basis of a moral duty. The micro-climate in which hypothetical choices are made has to be controlled by, in addition to rationality, ethical assumptions that bring flesh to the bones of logical thinking before we can reach towards enduring moral principles. The ethical assumptions bringing in the flesh have to be those which reflect our basic human nature as beings of flesh and blood – otherwise we get lost in the endless space of idealistic escapism.

Against this background Rawls is able to do better. His principle of fairness gains credibility from having been chosen in a carefully designed original position:

> Finally, we may remind ourselves that the hypothetical nature of the original position invites the question: why should we take any interest in it, moral or otherwise? Recall the answer: the conditions embodied in the description of this situation are ones that we do in fact accept.[14]

The ethical characterizations embedded in Rawls' original position make the principle of fairness immune to the self-interested inclinations of the actual promising agents. They comply because they are persuaded that, given their nature and the nature of the parties in the original position, the principle of fairness is the right one. As Rawls puts it: 'Each aspect of the original position can be given a supporting explanation.'[15] In Rawls' theory, unlike in Scanlon's, self-interest promoted through the recognition of promisees' interests is not the dominant reason for compliance. Compared to Scanlon, this takes Rawls' principle of fairness one step further in solidifying the moral stature of conventional and institutional practices.

Contract theory, as Rawls employs it, is an illuminating model with which to work out ethical principles from Kant's fundamental moral notions. However, a procedural theory cannot help relying upon some assumptions, tacit or explicit, which are of a metaphysical nature, if it wants to have bearing on an actual moral discourse when its values are opposed to the rational self-interest of living people whose actions those values are supposed to guide and measure.[16] Metaphysical concepts are needed because, even after all the reference to social conventions and all the hypothetical procedures, questions such as 'Why should we pay respect to conventional practices even when we find them unbeneficial to us?', or 'Why should we treat human beings as ends in themselves?' remain haunting. Therefore, it is a legitimate aim of moral research to expose the metaphysical concepts which are least contentious, instead of rejecting all metaphysics as chimerical.

I think that autonomy can be made plausible outside a contractual framework, and without severing all the ties with Kant's metaphysics. Success in this would add to the philosophical appeal of Rawls' hypothetical original position, not make it irrelevant. For this reason, I will soon revisit Kant. My purpose is to give one more supporting explanation for the ethically relevant aspects of human nature imposing constraints on self-interest, to penetrate a little deeper into the contentious realm on which ethical principles rest. It is a sensible aim, although with it arises the need to revive some of Kant's metaphysics of morals.

Kant's original idea of autonomy is that it is the characteristic of moral agents which enables them to shape the world through their choices. I hope to use this idea to anchor the duty to keep promises more firmly to the ontological fundamentals of the world we live in, and to the epistemic fundamentals of the experience we live through. A favourable outcome would give strong support to the claim that the hypothetical choices made in the original position, including the choice of the principle of fairness, are relevant to us as actual persons.

I make the effort aware of its controversial nature: it will lead to clashes with the mainstream metaethical position of contemporary analytical philosophy. To mitigate the potentially adverse effects of these metaethical controversies to the applied part of this study, I want to emphasize that the ethics of bankruptcy that will be developed in the subsequent chapters is able to stand on its own merits. Autonomy is a powerful axiom of moral philosophy even when it is not accommodated into a Kantian context. As long as it is recognized that we are autonomous agents, my ethics of bankruptcy should remain viable. On the other hand, if autonomy is denied then it is denied that we are able to pay respect to moral principles, which would mean that ethical debate in general is a pointless exercise.

Chapter 3

In search of the ultimate obligation
Why a metaethical affair?

Moral principles have to be argued for, not drawn out of a hat. In this chapter I purport to show that there is room for reasoning that seeks to extract autonomy from Kantian metaphysics without drifting into conflict with the empirical account of the world, and without sliding into murky noumenal insights. Any advance in this endeavour will increase the ethical weight of autonomy as the foundation of moral laws, while a failure would only provide a reason to maintain some distance between Kantian virtues and their historical roots. Hence, if I achieve my purpose I may increase the rational appeal of Kantian values, and if I fail, everything modern, metaphysically disentangled philosophy has seen as precious in autonomy remains intact and capable of supporting the more practical part of my inquiry. Because a revision of Kant's metaphysics of morals has a chance to win a lot but lose only a little I am happy to throw myself into the adventure.

Against some basic tenets of analytical philosophy, my view is that value judgements can be defended to the point where they get truth-value. I suggest that a normative theory can be proved viable if it manages criticism on three levels: empirical plausibility of the first premises, logical consistency of the argument and intuitive credibility of the conclusions. This leads to a three-part test which any moral theory should satisfy before it can gain approval on a rational basis.

The first stipulation of the test is that the premises of the theory should have empirical plausibility. An ethical theory should not add any objects or entities to the empirical world, or alter the empirical contents of descriptions given to the objects. However, an ethical theory may supplement the empirical descriptions, with the purpose of altering future human behaviour, by adding to them non-empirical terms which do not contradict the empirical truth. A moral theory is, according to the first stipulation, a rational theory to the extent that the supplementary terms are compatible with the true empirical descriptions of objects, and increase the explanatory force of those descriptions by introducing into them an ethical dimension which suggests why we should act in a particular way in the future empirical environment arising out of the present world.

The first step of the three-way test is needed to keep our feet on the ground, to confine ethical principles to the realities of the world we live in. Ethics is not limited to descriptions of observations, but we are required not to escape from the world of objects when we seek to guide the behaviour of human objects in that world. This is a very loose requirement. Many conflicting ethical theories can satisfy it. As such, it is a necessary but not sufficient condition for the correctness of an ethical argument. It needs to work together with other criteria.

The second condition insists that the internal logic of the argument is consistent. This should be self-evident; without internal consistency a theory can hardly be a rational one. In order to be a rational theory ethics must satisfy the formal requirements of rationality. The third condition is that an ethical theory should not produce strikingly counter-intuitive outcomes. This is more puzzling. Reconciliation of reasoning and intuition might seem to involve mixing two elements foreign to each other. Reasoning is objective, while intuition is subjective.

However, ethics is not restricted to logical conclusions from empirical facts. The first stipulation did not rule out philosophical elements from ethical principles – all that was stipulated was that their non-empirical contents should not alter the substance of the present empirical picture of the world. Since the first premises of a theory may – and in order to produce an ethical theory seeking to influence our future behaviour must – contain concepts explaining the empirical world in non-empirical terms, we need additional safeguards to guarantee that the resulting theory remains within the limits of human possibilities and understanding. This is achieved once we demand that the ethical conclusions pass the test of consistency with our intuitions.

The practical results of an ethical theory are often counter-intuitive. This is to be expected since in ethics the point is to influence our behaviour, which can be achieved only by shaking our intuitive convictions; no argument is needed to persuade us to act as our intuitions suggest. As far as we are rational agents, we can compare the apparently counter-intuitive conclusions of a theory with the argument it forwards, and decide whether the argument is convincing enough to override the intuitions. If not, if the conclusions are, even after thorough reflection, consistently and deeply at odds with widely shared intuitions, we have a reason to suspect that the non-empirical elements of the theory – although the theory has cleared the first and second steps of the three-way test – are somehow wanting. The abundant examples that counter utilitarianism, such as those permitting a utilitarian to kill one unhappy person quickly and painlessly in order to cause joy to thousands, are a good case of intuitions shaking an apparently sound moral theory.

Intuition is not the key to moral truth because morality is derived from a rational faculty of knowledge in the inter-personal sense. Nevertheless, intuition has a place in the rational pursuit of moral truth because the starting point of the pursuit is not limited solely to empirical concepts, and because ethics is bound to take into account everyone's subjective interests.

Ethics represents an individual reason's endeavour to accommodate its corporeal extension with the corporeal extensions of other living beings. It engages both reason's impersonal characteristics (objective rationality), and the world in which these characteristics prevail (empirical facts), but it cannot be dictated by either of them alone, not even by both of them together. Intuition, that is each individual reason's spontaneous response to moral stimulus, has to be accounted for as well, because spontaneity reflects our fundamental human capacity for autonomy. The three elements that have to work in balance in a theory in order to arrive at rationally established moral principles are world, logic and intuition. The three-way test I have proposed seeks to assess the working of this balance.

What I have just said about moral judgements may sound like chimerical metaphysics, but in fact it is only an application of the rationality of empirical methods to ethical knowledge. As an example, think about our perception of a pink object in a dark room. The object appears to us as grey, nevertheless we consider it rational to conclude that the object is a pink one. We reach the conclusion by means of a hypothesis that the perception is affected by a change in the circumstances of observation, rather than by a change in the physical properties of the object. The hypothesis may be corroborated by the perceptions of other people, and by varying the circumstances of perceiving.

Now, these procedures are analogous to the ones we use when we seek to reach rational moral judgements. An empirical description of the moral problem is the starting point, like perception in the analogy. The next step is a moral theory binding the empirical description of the problem together with philosophical concepts employing the universal characteristics of human beings and universal features of moral problems of the type under consideration. When a moral theory is empirically and logically consistent, it is ready for the final step: a check-up by intuitions.

In our empirical example the hypothesis of the unchanged physical nature of the pink object is validated by shared inter-subjective judgement about the physical properties of the object, reached after reflection on the actual perception and matters affecting its contents. Likewise, a moral theory obtains its validity through an account of the morally relevant properties of the problem and the agents involved, and leads to a judgement as to the proper course of behaviour in particular situations. In the empirical case it may well be that some people go on claiming, after the apparent greyness has been given an explanation, that the pink object actually turns grey in a dark room rather than accepting that our perceptions get affected by a change in circumstances, but we are entitled to consider their claim to be an irrational one. However, if there were many of these people we might suspect that the object really is grey, and that the pinkness was just caused by pink blinds that filtered the sunlight entering the room in the daytime. Whatever way the verdict goes, we are confident that we have a rational way to establish the truth of perceptions regardless of the possibility of a few discordant notes.

In a like manner we are able to establish the truth of moral judgements regardless of a few discordant notes. When a moral theory leading to practical judgements is in accordance with empirical descriptions of the world and with the requirements of formal rationality, it gets its final corroboration from intuitions. If a moral theory consistently contradicts intuitions, it needs to be revised. However, we should remember that an empirical theory may not lose its validity even in the face of significant opposition relying on immediate experience, if there is a rational explanation as to why the immediate experience appears not to support the theory. A hundred thousand people may claim that the object in the dark is actually grey, yet if we have a theory giving a rational explanation of its actual pinkness and apparent greyness we are entitled to consider the object to be pink. Hence, an empirical theory may carry relevance independent of individual empirical judgements, but not independent of empirical judgements altogether.

Moral theories have the same property. They can stand the attack of many intuitive judgements, but cannot resist a massive verdict by intuitive judgements. Where the exact line between 'many' and 'massive' lies is impossible to define in general terms. It is a matter for judgement in particular cases, just as the exact point at which a particular scientific theory is confirmed is not up to philosophers but for scientists to decide. Judgements on the validity of a theory are, ultimately, judgements – both in the case of an empirical theory and in the case of a moral theory. As such they are open to argument and to differences in perception and opinion, a fact which should not prevent us from taking them to be true or false.

Thus, I do not think that theories relating to facts and theories relating to values are as different as it has been fashionable to assume. The truth of both rests on rational judgements derived from the particular facts of the problem at hand, and general facts about the world and human beings. Even those who deny that the three-way test could prove a moral theory true or false should acknowledge that it provides a useful first heat eliminating the more freakish candidates from the finals. If a theory fails the test, we are entitled to consider it as inferior to the competitors who pass the test successfully.

All natural law philosophies fail the first step. Their premises rely on pure intuition in the Lockean sense of the term,[1] scorning empirical information about the world and our place in it. In its various forms natural law adds non-empirical entities to the world of objects (e.g. rights and duties which have an independent ontological existence), or postulates a reality independent of the world of objects but able to command it (e.g. God), or attributes properties to the objects that are not supported by our perceptions (e.g. pantheist values). Classical naturalism is not an empirically plausible approach.

This dead-end of natural law has contributed to empiricist and analytical teachings of values. The empiricist-analytical tradition may allow for 'autonomous norms', to use the terminology introduced by my famous compatriot G.H. v. Wright as an example,[2] but only after leaving the contents of these norms dependent on the accidental will (e.g. Hume's psychological naturalism) or immediate intuition (e.g. Moore's ideal utilitarianism) of the agents.[3] It renders the moral force of autonomous norms relative to whether they are actually wanted or not.[4] Values become, in v. Wright's words, first-person practical syllogisms. As such they are valuations, and may deserve the qualification 'well-grounded',[5] but cannot be true or false.[6]

V. Wright opened to analytical philosophers a gate that logical empiricists seemed to have shut permanently – a meaningful way to speak about values. However, he leaves unanswered a fundamental problem: if there is, ultimately, no criterion to validate value judgements except the fact that they are actually wanted, most deplorable judgements may gain the status of autonomous and well-grounded moral principles on the basis of being widely accepted as ends in themselves. We are left without benchmarks of reasonableness and rationality which would be capable of differentiating between conflicting judgements. In this sense v. Wright belongs to the tradition John Rawls has called rational intuitionism:

> It is important to see that the contrast between rational intuitionism and Kant's moral constructivism is not a contrast between objectivism and subjectivism. For both views have a conception of objectivity, but each understands objectivity in a different way.
>
> In rational intuitionism a correct moral judgement, or principle, is one that is true of a prior and independent order of moral values. This order is also prior to the criteria of reasonableness and rationality as well as prior to the appropriate conception of persons as autonomous and responsible, and free and equal members of a moral community. Indeed, it is that order that settles what those reasonable and rational criteria are, and how autonomy and responsibility are to be conceived.
>
> In Kant's doctrine, on the other hand, a correct moral judgement is one that conforms to all the relevant criteria of reasonableness and rationality.[7]

I do not want to go into detailed examples to show the counter-intuitive outcomes the analytic position would yield when applied to practical life. Here I will just make my disagreement with it explicit: a moral inquiry lacks philosophical sense if it is unable to produce arguments that verify its doctrines.

The best way to show that a philosophical argument can support the truth-value of an ethical principle is to show it:

If we are interested in the final resolution of meta-ethical questions – in whether or not there *really are* any moral facts – then it seems to me that we therefore have little alternative but to engage in normative ethical debate and see where the arguments that we give ultimately lead us.[8]

Hence, even in this study, which mainly falls under applied ethics, I have seen a short metaethical deviation to be appropriate because the applied argument for an ethics of bankruptcy, in so far as it is sound, is a contribution in favour of Kantian constructivism as well.

Since v. Wright wrote his theory allowing normative discourse to squat in the empiricist and analytical quarters, the squatters have sprawled out to create a well-established settlement. As long as normative ethicists have not challenged the basic relativist axiom of their analytical patrons, i.e. the claim that values are not truth-functional, moral philosophy has been allowed to toil with arguments that try to draw a distinction between right and wrong, good and bad. This tacit subdivision of the perimeters of philosophy has been subsequently sealed by allegiance to reflective equilibrium.

Reflective equilibrium is a notion developed by John Rawls, and it describes a procedure whereby we start ethical arguments from weak and generally held propositions, and arrive at a set of substantial ethical principles. R.P. Ebertz has summarized it in the following manner:

> Reflective equilibrium is the state of one's beliefs (about justice, in this case) when 'principles and justice coincide'. When a person's beliefs are in reflective equilibrium, the structure of those beliefs, from the particular to the most general, cohere. I find it helpful to speak also of 'the reflective process' to refer to the activities which lead one to reflective equilibrium. These include carefully considering individual beliefs, comparing them with one another, considering the beliefs of others, drawing out consequences of beliefs, and so forth.[9]

Thus, reflective equilibrium makes rational justification of ethical principles a plausible exercise without requiring that the principles gain truth-value. It avoids both the unempirical pitfalls of natural law theories, and the empiricist tendency of artificing all moral virtues and rights by rendering them relative to social practices. This is a great achievement, and we have every reason to grant reflective equilibrium a prominent place in the plan of philosophical research.

But must a normative argument keep strictly within the perimeters of reflective equilibrium if it is to preserve its rationality? Are commonly shared presumptions, which are ideas rather than facts,[10] the ultimate starting point of moral reasoning as reflective equilibrium suggests? My claim is that commonly shared presumptions, ideas which are weak and commonly held, cannot totally exhaust the foundations of normative ethics. In addition to these ideas a moral inquiry has to account for autonomy, the moral agency in us. This takes the inquiry beyond conceptions that merely happen to be held. Noumena, causality of reason, has a role to play – although that role is much more limited than Kant originally proclaimed.

Ebertz refers to M. DePaul's distinction between reflective equilibrium, which is a method of theory construction, and foundationalism, which is an account of the epistemic status of our beliefs.[11] Foundationalism in its modest form argues that justified beliefs are not only coherent with other beliefs, but have special epistemic status. Ebertz defines modest ethical foundationalism

> as the view that ethical beliefs are justified when (i) some of these beliefs have a prima facie direct justification and (ii) all of the other beliefs are justified in a way that depends on their relationship to these directly justified beliefs. To say that a moral belief is prima facie directly justified, is to say that either (a) its justification is not derived solely from inferences from other beliefs, or (b) it is justified by inference from some *non-moral* belief(s). Thus, modest ethical foundationalism contends that some beliefs must be justified in virtue of some source or sources of direct prima facie justification.[12]

Next, Ebertz goes on to define ethical coherentism:

> as the view that (i) one's ethical beliefs are justified by their systematic relationship to other beliefs, and (ii) none of these beliefs receive any direct justificatory support apart from these systematic relationships. Coherentism, as defined here, holds that a belief can *only* be justified by coherence considerations, and that it is coherence *alone* which justifies.[13]

In short, ethical coherentism – unlike at least some strains of ethical foundationalism – does not challenge the metaethical axioms of empiricist-analytical tradition. Ebertz's claim is 'that the reflective equilibrium method Rawls describes is in fact best construed as involving modest foundationalism'.[14] I shall not go into a detailed discussion of the nature of Rawls' theory. For my purposes Ebertz's important observation is that principles which are coherent with considered judgements and common presumptions may call for further justification.[15]

Ebertz then moves to the analysis of considered moral judgements. I find particularly interesting his third alternative as to why considered judgements are capable of serving as the foundation of normative pursuits:

> A third approach resists the attempt by constructivists to sever moral justification from epistemological justification. On this view, the justificatory task is not to show how principles can be constructed out of our convictions, but to show that we have reason to believe that they are in some sense objectively true. Adding this approach to the foundationalist interpretation of reflective equilibrium . . . results in *modest objectivist foundationalism*. Within this framework, considered moral judgements and common presumptions are taken to be, in some sense, indicators of moral truth. It is this which enables them to play the special justificatory role that they do. Yet the modest objectivist would seek to avoid the pitfalls of classical ethical foundationalism, emphasizing the fallibility of these 'foundations'. Because of this, the reflective equilibrium model becomes quite important. Since the 'foundations' provided by our considered judgements and common presumptions are weak and fallible, they must be tested against one another, and against principles and background theories. The reflective process is aimed at finding principles and considered judgements which reinforce one another, building a solid structure on foundations which are independently very weak. Although coherence alone is not a reason for taking principles and judgements to be true, seeking reflective equilibrium can be an aid for sorting out accurate from inaccurate input.[16]

In the following text Ebertz points out the main problems for modest objectivist foundationalism:

> By far the most central of these is the difficulty of providing a plausible account of why considered moral judgements should be taken as indicators of moral truth, even if they are only fallible indicators. . . .
> Unlike sense perception, there does not seem to be an obvious

causal connection between objective moral truth and our moral beliefs and judgements.[17]

This puts my purpose in the next chapter well into perspective. I want to try to work out of Kant's central philosophical notions a plausible form of modest objectivist foundationalism. My answer to the difficulties pointed out by Ebertz is that considered moral judgements and shared presumptions should be taken as indicators of moral truth for the same reason as considered and shared empirical judgements are indicators of empirical truth. Ultimately, our autonomy provides the causal connection between objective moral truth and our moral beliefs and judgements.

The controversies surrounding moral judgements may seem greater than those surrounding empirical judgements. Nevertheless, I think that this is not quite the case. We should remember that in ethics, unlike in science, distortion and oppression of rational justification aiming at truth can be used to promote the interests of distorters and oppressors. The pursuit of moral truth is all too often deliberately and systematically discouraged because it involves impartial and equal consideration of interests. And finally, ethics is an area where social behaviour is at stake. All social sciences are still teething because of the immense complexity of our social behaviour. This complexity is not merely a matter of degree. In addition to the causality of nature, explanations of social behaviour have to account for human autonomy too; they have to account for the causality of free human choices.

The next chapter will detail my modest objectivist foundationalist interpretation of Kant, or modest Kantianism. It is an account of moral principles arising out of autonomy, which is seen as a property shared by human beings. I hope that Ebertz's groundbreaking distinctions have helped to put my metaethical endeavour into perspective. Logical empiricism denied meaning to normative discourse. Analytical philosophy allowed that discourse some breathing space, but kept the leash tight. For decades there has not been a way to get over the queerness of entities which contain moral truths. Ebertz has made a laudable effort to restart the metaethical product development halted by the failure of classical naturalism.

In response to the objection that the affirmation of moral truths implies a commitment to 'queer' entities, moral realists are seeking to develop more plausible accounts of how moral judgements could be 'true' which do not involve the positing of new entities. . . .

What must be emphasized is that all of these contemporary suggestions differ from many earlier versions of foundationalism in that they recognize the fallibility of the foundations.[18]

My modest Kantianism accommodates the fallibility of its foundations by focusing on anthropocentric universality, on us as we are. It is we who introduce to the world the effects of our free choices. Those effects are known to us, but the ultimate noumenal self bringing them about, the thing in itself, remains inexplicable.

There is nothing that guarantees that our noumenal self may not change. So far the empirical expressions of that self have witnessed for autonomy, but if the self changes, its empirical expressions may change and force the ethics relying on those expressions to change too. As long as we allow for the possibility of that change, and construct an ethics which captures the universal characteristics of our value judgements and the ways we make them, we can reach the moral truth. An ethics reaching for the truth does not make reflective equilibrium redundant as a philosophical tool, but completes and supports it:

> In whatever area of philosophy it is applied, the proponent of reflective equilibrium must also spell out why it is that the 'considered judgements' in that domain can play the role they do in reflective equilibrium. Without such an explanation, appeal to reflective equilibrium supplies an incomplete view of justification.[19]

Let us proceed to see whether a modest objectivist foundationalist revision of Kant can increase the appeal of considered judgements about the autonomy of human beings.

Chapter 4

Ethics founded on autonomy
A modest objectivist foundationalist interpretation of Kant

Like Hume, Kant made a powerful attack on classical naturalism. However, at the same time he fought Hume's empiricist consequentialism. In building his philosophical edifice Kant started from two basic facts that are immediately available to us:

> Two things fill the mind with ever new and increasing admiration and awe, the oftener and the more steadily we reflect on them: *the starry heavens above and the moral law within*. I have not to search for them and conjecture them as though they were veiled in darkness or were in the transcendent region beyond my horizon; I see them before me and connect them directly with the consciousness of my existence.[1]

In this eloquent passage the starry heavens stand for the empirical representations of external objects. We are immediately aware of these and, Kant proclaims, by means of philosophical analysis are able to proceed from them to understanding the nature of our knowledge. The result of Kant's analysis is an epistemology where the active mind conceptualizes the chaos of sensibilia into a coherent external world of objects. This world is, in the ontological sense, only appearance, but it is, nonetheless, the real and objective world.[2] There is also the noumenal world of 'things in themselves', but it is beyond all possible experience, and as such meaningless to us. We only know its possibility as a result of philosophical analysis, but never gain any knowledge of it.[3]

Kant attacked naturalist conceptions by making sensual perception the condition of all knowledge. By the same token, he criticized empiricism for taking the perceptions as unproblematic. Kant's postulate is that, in order to provide us with a representation of the external world, it is necessary that the perceiving mind introduces unity and order to the random chaos of perceptions. The causality of natural laws is the outcome of our cognitive faculties, a result of the only means which we, as human beings, have at hand to observe objects in the world, including ourselves. The causality is, nevertheless, necessary because without it there would not be any knowledge of the world.

Here Kant achieves his most important goal: he establishes the causal necessity of the laws of nature while leaving a gate open for freedom of will. The gate opens through the thesis that causality is a result of the mind's activity. Being the source of causality, the mind can also accommodate its own initiative, which Kant calls the causality of reason, as the source of human action: when a rational agent's actions are explained, they can be explained both from nature's causality and from reason's causality. The latter safeguards the freedom of our will, the possibility of which is given by the fact that we observe moral laws.

To summarize, Kant acknowledges that beyond perceptions of external objects there are 'things in themselves' of which we can know nothing. Beyond perceptions of ourselves are 'things in themselves' too, but the existence of moral law gives our noumenal self some immediate exposure in the world of empirical objects. We are forced to accept freedom of will because moral law would not make sense otherwise.[4] This makes us the cause *a priori* of our actions – the ultimate cause without any further empirical connection – rendering freedom of will the one and only instance in which we can know the direct effect of 'things in themselves' in the world. But freedom of will, or the causality of reason, always coexists with the causality of nature. When our action falls under the moral law, the mind perceiving the action labels it as one caused by our will, while continuing to explain the same action in terms of causal necessity as far as its relation to other empirical objects is described.[5]

After establishing freedom of will Kant moves to the central piece of his normative ethics, to the concept of autonomy: 'when we think of ourselves as free, we transfer ourselves into the intelligible world as members and recognize the autonomy of the will together with its consequence – morality'.[6]

The ultimate cause of our actions is within us: our will. The capacity to master our conduct makes us autonomous beings. This brings in responsibility. We cannot put the blame for our deeds on anything or anybody other than on our own will, therefore, as autonomous beings, we are morally responsible for our actions.

As Kant said, we apprehend the moral capacity innate in us as immediately as the starry heavens above us. We are more than bodily organs, a fact which makes us morally responsible. But moral responsibility alone does not amount to substantial normative rules. It is a necessary condition for the existence of ethical principles, but not sufficient to determine their contents. Ethics does not only rest on freedom to choose. If it did, nothing would prevent us from choosing as ethical whatever principles that may occur to our minds. Applied to promises, this would mean that we could decide to have moral responsibility for our undertakings, until we chose to cancel it. Kant would scorn this attitude. How does he establish the contents of right and wrong, good and bad? We have noted that he does not accept naturalism in its classical form, that is, the derivation of values from an authority or entity external to ourselves. Nor can they follow from the consequences of our actions. Kant rejects utilitarian versions of ethics because 'the motives of virtue are put in the same class as those of vice and we are instructed only to become better at calculation, the specific difference between virtue and vice being completely wiped out'.[7]

His rejection of utilitarianism, long before the school obtained its name, is, in effect, based on the same fundamental argument that is used by modern critics of utilitarian ethics.

REVIVING THE METAPHYSICS OF MORALS: A KANTIAN BRIDGE TO DEONTOLOGICAL VALUES

Kant establishes values in our peculiar nature as human beings: in our capacity to observe the moral law. We saw that it secures autonomy by proving the freedom of will. Next, he continues to the normative contents of his theory. This is critical, as it is a move from a statement of fact (our capability to govern our actions) to a statement of value (what course of action we should follow). This move from 'is' to 'ought' has been rejected by most of modern philosophy.

I shall make an effort to revise Kant's argument so that it is less open to attacks, while preserving its essence. Those ingredients of Kant's epistemology and ontology that do not clash with our empirical conception of the world may be used as a platform to launch ethical principles. The analysis of promising that follows seeks to illustrate that there can be a productive connection between metaphysics and autonomy, and shows how a modest objectivist foundationalist interpretation of Kant can provide tools for a normative argument in applied philosophy.

I shall start my moderation of Kant by acknowledging that he makes an error in assuming that we have a noumenal insight which reveals moral truths to us.[8] We have no such access to the noumena. However, we should anchor the ethical value of autonomy in something. If neo-Kantianism tries to strip off the metaphysical burden of Kant's ethics by axiomatizing the goodness of autonomy without any further argument, then it either falls back to the dubious idealism of noumenal insights, or leaves ethical principles only the meagre status of an opinion or emotion backed by institutional arrangements. Once autonomy as the ethical fundamental is mounted on nothing, it is deprived of the power to raise values above beliefs and prejudices.

Let us consider Kant's attempt to arrive at 'ought'. He claims that the idea of freedom makes us members of an intelligible (noumenal) world, while at the same time we remain members of the world of the senses. The better, noumenal, person in us forces to our consciousness the knowledge of what we would do if we were bound only by free will. This knowledge we observe as an 'ought' inasmuch as we consider ourselves to be members of the world of senses. Simultaneously, we are under the influence of our lousier, sensual selves trying to distract us from toeing the line. Whether 'ought' and the freedom of the will, or sensual attractions and the causality of nature, get the upper hand determines how ethical we are.[9]

I do not think that Kant here has enough material to build the bridge he wants. It is too strong an assumption that only when we follow the moral law are our actions the products of free will. Besides, if free will is equated with right and good, how can it be used to sort out what right and good are? Once right is defined in terms of actions guided by free will, and free will is expressed only in right actions, the definition is a circular one which does not leave room for normative conclusions. Kant's theory could work if we had, as Kant assumes, a direct access to the noumenal world unearthing for us the true moral laws. However, this goes too far into the realms of idealism. We do not have any special sense forcing the eternal values to our consciousness, although it is sensible to recognize that we all share the capacity to observe at least some values.

My suggestion to break this circularity is that deliberate actions which are against the requirements of morality result, nevertheless, from free choices. We do not have to deny Kant's observation that moral law is a fact that we are immediately aware of, even if we want to deny his claim that only morally correct actions are initiated by free will. The immediate awareness of *some* moral law still serves a useful purpose: it establishes the general possibility of freedom of will. My moderation of Kant rejects his postulate that *only* the moral law represents *causa noumenon*, and postulates instead that all deliberate human choices are manifestations of freedom of will, the existence of which is implied by the existence of moral laws in general.

We have to determine separately what actions fall under the concept 'deliberate', but the problem is not a difficult one. We constantly deal with it in discourses over moral and legal responsibility, and arrive at satisfactory outcomes. Actions caused by our intentions and desires are taken as the results of free will, at least unless some particular circumstances or reasons prove the contrary. These discourses reveal that it is easier to reach an agreement over what constitutes a deliberate action than over what constitutes right or good action. Therefore, freedom of will, as a characteristic of deliberate human actions in general, has more explanatory force, and is less open to criticism, than freedom of will as a property solely attached to morally correct actions.

Kant bundles together freedom of will, autonomy and obedience to the moral law with the effect that only morally correct behaviour expresses free will and autonomy. I have wanted to break the connection, but have allowed moral laws a place in establishing the general possibility of free will. They suit the purpose well because they are, as empirical patterns of behaviour, in some form present in every human community and, as theoretical axioms, a necessary condition for any normative pursuit. In addition, I find Kant's concept of autonomy worth preserving, but with a broader connotation. Now it stands for the uniquely human capacity for free choice, including the choice to be ethical.

The resulting modest Kantianism rests on two premises. First, free will is the cause of our deliberate choices. Second, we are autonomous in so far as we have the capacity for free choice. My revision moderates Kant because it is a pragmatic and anthropocentric one. It focuses on our capacities as we are, on ourselves as empirical rather than noumenal beings. We can employ the resulting broader, but still Kantian, concept of autonomy, understood in the pragmatic sense as a capacity for free choices, to fill the gap between 'is' and 'ought'. At the same time, Kantianism is brought closer to the contemporary mainstream conception of autonomy as authority over one's own world and life.[10]

While we get rid of Kant's peep into the noumena, we should, nevertheless, preserve some central notions of his epistemic and ontological system. Kant's things in themselves could, in relation to external objects which are perceived by us, be as well called non-things. He emphasizes time after time that to us the real world is the world of empirical objects. This leaves the noumenal entities behind empirical objects only the status of 'ontology-bearers' – they are a constitutive substratum we have to assume in order to explain the fact that we are given from outside the raw material, sensibilia, out of which mind organizes the perceptions.[11]

Why not preserve the noumenal veil in regard to our moral self as well? We could still recognize the fact that some moral law exists, take freedom of will to be the necessary condition of its existence, and as a consequence regard autonomy as fundamental to human nature. The noumenal constitutive substratum for the purpose of ethical choices, the ultimate mover behind our acts, would still be there, but would now remain beyond our cognitive capacities. Like the noumenal thing in itself which supports the ontological reality of empirical objects, the noumenal will as the cause of our choices would be only a conceptual tool necessary to explain the existence of moral laws.

We could compare noumenal will to the speed of light, which cannot be the direct target of sensual perception as it is the ultimate measure which carries the sensibilia to us. Our sensory experience simply cannot go beyond the means for perceiving, but our reason has established, for theoretical purposes, the speed of light by agreement, and the rationality of the agreement has been confirmed by the conformity of empirical laws to it. In like manner it is rational to agree that we have a capacity for freedom of will, that the source of the capacity cannot be an object of perception, and that free will is the cause of our actions, no matter what those actions are – unless in a particular case there is enough evidence that external reasons forced us to act against our will.

Thus, the centrepiece of my revision of Kant is a blocking-up of the holes Kant left in the transcendental wall. The result is that the wall becomes like a semi-permeable membrane. It allows the noumenal entities philosophical relevance in our world: they sustain the ontological reality of empirical objects external to us, and the metaethical reality of moral values emerging from us. At the same time, the traffic to the noumenal side is totally blocked, permitting a broader concept of autonomy. One-way traffic also reveals how misleading the name 'transcendental idealism' is for Kantianism. Transcendental empiricism would better describe where Kant laid his emphasis when he mapped out the relations between the noumenal realm and the world in which we live.

So, how does the moderated, still Kantian but more pragmatic and anthropocentric, concept of autonomy assist us in filling the 'is'–'ought' gap? Philosophical analysis, which Kant engaged to prove the general possibility of the moral law, is the key to working out normative issues as well. Two facts provide a starting point. First, autonomy is a universal property of human beings. Second, freedom is a necessary condition for autonomy. Every human individual has the potential for autonomy, and autonomy includes the capacity to obey the moral law or, in other words, to make moral choices. Hence, a moral law – if there exist any, and we have no example of a human community without any[12] – has to embrace all individuals. This means that a moral law has to be of universal application. So far we are on a beaten track. The real challenge lies ahead. There is no widely approved way of moving from universality to normative conclusions. How can we, then, sort apples from oranges?

My suggestion to get over the perpetual stumbling block is that a shared capacity, like human consciousness or human autonomy, inevitably produces uniformity in the rational judgements that are initiated by the external stimuli which activate the capacity. Sensibilia are the stimuli which cause consciousness – our capacity to be aware of the world and ourselves – to form empirical perceptions and judgements. For example, when we feel hungry our rational judgement tells us to look for food.

As for autonomy – our capacity to make choices and comprehend the moral law – conflicts of interest act as the stimuli leading to value judgements. When two hungry agents are looking for food and find the same nourishing object, a conflict of interests arises, at least if the object cannot satisfy all the needs of both agents. This conflict is not normally solved by using force, but by value judgements which carry uniformity in their treatment of conflicts; they show at least some consideration for the interests of others. Always placing one's own immediate aspirations first would only return the conflict back to the use of force. This is not how most conflicts are resolved, and it is not in accordance with the fact that we are capable of observing moral rules. Of course, value judgements arising out of conflicts of interest may themselves clash, but our experience is that they possess common features.

Thus it would not be rational to claim that a capacity, shared by a species, yields fundamentally opposite outcomes in the case of different members of that species. Sensuous stimuli produce empirical judgements that are sufficiently coherent to tell us that the world in which we, as separate individuals, live, is one and the same world. Conflicts of interest lead to value judgements that are sufficiently coherent to enable us, as separate individuals, to share the one and the same world.

In an important sense autonomy is similar to our perceptional capacities. We may have different sensual representations of one object, and we do actually hold different moral standards in regard to most, if not all, social practices. However, we readily admit that it would be irrational to accept two conflicting scientific explanations of the nature of an object. My claim is that there are situations when it would be just as irrational to say that two contradictory moral principles are both valid. What are these situations? How do we identify which among the clashing principles are the valid ones?

A merely formal requirement of universality does not rule out all sources of contradiction. For instance, consistently egoistic principles could pass the test. If each member of a group held that true moral principles are those which always promote only her own interests we would have a pot pourri of egoistic rules that were universal yet conflicting. Nevertheless, accepting that any universalizable principle could serve as moral is clearly contrary to the fact that we are able to comprehend moral laws as separate from other types of universal principles guiding our behaviour. Add to this the fact that every law, which we comprehend in some sense as a moral one, gives consideration to the interests of others, and we have enough reasons to replace the formal condition of universality with what I will call anthropocentric universality, which is meaningful for the purposes of human moral reasoning.

Our experience is that totally arbitrary and conflicting rules cannot emerge out of autonomy. I have already emphasized that in every human community some moral laws are recognized. The quality in virtue of which these laws can be identified as moral is that they have other regarding aspects. They give at least some consideration to the interests, which are expressions of a person and her choices, of more than one individual. Even the most monstrous tyrant has to involve other regarding elements in her despotism if she wants to save it from immediate and inevitable destruction.

Since the distinctive characteristic of existing moral laws is that they pay attention to other people's interests, this characteristic has to be taken into account in the theoretical analysis seeking to draw normative conclusions. Other-regardness being the only universal feature of these laws, universal in the sense that it is the only quantifier that ranks competing interests and can be found in any system of moral rules regardless of their particular contents, we have no reason to prioritize any particular individual's preferences at the beginning of a theoretical ethical inquiry.

This means that the starting point of an ethical argument must be equal consideration of interests. We have good reasons to accept that moral principles have to give consideration to everyone's interests, and that they have to apply equally in similar situations and to each of the individuals. Hence, my modest Kantianism has, already, found three substantial cornerstones for our moral inquiry: autonomy; the fact that the moral law emerges from within ourselves; and equal consideration of interests.

The reconciliation of interests, competing from an equal standing, is the task of moral laws. A moral inquiry may well turn out to justify preferential treatment of some persons and interests, but this can never be the undisputed premiss of moral reasoning. This normative conclusion has not been arrived at by smuggling in the accidentally held moral beliefs of any particular person, but by introducing into the argument the element common to every belief recognized as moral.

Like Kant, I have relied on the claim that we are immediately aware of the existence of some moral law. Since 'we' covers all humans, that is, all humans have the potential to act in accordance with some moral law, moral properties are of universal nature. This claim is supported by the empirical fact that a human community cannot exist without rules which have at least some other regarding aspects. For the purposes of moral theory these facts form the core of anthropocentric universality, providing enough material to upgrade the merely formal necessity of universalizability to a sufficient condition implicating normative conclusions that are relevant to human beings. After extracting from the facts of the empirical world – 'is' – the characteristics which are endemic to value judgements and to agents making those judgements, we arrive at a moral conclusion – 'ought': the first premisses of an ethical theory cannot prioritize any particular individual's interests.

I admitted above[13] that if only formal universality is required for moral laws it would not exclude the logical possibility of sharply contradictory or intuitively outrageous moral laws, like consistently applied egoism. Now it should be clear that these logical possibilities have as little bearing on ethical theory as unicorns have on the theory spelling out the characteristics for an object to fall within the domain of zoology. The logical possibility of unicorns does not blow life into them, nor does the logical possibility of consistent egoism turn it into a valid moral theory.

Some more clarification is needed in regard to my sympathy for Kant's initial point that we are immediately aware of the moral law, as of the starry heavens. I have denied that we have a direct perception of the contents of moral laws. Instead, I claimed that our capacity to gain knowledge of moral laws is, in a certain respect, similar to our capacity to know empirical objects. This may seem to involve a contradiction with Kant's emphasis on immediate awareness, but there is none.

We do immediately perceive the starry heaven as something which is external to us. Having granted this, it is up to rational examination of the perception to find out the empirical nature of the stars and the heaven: are they concentrations of mass in the universe or shiny lights on the arch of the sky. Likewise, we are immediately aware of the general possibility of moral laws, yet we need rational inquiry, not noumenal insight, to determine their contents. A moral inquiry neither takes us beyond human experience, nor leaves us at the mercy of arbitrary claims arising out of the blue.

Universality of moral laws does not mean that there is no room for a diversity of ethnic and cultural values. Rather, it is an indication that moral laws savour of inalienable human rights shared by everybody in virtue of their human nature. Human rights fall into the domain of fundamental moral principles, behind which there is a myriad of lesser ethical rules generated by diverse conditions. The former are of universal application since they rest on a universal property; the latter may conflict and vary since they depend on the specific properties of particular communities.

So, being a universal property of human beings, autonomy is part of the foundation for inalienable moral rights. Moral agency underpins moral principles, which appreciate their genealogy by employing rights to safeguard each agent's participation in humanity. I shall, from now on, reserve the term 'moral law' exclusively for this fundamental category of principles.

What are the inalienable rights? The answer can be found by means of rational moral inquiry, and we have just seen how autonomy stipulates that impartiality has to be the ultimate starting point of any reasoning leading to normative conclusions. In addition, autonomy is capable of delivering even more substance. Freedom of will is embedded in autonomy; it is, therefore, a uniquely and universally human property as well. Since freedom of will is the characteristic making possible the existence of moral laws in general, they have to leave room for it.

Arising from ourselves and applying to ourselves, the moral law itself is a result of choice, a result of exercising our autonomy by defining the law and respecting it. Therefore, the moral law can only exist if freedom of choice exists. Or, as Kant puts it in the *Critique of Pure Reason*:

> A constitution of *the greatest possible human freedom* according to laws, by which *the liberty of every individual can consist with the liberty of every other* (not of the greatest possible happiness, for this follows necessarily from the former), is, to say the least, a necessary idea, which must be placed at the foundation not only of the first plan of the constitution of a state, but of all its laws.[14]

And in *The Metaphysics of Morals*: '*Freedom* (independence from being constrained by another's choice), insofar as it can coexist with the freedom of every other in accordance with a universal law, is the only original right belonging to every man in virtue of his humanity.'[15]

Now we have reached the culmination of my revision of the Kantian edifice. Autonomy, and its necessary condition, freedom of will, induce substance to ethics: moral laws have to be derived from premises giving individuals impartial consideration and safeguarding freedom. Although autonomy stands for the capacity to choose, including the choice to observe the moral law, the moral choice is not an arbitrary one. We can provide reasons for respecting the ideal Kant expressed in the categorical imperative: 'I ought never to act except in such a way *that I can also will that my maxim should become a universal law*.'[16]

An ethics that claimed that we could not be responsible for our actions, and that we had no capacity to create and observe moral laws, would be self-contradictory. One suggestion to avoid this contradiction is soft determinism, but it is philosophically unsatisfactory unless the softness is given an adequate metaphysical and epistemic explanation. My modest Kantianism should be seen as an effort to this end. It is modest because it focuses on the empirically conceivable common nature and social structures of humans. It is Kantian because it finds autonomous agency to be at the heart of human nature and behaviour.

I have expended much effort to derive autonomy from its Kantian pedigree, and admit finding his epistemology and ontology, what he confusingly calls transcendental idealism, to be a very appealing account of the world. Contemporary philosophers prefer to assume autonomy without the Kantian extras, and there is no doubt that the concept can serve as a firm foundation for normative ethics even outside of Kant's general philosophical framework.

Autonomy is always a useful theoretical notion which focuses on the morally relevant essence of human nature: freedom of will, moral responsibility following from that freedom, and, ultimately, the fact that we have the capacity to create and observe moral laws and that we use this capacity. This shared agency is a precondition for moral laws which any ethical inquiry has to accommodate, with or without metaphysics, because without it ethics would be left short of a rational basis. It is not uncommon for philosophers to contend the statement 'That freedom is of inherent value cannot be proven'[17], but, as Rawls admits, 'we long to derive its law'[18]. My longing has resulted in an affair with metaethics, and its offspring is the derivation of autonomy contained in this chapter.

Where is ethics led by our common nature? A shared essence implies a shared interest. As long as we want to live we have an interest to be what we are. More than anything, humanity is earmarked by autonomy. Thus, ethics has to value autonomy highest. Our interest to be what we are is best looked after by giving the highest moral protection to the features that make us humans.

Human rights are the elite force safeguarding our autonomy. A moral inquiry, giving equal consideration to everyone's interests, is bound to prioritize human rights, protecting our most valuable ethical asset. They are, to use Ronald Dworkin's term,[19] trumps which can push aside other moral obligations arising out of contingent interests, arrangements and undertakings. Here we have a modest Kantian ethical platform which supports the forthcoming normative arguments.

Chapter 5

Autonomy and promissory obligations

KANT ON PROMISES

Back to promises. Kant sees that the duty to keep promises arises out of a merger between the promisor's and the promisee's will: 'But what belongs to the promisor does not pass to the promisee (as acceptant) by the *separate* will of either but only by the *united will* of both, and consequently only insofar as both wills are declared *simultaneously.*'[1]

Kant claims that the simultaneous declaration cannot take place empirically but, rather, consists of the creation of a kind of united noumenal will. This new noumenal joint venture is to him the basis of the duty to keep promises and, consequently, of the moral binding-ness of contracts.

> Here both acts, promise and acceptance, are represented not as following one upon another but . . . as proceeding from a single *common* will. . . .
>
>   That I ought to keep my promise is a postulate of pure reason (pure as abstracting from all sensible conditions of space and time in what concerns the concept of Right).[2]

Kant's account requires too much charity to accept that in promising we create a joint noumenal will which immediately raises to our awareness the obligation. I want to find a less cumbersome manner in which to move from the autonomy of human nature to the duty to keep promises.

Let us have a closer look at Kant's explicit example of the duty to pay debts. It is offered in *Groundwork* as a test case of false promising. However, I do not think that it successfully establishes why debts should be paid. Kant tells us about a man who borrows money knowing that he will not be able to pay it back, and the point is that this position would contradict itself as a universal maxim:

> For the universality of a law that every one believing himself to be in need can make any promise he pleases with the intention not to keep it would make promising, and the very purpose of promising, itself impossible, since no one would believe he was being promised anything, but would laugh at utterances of this kind as empty shams. . . . [3]

> This incompatibility with the principle of duty to others leaps to the eye more obviously when we bring in examples of attempts on the freedom and property of others. For then it is manifest that a violator of the rights of man intends to use the person of others merely as a means without taking into consideration that, as rational beings, they ought always at the same time to be rated as ends – that is, only as beings who must themselves be able to share in the end of the very same action. [4]

These passages offer us at least three ways to interpret Kant's justification for the axiom 'debts should be paid'. First, Kant's own stand takes us back to his metaphysics, to the noumenal insight which is the ultimate resort distinguishing good from bad and giving credibility to the categorical imperative. I have dismissed this path as too chimerical.

Second, we could adopt a neo-Kantian approach, push the metaphysics aside and focus on the latter passage which puts the emphasis on treating persons as ends in themselves. But this would help us only a little towards a justification for the duty since neo-Kantianism shelves the metaphysical foundation of personhood, which for Kant establishes a person's intrinsic moral value as an end in itself. After metaphysics is rejected, praising the value of persons as ends in themselves is just an unsupported axiom: we have to keep our promises because they are made between persons, and persons have intrinsic value which will be violated if we do not honour the duty to keep promises.

Despite the intuitive appeal of the intrinsic value generated by membership of our species, the question of the origin of the moral force of this value is left open, and therefore the axiom stating the duty becomes vulnerable. For instance, our inquiry is dealing with explicit promises, financial contracts which the parties undertake with the particular purpose of benefiting themselves. These promises are made in order to use the other parties as means to obtain benefits, yet there is nothing wrong with it.

Financial contracts may, after they have been entered into, trigger respect for obligations that would meet Kant's postulate that the other party ought not be treated merely as a means. However, since the parties' motivation for entering into the contract is usually purely self-interested, from where does the respect for obligations come? What introduces, all of a sudden, sanctity into promises we routinely make with the purpose of using others as means to our own ends? I find it difficult to see in the contract any such characteristic which would be capable of doing the job, and noumenal insight, natural law and consequentialism have appeared as more or less wanting explanations too.

We have to establish the value of persons as ends in themselves outside of the actual sequence of the contractual events if we want to say that promises must be kept because persons are to be treated as ends in themselves. Neo-Kantians beg this problem. Hence, the second interpretation leaves the argument deficient. When the metaphysical foundation is in tatters all a neo-Kantian has is a blunt assertion of the intrinsic value of human beings. However, this value is the centrepiece of normative pursuits, and as such it is the principle calling for justification rather than the tool to churn out duties.

Next, let us proceed to a third alternative with which to explain Kant's example. It regards the act of promising as a social practice generating rationality in human behaviour. I shall quote R.P. Wolff on this:

> The key to correct understanding of this example, and thereby to an understanding of Kant's moral philosophy as a whole, is the concept of social activity governed by rules which specify a system of expectations, commitments, burdens, and rewards attached to the roles defined in the activity.[5]

According to Wolff, the duty to keep promises flows from the categorical imperative, which lays down a criterion for practical rationality: 'What this means, concretely, is that it is irrational to adopt a set of policies which so conflict with one another that it is logically impossible to carry them out in toto.'[6]

I think Wolff gives us an elucidating explanation of the nature of the categorical imperative as a medium for rational judgement, but as an account of promising he fails to take us far enough. Kant's example shows us why it is wrong intentionally to make a false promise. The core idea is that if we promise something while knowing, or having decided, that we will not keep the promise, our promises become meaningless.

Wolff presents Kant's position in more understandable terms. However, Wolff's account, focusing on the human rationality, leaves me wondering why we would not be entitled to change our mind when we have sincerely promised something, and later develop a new state of mind which is as sincere and expressed as explicitly as the original promise was. This sequential process would guarantee that at any one moment there would be no inconsistency in the adopted set of policies. Hence, we would be able to preserve our rationality – the logical consistency of our intentions – even without keeping our promises. It would remain true that the totality of a promisor's shifting commitments, adopted over the course of history, could not be carried out. But why should this matter? The totality of historical commitments will always be contradictory anyway.

The ethical criterion requiring logical consistency to prevail between making a promise and fulfilling it cannot be the mere existence of a contradiction. History is full of contradictory statements and actions, yet it may depict a rational course of events. It may be rational for me to want one thing at moment A, and another at moment B, although the two intentions are contradictory. One day I prefer vanilla ice cream to chocolate, another day the other way round. Both preferences are rational ones because they reflect what I want. Only if I had preferred both A and B simultaneously would there be something irrational in my intentions – although not always, as I may want two things equally badly without being irrational. I cannot be in Europe and Australia at the same time, yet it would not be irrational to want to be in the two places if I happen to like them both a lot.

What is the ethically relevant variable that confines the temporal continuum over which contradictions are not allowed in rational ethical judgements and descriptions within the time which starts when the original promise is uttered, and ends when it is fulfilled? The ethically relevant variable cannot be the utterance, since that is what we seek to explain. It cannot be persons as ends in themselves because the contractual context, most often, is that of using others as means for our own ends. A noumenal insight has already been dismissed, and autonomy is excluded too if it is understood only as a capacity to master one's own life: why would we not be able to master away the promise?

I accept that ethics is more than a matter of mere preferences, it is subordinate to rationality. Therefore, rationality provides a criterion to draw some distinctions between ethical and unethical behaviour: intentions behind an ethically sound course of action should be non-contradictory in the sense that they should be consistent with a set of non-contradictory ethical principles. Hence, two ethically conflicting intentions cannot be correct simultaneously. Against this requirement it is evident that something is wrong (i.e. I commit a wrong) if I, through promising, adopt a policy to pay a debt while knowing that I will not pay it. However, this does not give us an explanation as to why it would be a wrong if I sincerely made the promise and later changed my mind. The outcome of my criticism is that Wolff's rewriting of Kant is unable to explain the general bindingness of promising, the duty that carries its validity over time and against the promisor's later desires. It is a serious defect which forces us to look for other ways to solve the problem.

After examining the three interpretations of Kant's example we are entitled to conclude only that insincere promising is wrong. That is, we have a reason to morally condemn fraud because it is irrational to act on two contradicting principles at one moment of time. However, we are after a broader theory which asks why promises are binding even when the promisor afterwards changes her mind. For two reasons Kant's example is not the key to the broader theory. First, it focuses only on fraudulent promises. Second, it focuses on the autonomy of the receiving party, the promisee.

I shall reject the much cherished view that the promisee's autonomy is the main moral entity supporting the promise. My suggestion is that we should shift the focus to the promisor: it is her autonomy that counts. The promisor's autonomy is the logical starting point for the inquiry because it is the acts of the promisor which bring into existence the promise. The promisor decides whether she comes to owe the duty to the other person or not. If she does not want the duty, she does not make the promise. It is true that after a promise has been made the promisee has a right to expect delivery. However, this right rests on the act of promising performed by a promisor.

This is significantly different from human rights, such as a person's right to bodily immunity. We are under the duty not to cause others bodily harm, regardless of whether we want to be obliged, because the duty is based on the rights of others as autonomous agents. Quite differently, we are under a duty to honour our promises only because we decide to be bound by them, and utter our decisions to the other parties. Without the promisors' own initiative the duties and rights related to promises would not exist.

The promisor's autonomy gives us an ethically relevant variable with which to mark out of a history infested with contradictions the temporal continuum over which promissory incongruities are not allowed: if it is my autonomy which makes my promises binding, it is the time from the utterance of the original promise to its fulfilment which is relevant to the application of the rationality condition expressed in the categorical imperative. Within this period of time my actions pertaining to the promise should not be contradictory. Thus, the soundest deontological basis for the duty to keep promises is the autonomy of the promising agent, which this study has extracted from a generally Kantian, but much weakened, ethical platform.

A THEORY OF PROMISSORY AUTONOMY

The discussion above has purported to show that there is room for a theory which mounts promises on the autonomy of the promising agent, rather than on social conventions or attributes relating to the promisee. I shall soon spell out the details of my theory of promising, but let us first add momentum to the argument by looking at the interpretation of Kant put forward by Charles Fried in his book *Contract as Promise*. The following quotations summarize Fried's account of autonomy as the basis of the obligation to keep promises:

> The obligation to keep a promise is grounded not in arguments of utility but in respect for individual autonomy and in trust. . . .
>
> An individual is morally bound to keep his promises because he has intentionally invoked a convention whose function it is to give grounds – moral grounds – for another to expect the promised performance. . . .
>
> To summarize: There exists a convention that defines the practice of promising and its entailments. This convention provides a way that a person may create expectations in others. By virtue of the basic Kantian principles of trust and respect, it is wrong to

invoke that convention in order to make a promise, and then to break it.[7]

These moral grounds cover contracts as well:

> since a contract is first of all a promise, the contract must be kept because a promise must be kept. . . . [8]
>
> The moral force behind contract as promise is autonomy: the parties are bound to their contract because they have chosen to be.[9]

So, in Fried's version, the binding force in promising comes from the fact that the parties, as autonomous persons, have chosen to be bound. But this still leaves open the same question that troubles the Humean empiricist: if the contract is binding only because the parties have so chosen, why cannot any of the parties at any time make a new choice and get rid of the obligations? I shall borrow from James Gordley to further illustrate this point:

> In contrast, it is hard to see how Kantian or utilitarian philosophy could give a reason why promises are binding other than the fact that the promisor has chosen to commit himself. According to Kant, to act morally one must act in obedience to the law that a rational being would freely choose as the measure of its own actions. Thus, Kant arrived at the 'categorical imperative' to which all moral action must conform: one must act only by those rules that one could will to be universal law. Promises are binding, he said, because one could not will, as a universal law, that promises should be broken. Promises would then be idle words. Thus, the categorical imperative brings us right back to where we were with the will theorists, and before them with Wolff, and before him with Hobbes and Locke: promises are binding because they have been defined to be.[10]

The problem Gordley spells out is, basically, the same which I raised above[11] as a reason for getting involved with the philosophical fundamentals instead of just taking for granted the intrinsic value of autonomy. It is true that Fried props up the binding force of promises with the notion of a convention supported by trust and respect. Nevertheless, this only amounts to explaining why promises are generally upheld. It does not say why someone would still be under the moral obligation if she, unilaterally, decided to throw over the promise, regardless of the mistrust and disgust cast upon her.

My modest Kantianism advances one step further from Fried's position and can deal with Gordley's criticism. We have to focus on the fact that the promisor creates expectations in regard to her future behaviour. She does this by expressing a plan of future actions which she undertakes to bring about. The promisor deliberately sets limits upon the future exercise of her capacity to make choices, that is, upon the exercise of her own autonomy, by committing herself to a particular future course of events.

A promise is an expression of a free will imposing restrictions upon its own freedom. The human will is free. It is capable of choosing. This includes a capacity for choices narrowing the scope of future choices. We call these choices promises when they are made explicit to other human beings and restrict our future liberty by our own volition. A promise binds us to the future we have declared by our will because we have decided so.

Mastering our own future through choices that bring into existence moral rights and duties is part of being an autonomous person and promising is a practice which realizes this capacity by shaping the future after our will. The future is not yet actual when we make the promise, but part of it gets determined: it becomes a true proposition in regard to the future that either we keep our promise, or we commit a moral wrong.[12]

The promisor exercises her autonomy when she conceives the moral duty to restrain her behaviour within the confines of the options she allocates to herself. A human will can establish the morally binding contractual obligations because as autonomous beings we are capable of doing so. The expression of an autonomous will is not just a contingent, ethically irrelevant moment in the endless sequence of events, but a demonstration of the capacity to reshape the future through the imposition and observance of moral principles. This statement amounts to more than just a definition. It is a true description of a uniquely human characteristic, and as such it is powerful enough to make true the moral principle that promises should be kept.

Contract theorists are right when they say that promisors narrow their future options by introducing moral meaning into their utterances in order to enhance their interests. I have now amplified the contractual account with an explanation as to why promises retain their moral bindingness no matter how the promisors' interests later evolve. The moral permanence of promissory obligations rests on the autonomy of the promisors, on their capacity to shape the future by introducing permanence which is valid independent of changes of mind and mood.

If the committing will was free unilaterally to revoke the commitment at any time, the commitment would be rendered meaningless. This would suggest that autonomous persons lack the capacity to impose binding limitations upon themselves. But persons lacking this capacity would not be autonomous. In an important sense they would not be able to master their conduct: they would not be free to choose that they narrow their future options. Therefore, as far as we are autonomous, we are capable of choosing to be morally bound by our promises no matter how much we would later want to get rid of them. And we are autonomous. We are born with the capacity to make binding decisions about our future behaviour.

This bindingness reduces our future freedom to shape the world, yet it does not, normally, reduce our autonomy. As concluded in Chapter 4, freedom is a necessary condition for autonomy. However, autonomy is not equal to freedom but stands for the agency in us, for the capacity to make choices – including ethical choices which constrain our future freedom. Although *some* freedom is a necessary condition for autonomy, a *total* freedom would destroy it because ethical choices would no more be possible: if we were at liberty to do whatever might please us at any particular moment, then moral obligations would be void.

The dependence–destruction relationship between freedom and autonomy leads to moral constraints on freedom on two fronts. First, human rights safeguard autonomy as the inherently valuable source of morality and humanity. They guarantee each individual the minimum amount of freedom which is necessary for autonomy to exist, and impose a ban on total freedom which would negate autonomy. Second, our own choices, one category of which are promises, limit our freedom by determining the future according to our will through the introduction of moral obligations. These choices are exercises of our autonomy, a skill we are naturally endowed with, and as such they are subject to the more fundamental moral constraints of the first type, which arise directly out of the inherent value of autonomy: human rights override the choices that would violate our own autonomy, or the autonomy of others.

In other words, we can manipulate our freedom through our choices as long as we leave ourselves a minimum of freedom necessary for autonomy to exist, and disallow a total freedom which would destroy autonomy. I hope that these distinctions clarify the relationship between autonomy and freedom. In spite of embracing freedom, autonomy is a more complex and extensive human property. As agency it is a natural characteristic of human beings. It is absolute in the sense that all humans share the potential for it, and can realize that potential if their freedom falls within the range conducive to the realization.

If freedom were depleted altogether, we would not be able to choose. If it were all-encompassing, we would not be able to choose to be irreversibly bound by our commitments. These facts reveal that freedom is a relative concept. Its moral connotation depends on the interaction between the facts of the world and us as autonomous agents in that world. The most general facts affecting freedom are the scarcity of the world's resources, limitations of our skills, and competing claims of autonomous agents. After examining and weighing these facts against more or less rationally established values we, as autonomous agents, arrive at moral judgements. These judgements introduce moral constraints which take over the control of freedom from the less sophisticated factual constraints.

The metaethical thesis of this study has been that we are immediately aware of some moral law, which proves that we carry the moral agency within us. Our potential to moral agency excludes the total denial of freedom, as well as total freedom, from our moral options. It explains why we cannot avoid the conclusion that autonomy has intrinsic ethical value: autonomy includes the capacity for moral judgement and that judgement has to protect the capacity which produces it.

Autonomy would generate its own destruction if it spawned moral judgements that did not value autonomy. It is rational and logical to claim that any agency seeks to survive. This is also the natural aim of an agency: survival is what living organisms do for their living. Agency is absolute and counts first because without it there would be no agents, there would not be us as we are.

It is nothing but natural, logical and rational that the agency in us seeks to safeguard its existence and operations, and it is also what we intuitively strive for in our lives. This means that my account of autonomy, freedom and promising fares well in the light of the criteria Chapter 3 suggested for the testing of the viability of an ethical theory. It is reasonable that ethics sets limits as to the minimum and maximum amount of freedom we ought to have, and that within the set range we may choose to introduce further constraints on freedom by promising.

We have explained why our promises which shape the future by restricting our freedom do not erode our autonomous agency, and why autonomy is the primary concept of the two ethically. Freedom may be eroded within the minimum/maximum range, autonomy may never.[13] It is another moral issue what the exact minimum amount of freedom necessary for autonomy is, and when exactly freedom becomes so total that it threatens autonomy. These are problems which have to be settled separately in each particular area of life. In this study I shall suggest answers only in relation to insolvency.

Finally, a number of objections may be raised against my theory which takes the promisor's autonomous choice as the source of moral obligations in promising.[14] One objection is that it makes promises absolute: they are binding until fulfilled, or until the promisee grants a release. It would be counter-intuitive if we were never justified in breaking our promises, even if they turned out to be fatal to our autonomy (voluntary slavery), immoral (promise to thrill-kill), cause great harm (an election promise to turn a suburb's last tract of park into a car park) or absurd (promise to deliver a dead person a bottle of milk each Tuesday).

However, promissory autonomy is able to steer clear of these anomalies. In the subsequent chapters it will become more explicit that if a promisor's autonomy collapses as a consequence of her promise, that promise turns void. A promissory obligation is a derivative of autonomy: it cannot cause the collapse of the very property which is necessary for the obligation to exist in the first place.

The principle that promises must be kept may also be overridden by other moral principles. Far from being absolute, promissory obligations must often give way to more fundamental moral considerations which may rest on the autonomy of the promisor, promisee or third persons. The more fundamental considerations may intervene because human rights are trumps that are capable of overriding lesser rights and duties. These trumps have the power to deal with immoral promises.

It should be noted that promissory autonomy allows for different kinds of promises. Some may be made to promote a particular good. If a better way to promote that good is later found, it may be reasonable to reconsider the original promise. Yet

the onus is clearly on the promisor to show that it is more beneficial to all of the parties involved that the original promise is
discharged than that it is beneficial only to herself. My theory does
not exclude consequences from affecting the bindingness of a
promise, but it requires that, other things being equal, promises
cannot lapse only because promisors' preferences in regard to
consequences happen to change. Thus, the threat of great harm can
expunge a promissory obligation.

As for promises to a dead person, my reply would be that after a
promisee's death the relationship between the promisor and
promisee changes. When the promisor exercises her power to introduce moral bindingness by promising, the promisee obtains the
power to require performance or grant release. If the promisee dies,
the promisor must deliberate what the will of the deceased would
have been in the new circumstances: would she have demanded
accomplishment, or would it have become so trivial that it makes
sense to assume that she would have released the promisor? Thus,
we have flexibility as to promises to the dead without having to
presume that all their interests become meaningless.[15] The flexibility
may be more constrained if the contents of the promise are such
that a third party, for example the promisee's descendants, are
involved. In that case their interests could assume the place of the
dead promisee's interests, and preserve the moral bindingness of the
original promise.

Overall, there is nothing in my theory which would compel us to
take promissory moral obligations as absolute. On the contrary, it is
well-equipped to explain the various degrees of bindingness that
our intuitions and practices attach to promises in real life. What the
particular answer is in each situation depends heavily on the facts
involved. Therefore, I will not get involved any deeper in these
issues, except for the problems surrounding bankruptcy. For my
purposes it is sufficient that the theory is able to keep the counter-
intuitive examples at bay. It allows, roughly, for the same amount of
resilience to promises as our intuitions, common sense and legal
practices do.

Another way to object to my argument is to return the focus to
the promisee's interests. It could be emphasized that they have to
count because promisees have the power to grant a release to the
promisors. I accept the validity of this point, yet it does not refute
my theory. From where do promisees get this power to release
promisors? They do not have it before promisors exercise their

autonomy by making a promise. Therefore, the power of release is handed over by the promisors, who both incur the obligation and provide promisees with a proxy to delete it. The promisees' interests count, but they count only because promisors make them count.

Promissory autonomy as the source of moral obligations in promising clears the difficulties which were summarized in the above quote from Gordley. He thought that the older naturalist concepts were needed because any theory seeking the ultimate source of law or morality in human choice could not resolve the moral bindingness of promising.[16]

I think that Gordley makes a mistake: it is just the *human* capacity for autonomous choices, understood as a characteristic typical of the species, that forges the chain of moral obligation in the bond established by a promise. The act of promising calls this capacity into service and establishes the duty to keep the promise, and the duty is sustained even against our will because we, as autonomous persons, took the initiative to establish it. To claim otherwise would be to claim that we do not have the potential to narrow the scope of our future choices at our will. This would be a gross understatement of our mental competence and a false description of our everyday moral consciousness.

We have now found why moral responsibility, made possible by the freedom of will, has permanence over time even with respect to promissory obligations which we bring into existence by our own will. Being autonomous agents, we are capable of choices which limit our future choices. Rawls has pointed out that an

> essential feature of Kant's moral constructivism is that the first principles of right and justice are seen as specified by a proce- dure of construction (the CI-procedure) the form and structure of which mirrors our free moral personality as both reasonable and rational.[17]

I have applied the procedure of construction, which mirrors our nature as autonomous agents, to establish the duty to keep promises with the effect that debts should be paid.

SHOULD DEBTS BE PAID?

The moral force behind a contract is a promise. Hume's and Kant's theories represent the two major ways to justify public enforcement of contractual debts. The Humean, and utilitarian, point is that debts should be paid because it is in the interest of the parties involved. Consequently, society should support this aim. The Kantian thesis is that our autonomy supports the moral duty to keep our promises. Laws should adhere to this duty and enforce debts. The third historically influential normative tradition, natural law, has also put its weight behind the duty. However, I have paid little attention to natural law theories because they have been subject to crushing philosophical criticism.

We have now reached an important conclusion: ethics requires that, as a general rule, promises should be kept. Whether this principle spells out a moral duty or not, and whether the eventual duty is an absolute one or allows for exceptions, the theories disagree. I find the criticism invalidating Hume's argument powerful against utilitarianism as well. On the other hand, Kant has been attacked on the basis of his peculiar metaphysical views, and on the lack of bindingness of the mere act of human choice. I have tried to free the Kantian concept of autonomy from some of its dubious metaphysical burdens. Also, I have formulated a theory of promissory autonomy that explains why the promises of autonomous persons impose moral obligations upon them.

After these revisions it seems to me that autonomy is the superior source of promissory moral obligations. It gives good deontological reasons for the duty to pay our debts. The appraisals of hypothetical contractors and utilitarians increase the credibility of this duty: we should find it easy to comply with it because the consequences of compliance are good. We have established why debts should be paid; it is now time to look at the ethical problems we face when debts turn sour.

Part III

Ethical principles of insolvency
Should debts always be paid?

Chapter 6

Going broke, breaking promises

Moral philosophy tells us that we should stick to our promises. This is the starting point of contract law as well. The principle being sound and clear, what could be said for breaking promises in going broke, and for an institution which grants the discharge to breachers? Ethics is often riddled with discordances. Against this background it may be surprising to discover that from different sources springs a widespread unanimity favouring the release of insolvents. Before going to the deontological tangles, I shall group together some less knotty points.

FORGIVENESS

Christianity has played an important role in Western culture and societies. One of its central doctrines is forgiveness. In tracing the historical origins of bankruptcy we noticed that the Bible advises us to forgive debts every seventh year:

> At the end of *every* seven years thou shalt make a release.
> And this *is* the manner of the release: Every creditor that lendeth *ought* unto his neighbour shall release *it*; he shall not exact *it* of his neighbour, or of his brother; because it is called the LORD'S release.[1]

The Biblical cancellation of debts is an act of mercy toward the debtor, the poor brother.[2] This attitude has left its mark on present day language: we often call discharge in bankruptcy the forgiving of debts. But, as a moral concept, forgiving requires that the agent who forgives contributes to the act.

Can a legal institution grant an excuse? I do not think so. When discharge is called excuse or mercy or forgiveness the meaning is normally well understood: the debtor gets rid of the debt. But legal institutions enforce rights, which are supposed to apply in a similar manner to every individual, while forgiving is based on the sympathetic will of the person excusing. Sympathy is a subjective attitude of mind, it cannot be brought about by decree.

Creditors may, by virtue of their position, decide to give up their claims whenever they want. Nothing prevents them from observing the duty to give mercy, if we assumed such a duty, but they cannot be forced to forgive. Therefore, an institution discharging the debt against the creditor's will does not represent forgiveness, which can be a morally meaningful term only in relation to persons willing to forgive, and forgiving does not amount to a justification of the institutional revoking of contractual debts.

IMPOSSIBILITY

Even if the duty to keep promises is given the strictest possible interpretation, to the effect that promises must always be kept, there are circumstances when the duty simply becomes void. If the duty requires an agent to perform impossible acts, it would be absurd to say that the agent has to perform them. A human being cannot do what is impossible for her to do: 'ought' implies 'can'.

Bankrupts are often in a situation in which there is no way they can meet their financial liabilities. The absurdity of imposing moral duties requiring the performance of impossible acts entails, in this particular case, that there is no sense in saying that insolvent debtors are under a moral obligation to pay all that they owe. Thus, there is nothing ethically suspicious in relieving from their excessive burden those debtors who do not have any chance of paying.

This ethical point is recognized in the theory of contract law. The doctrine of impossibility overrides contractual rights in two senses. First, it is seen as a supervening rule of law capable of annulling contractual obligations: 'the impossibility doctrine says that in certain instances a contract obligation which would otherwise create a liability will be excused because some sort of performance is impossible in some sense'.[3]

The second way of understanding the doctrine makes it a tool for exposing all the consequences of a contract. It determines how the unexpected risks and damages should be shared between the parties when no explicit clause in the contract can be used as a guide: 'The impossibility doctrine may be a method of interpreting what was implicit in the agreement from the start'.[4]

Charles Fried favours the first interpretation in his *Contract as Promise*. According to Fried, the parties have had no will on all of the issues arising from circumstances of impossibility. The gaps are covered by the general legal framework, including bankruptcy laws. Instead of letting the losses lie where they have fallen, the law has moved to support the principle of sharing: contracts create a common enterprise in which accidents have to be shared too.[5]

The legal reasoning described above reflects the fact that if moral obligations arising from promising were absolute and, as a consequence, contractual obligations were absolute, contracts would be generally impossible because no contract can explicitly state obligations in every potential situation. If we have contracts, there must always be interpretation from more general principles. The impossibility arising from insolvency is one example of the circumstances calling for reassessment of contracts.

It seems evident that impossibility to pay the debt relinquishes an insolvent's moral obligation to perform. This leaves the question open in cases where debtors might, at some later instance, have enough income or property to satisfy at least some of their creditors' claims. We must go further in the analysis to find out if the duty to pay bounces back when the debtor's financial situation improves.

LEGALISM

One could say that an insolvent debtor is under no obligation, moral or legal, to pay her debts in a society where there is a bankruptcy law allowing a discharge. Versions of this argument have been offered by Elizabeth Warren[6] and Philip Shuchman.[7] According to Warren, a debt contract requires us to pay, *or* to discharge the promise to pay through bankruptcy. What this means, in effect, is that a contract as a promise includes implicit side conditions which stipulate the revoking of the promise.

Warren explains why, in particular cases, discharged bankrupts should not feel any moral stigma, but I do not think that her thesis amounts to an ethical justification for the institution, for the laws granting the right to discharge. The ethical justification has to go beyond the positive law and explain what ethical sense it makes to have the law in the first place. Otherwise it could as well be said that, in the absence of the discharge laws, it is completely morally unproblematic to uphold the insolvent's obligations till her death, or even extend them to her family.

Philip Shuchman sees promising in terms of actions defined by rules which are a set of constitutive conventions. These rules may have a moral element when the promising parties in a contract are natural persons, but contracts with corporations are only constitutive. Business lending lacks any moral component. Therefore, relinquishment of debts to corporations is only a matter of legal and economic expediency. At least in these cases a legalist justification for discharge is all we need.

I see much appeal in Shuchman's argument. Businesses give credit in order to make profits and they should be aware of the risk. If they do not get their money, that is just part of the business. In the final chapter I shall return to the question whether we owe any moral duty to pay back to our corporate lenders, or whether it is just the fear of public enforcement that makes us perform. In regard to debts owed to natural persons, Shuchman thinks that a promise to pay tells that one is to pay unless certain excusing conditions are present. He also sets out a utilitarian account of the excuses. It takes us to the next justification for the exoneration of bankrupts.

UTILITARIANISM

The most common argument for laws protecting the debtor is that their consequences are favourable. They are seen as producing the best outcome, at least from the debtor's and society's point of view, but often from the creditor's perspective as well. Utilitarian ethics is observed, for instance, in the committee reports which have formed the basis of recent insolvency or bankruptcy law reforms in England, Australia and Finland.[8]

It is obvious that to the debtor the discharge is a fortunate event. So far the utilitarian argument seems evident. It is also widely accepted that indefinite enforcement of the insolvent's debts has harmful effects to society as a whole. If the debtor's income is bound to go to her creditors, without any hope of satisfying them within a reasonable time, it becomes irrational for her to have paid employment.[9] A more attractive alternative is, at least in a Western welfare society, to obtain from social security the minimal income she needs to subsist. Without a discharge, people who could be taxpayers contributing to the community easily become only consumers of common assets. Hence, in the utilitarian account, it is not in society's interest to prop up an overwhelming burden of debt, even though debts, as a general rule, ought to be paid.

What are the positive consequences of a discharge to the creditor? Does she not incur a loss, and should not the generation of loss be discouraged? This is the crucial question a utilitarian, propounding discharge, has to answer. However, she has a way around the problem. Normally creditors do not have any hope of getting their money from bankrupt debtors – whether bankruptcy laws contain provisions for discharge or not. Most debtors are so poor that in no circumstances could their income and property fit the bill.[10]

In addition, it has been argued that the supply of credit is fully elastic.[11] This means that credit losses increase the price of credit. In the end the cost of bankruptcies is borne not collectively by the creditors but by the debtors as a group. The debtors should not complain of this extra levy, rather they should consider it as a kind of insurance premium for the cover of limited liability. Hence, from the utilitarian point of view, it normally makes no difference to the creditors as a group whether a discharge is granted or not. The amount of loss will be the same anyway, and whatever has gone down the drain will be recovered from other debtors. Creditors may even get some advantage from letting bygones be bygones. Instead of the futile pursuit of past interests they are freed to concentrate on exploiting the opportunities of the future.

Even if the losses to creditors, as a result of discharge, are greater than the gains to other parties, a utilitarian might argue that the outcome is ethically just. The principle of diminishing marginal utility tells us that money creates more beneficial effects in the hands of those in need than in the rich lender's bank account. In the final count of the units of utility a better overall result is achieved if the law protects the interests of the bankrupt, the financially weaker party. A discharge brings about distributive justice: the bankrupt has lost everything, and is poorer than her creditors. She should be brought to more equal standing with her fellow citizens.[12]

Bankruptcy laws providing relief from unbearable debts appear to be ethically just in the utilitarian sense. This conclusion may, nevertheless, be criticized on the same basis as utilitarianism in general. The first source of criticism is the problem of calculation. Insofar as discharge causes damage it is borne by the creditors. How can we be sure that the harm to creditors is not greater than the benefits to other parties? We have found strong evidence in favour of the beneficial effects of discharge, but theoretically this question could still be raised by the opponents of liberal bankruptcy laws.

The other target for criticism may be the utilitarian view that no moral obligations exist independent of the principle of utility. Whether there are any non-consequentialist obligations is an unresolved dispute in moral philosophy. However, all deontologists allege that at least some obligations cannot be overridden by utilitarian calculations. An example is the duty to keep promises, the parent of the duty to pay debts. A deontologist defending this duty may oppose discharge, no matter how beneficial it appears to be. Would insolvency laws be different if they were shaped by deontological ethics instead of utilitarian thinking? Next, we shall enter the non-consequentialist debate on discharge of debts.

Chapter 7

Deontological ethics and insolvency

It would be easy to assume that deontological theories are hostile to discharge of debts. The debtor has promised to pay and, as a matter of principle, promises ought to be kept; therefore it would be wrong to release insolvents against their creditors' will. The reasoning is simple and palpable, yet a closer ethical scrutiny reveals its hollowness. Deontological ethics not only allows for discharge but accentuates it as a right which safeguards the most fundamental human values.

A deontologist does not have to stand for unqualified obligations. Indeed, one of the reasons why natural law theories proved unviable was the absolutism they propounded. This chapter looks at two deontological ways to justify the discharge of insolvents' debts: we shall apply John Rawls' principles of justice to the ethics of bankruptcy, and examine what implications my theory of promissory autonomy has when a promisor goes broke.

DISTRIBUTIVE JUSTICE

In discussing the philosophical fundamentals of credit in Chapter 2 we noted that, according to Rawls, the duty to pay debts rests on the principle of fairness, chosen in the Rawlsian[1] original position and making it a duty to do one's share in a social practice established to further one's own interests. However, the principle of fairness only applies if the social practice satisfies Rawls' two principles of justice.[2] Hence, the duty to keep promises has a subordinate status. It is inferior to the two principles of justice which guarantee the political rights of all the members of a just society, and maximize the distributive entitlements of its worst-off members.[3]

I will try to avoid going into Rawls' theory in any detail, but it is

clear that it can be used in favour of discharge. A bankrupt individual is in the worst-off wealth bracket; she has more debts than
property. At least at the moment of bankruptcy no one can be
worse off financially. She is also denied many civil rights and liberties enjoyed by her fellow citizens. Assuming that Rawls is correct,
social justice requires that the life prospects of bankrupts are
improved. If this is achieved by annihilating their debts, the
measure is ethically just.

Rawls adds a qualification to the principle of fairness which tells
us that the choosers in the original position reject an absolutely
binding duty to comply with promises. This qualification should be
relevant to other procedural accounts of promising as well. For
instance, in Thomas Scanlon's paper, 'Promises and practices',[4] the
potential promising parties generate moral bindingness to promises
by agreeing to the principle of fidelity because fortification of the
institution serves their interests. In particular, the introduction of
morality is in the promisors' interest since it strengthens the
promisees' expectations of getting their assets back, thus making
the promisees more willing to enter into the contract.

However, it is hard to believe that promisors would agree on a
principle of fidelity that would make promises morally binding even
in the face of unexpected hardships such as insolvency. Therefore,
as Scanlon's principle was validated by the hypothetical acceptance
of both the promising party and the receiving party, it would be
adopted only in a form which revokes the moral duty when insurmountable obstacles impede the performance. In summary, theories
seeking the moral meaning of promises from hypothetical contracts
and conventions cannot make non-payment due to insolvency a
moral wrong if the interests of the potential contractors are taken
as equal – and we have seen that there can be no morally relevant
reasons for unequal treatment of interests on the level of first
premisses of an ethical theory.

Here we should also recollect Philip Shuchman's view that
bankruptcy makes utilitarian sense as a tool for social justice. His
points are that debtors may make more beneficial use of the money
than their creditors, and that the wealth transfer effect of
bankruptcy is relatively minor. Even in the United States, the
country with the most liberal bankruptcy laws, the wealth transfer
effect has not amounted to more than 1 per cent of the funds used
annually for social welfare and business subsidies. Shuchman

concludes that the distributive function should not make bankruptcy a morally disapproved institution.[5]

Yet another way of seeing bankruptcy in the context of distributive justice is offered by Charles Fried. According to him, a contractual relation establishes a morally meaningful bond between the parties. This means that, in the case of unexpected difficulties, they have a duty to share the burden.[6] However, I am not convinced that the duty to share could be established from the fact of contract alone. Most contracts are made in order to seek economic benefits. They are technical devices for promoting the agents' self-interest. As such, I do not see in them any characteristics which would impose upon the parties a general social responsibility to look after one another's welfare. I think Fried's idea of sharing the burden can be made more meaningful morally if it is explained in terms of a common misjudgement: that things did not go as was expected indicates a misjudgement by all of the parties. Therefore, in virtue of being responsible for their deliberate choices, they should all share the damage, rather than letting it lie where it falls.

Distributive justice provides good reasons for the discharge of debts in bankruptcy, which can be seen as a means to promote social equality. In this sense deontological ethics employs debt-clearing much the same way as utilitarianism: it is a strand in the safety net of the market economy. Yet, this does not exhaust the deontological vision. The theory of promissory autonomy can give further backing to discharge.

AUTONOMY AND DISCHARGE

The discussion about promissory autonomy has drawn on Kant. His ethics has often been associated with absolute duties. Nonetheless, there is plenty of material in Kant's works to prove that this is a mistaken interpretation.[7] Kant allows exceptions: a rule can be overridden by other rules. I shall now show how my modest Kantian account of promissory autonomy applies this feature to the problems surrounding insolvency. If I am successful in proving that, *prima facie*, no moral wrong is committed when the insolvent does not pay her debts, then we will have concrete evidence that Kantian ethics does not lead to absolute moral rules. More importantly, my success would deliver a sound deontological ethical theory which respects the moral duty to keep promises and pay debts, whilst leaving room for exceptions in certain well-defined circumstances, such as insolvency.

We are autonomous agents, furnished with free will. From the Kantian concept of autonomy I deduced, in Chapter 5, the capacity of the human will to make choices which exclude some future choices from the options available to the choosing agent. This means that we are capable of introducing morality into our behaviour. When we make a promise we employ this uniquely human capacity. Promises express our autonomy by imposing restrictions upon our freedom; we deliberately ban some choices which otherwise would be within our means. The ban is a moral one: we say that we have a duty to keep the promise. Albeit a moral notion, the duty is a permanent reality. We are not at liberty to choose a banned option.

If our will were capable of establishing the duty only in a contingent sense, meaning that a duty to keep the promise existed only as long as we actually wanted to keep the promise, we would be – regardless of the promise – morally free to choose any course of action which we might find preferable. There would, of course, be other pressures pushing us to live by our word – such as resentment from our peer group or fear of public enforcement. But if we found, all things considered, that breaking the promise brought us overwhelming benefits, there would be no moral duty whatsoever requiring us to act against our calculated interests. This would mean, in effect, that we were not able to make binding decisions concerning our future actions.

On the level of ethical theory the result would be that we would not be autonomous beings. On the level of contractual theory it would indicate that there are no inherent, or even *prima facie*, morally binding elements in contracts. These are clearly unacceptable outcomes. They do not correspond to the ways we conceive our obligations in a civil society, nor can they provide a satisfactory explanation of the social practices and institutions we have created. Therefore, we have to accept that human beings are autonomous, and that this means they can impose moral obligations upon themselves by voluntarily limiting the future scope of their actions in a morally binding manner. The autonomy of the promisor implies that she has a *prima facie* moral duty to keep her promises, and to pay her debts.

But this duty is, indeed, a *prima facie* duty. There are circumstances in which the obligation is void even if the other party, who has received the promise, wants us to keep it. I do not mean only circumstances in which it is impossible to perform the required act. We have not even a *prima facie* duty to perform impossible acts, because a duty to perform an act which cannot be done is inherently contradictory.

What I mean is that, over time, the position of the promising agent may change in such a manner that the necessary attributes which constitute the moral bindingness of a promise are no longer present. I have spelt out autonomy as the crucial attribute from which the obligation emerges, and autonomy stands for the agent's capacity to make choices based on free will, including choices narrowing the scope of future choices. Now, if a promise narrows the scope of the promising agent's future choices, either intentionally or unintentionally, to the extent that she no longer has any choices left, but is bound in the foreseeable future to one course of action in order to meet the obligations evoked by her promise, the agent has lost her capacity to make free choices. She has lost her autonomy.

For the moral rules this is an unbearable situation: they cannot endorse the collapse of the very property which is their foundation. Put in another way, freedom of will as the capacity to choose is a necessary condition for moral responsibility. When an insolvent has no choice left in regard to her financial future her economic life becomes totally subordinate to her creditors' interest. She is denied her freedom of will in a core area of her personhood, therefore she cannot be held morally responsible for her promises relevant to that area either.

Losing one's autonomy because one has no material choice left is different from breaking one's promises – even from the consistent breaking of one's promises. In the first case one's future life is no longer dependent on one's will, in the latter case one can always decide to start honouring one's commitments. But for the person whose commitments have exhausted her choices, salvation comes exactly from the desperate and degrading nature of her ordeal: she has lost her autonomy. Since autonomy was the attribute bearing the moral obligation to keep the promise, and the autonomy has now ceased to exist, due to a total loss of freedom in organizing her subsistence, there cannot be any promissory moral obligation left either! The moral obligation generating the end of autonomy terminates its own life as well.

Insolvency being detrimental to autonomy, an insolvent's

contractual obligations cannot escape its pernicious effects either. All of her financial obligations go for the same equitable reasons which justified *pari passu* treatment of her creditors.[8] Money has no earmarks. Each and every penny an insolvent owes contributes to her misery. Although it may be the stick that breaks the camel's back, an insolvent is liable to pay all of her dues, and her property is distributed amongst all of the creditors. Within each class the creditors have a right to be treated equally, and their debtors have a right to put them all equally behind.

An insolvent does not commit any moral wrong when she does not pay her debts because the moral obligation to pay no longer exists. Here we have the deontological justification, from the defaulting agent's point of view, for the default in bankruptcy. From the point of view of society, the cessation of the moral obligation should be recognized by cancelling its legal enforcement. This is achieved through the institutional discharge of debts – a device which restores the personal autonomy of the debtor.

WHEN IS AUTONOMY UNDER THREAT?

There are two contractual relations which invalidate autonomy: voluntary slavery contracts and insolvency. Loss of autonomy can, of course, follow from various kinds of oppressive measures: imprisonment, disabilities, poverty and so on. But these differ from slavery and insolvency in the sense that they are not initiated by the free will of the agent who loses her autonomy, but are consequences of accidents of nature or actions of other people. Slavery can also be, and most often is, a consequence of other people forcing their will upon the slave, but I shall here speak only of slavery initiated by voluntary slavery contracts.

As voluntary slavery and insolvency are initiated by voluntary actions, the ethical problems involved are different from those related to, for instance, poverty or forced slavery. Nobody has a moral duty to be poor, but the presence of one's own free choice in the case of voluntary slavery and insolvency gives some apparent credibility to the idea that the unfortunate agent might be under some moral obligation to remain enslaved or indebted. My point has been that no such obligation exists, not even if we accept the *prima facie* duty to keep promises and pay debts.

The non-existence of moral obligations that would push one, as a result of one's choices, to servitude is recognized in international conventions. The supplement to the 1926 Slavery Convention of the League of Nations, resulting from a 1956 conference organized by the United Nations, includes – and condemns – debt bondage as a form of enslavement. It defines debt bondage as the status or condition where the value of the services of the debtor 'is not applied towards the liquidation of the debt or the length and nature of those services are not respectively limited and defined'.[9]

The convention's purpose was to target well-established practices in Third World countries, where generations of poor labourers were kept in virtual slavery by means of debt bondage. Recalling that most contemporary insolvent debtors in wealthy countries have no chance of paying their debts in the foreseeable future, the convention's criteria fit them as well. Although the hallmark of forced slavery – regarding slaves as private property, as chattels – is absent, the loss of autonomy amounts to factual slavery for insolvent citizens of those countries which do not have legislation granting discharge in a bankruptcy. Since their perpetually enforced debts can be bought and sold, control over their lives can be transferred as handily as if they were tangible goods.

In common law countries the threat of debt bondage has received some attention. Bankrupts are not seen as slaves who are under a duty to perform future work for the benefit of their creditors.[10] On a more general level of contract law, specific performance defined in a contract is denied if it would restrain the freedom of the agent who has agreed to perform: 'the courts are bound to be jealous, lest they should turn contracts of service into contracts of slavery'.[11] We can find this principle embedded in the bankruptcy laws. For instance, the Australian Bankruptcy Law does not pass to the trustee the rights under contracts which require the bankrupt's personal skill and ability in order to complete performance.

Another example of the legal recognition of the inalienable nature of rights related to autonomy is that in the United States the right to discharge is non-waivable. This means that a credit contract cannot contain a valid clause excluding the possibility of discharge in case of insolvency. Thomas Jackson has a thorough discussion of the different ways to justify non-waivability.[12] For him the problem is what justifies the special protection Federal laws grant to human capital in the form of a non-waivable right. One of Jackson's worries is that the protection interferes with human autonomy because it denies us the freedom to contract away the right to be cleared of debts.[13]

Jackson's answer is that the justification, if there is any, lies in the need to protect people from the consequences of their erroneous nature:

> Thus the question really is: why is the special trigger rule applicable to human capital a federal rule? . . .
>
> Perhaps the answer in federalizing the fresh-start law as it relates to human capital has to do with a belief that impulsive behavior, incomplete heuristics, and externalities generate a standard problem with respect to human capital.[14]

Jackson admits that to solve this problem, a uniform rule guaranteeing discharge may be needed. However, he does not see any particular characteristics in human capital which would make it distinctive from other forms of wealth:

> But there is nothing absolute about this particular balance. If it were thought that certain forms of wealth other than human capital shared particular attributes with it – such as non-diversifiability or representing a form of savings for the future – they, too, might be considered amenable to a nationwide solution.[15]

What Jackson fails to grasp is that the need for the uniform rule of discharge does not arise only out of the rational calculations of self-interested agents estimating what sort of law might best serve their interests in the uncertain future. Rather, it arises out of the necessity that in order to be autonomous we have to be capable of making choices. If this capacity is suppressed, even by our voluntary commitments, then there is nothing left to support the moral obligation that makes the commitment binding.

Freedom of choice is the essence of our morally relevant human capital. It makes human capital a distinctive category separate from everything else, and worth special protection also in bankruptcy. In modern times it has become common to exempt the corporeal side of human capital, the body and person of a debtor, from distribution to creditors. The obvious reason for this is that if an insolvent's body and person were distributable she could be stripped of her humanity, which would violate her human rights. My argument has highlighted the fact that the protection of human rights extends to the moral side of an insolvent's human capital as well – to her autonomy.

Laws recognizing inalienable legal rights to one's person are an empirical realization of ethics based on human autonomy and emphasizing human rights. It is a peculiarly human capacity to make morally meaningful decisions and to carry the moral responsibility for them. Creatures furnished with such a capacity have inherent moral value because there would be no morality without them. As a consequence, each individual has inalienable human rights which are of a political and material nature, and which support her existence as an autonomous agent. The material rights are also essential, since without them human existence is simply not possible. The necessity of at least some material rights for autonomy to exist should be taken into account by social institutions, including bankruptcy. This is neglected if bankruptcy proceedings are only confined to the distribution of the debtor's property to the creditors.

Perpetual indebtedness would control the insolvent's future life in a manner which would, *de facto*, extend the creditors' rights to the debtor's person. It would reduce the debtor to a mere means of satisfying her creditors' interests. As Kant has noted, a person's natural rights cease if she is nothing but a debtor.[16] The way out is to grant an insolvent a discharge of her debts, which can be seen as an expression of the Kantian concept of treating persons as ends in themselves.

I started by showing how autonomy, as the ground of the moral duty to keep promises, could be employed to explain the relinquishment of an insolvent's contractual obligations. Now the case has been strengthened to the extent that the discharge in bankruptcy appears as an inalienable human right. It safeguards autonomy, a human characteristic with moral worth similar to that of an individual's body and life. Laws enforcing contracts which exhaust the options of a contracting party totally, thereby destroying her life as an autonomous being, are morally bad laws. This should be enough to prove that a Kantian does not have to regard the duty to keep promises as an absolute one. The true Kantian position is that we cannot contract away our autonomy:

> a contract by which one party would completely renounce its freedom for the other's advantage would be self-contradictory, that is, null and void, since by it one party would cease to be a person and so would have no duty to keep the contract but would recognize only force.[17]

Here Kant explicitly adopts the interpretation I have wanted to give to autonomy as the basis of contractual obligation. The passage occurs, however, in the middle of a rather outdated discussion of marriage and family, and has gone largely unnoticed. Nevertheless, the Kantian message is clear: a promise that would destroy the autonomy of the promisor, the morally relevant essence of her human nature, is null and void in the moral sense.

Chapter 8

What kind of discharge?

We have ample ethical support for the discharge of debts in bankruptcy. But what should the discharge be like? A once and for all fresh start, as in the United States? Or should there be some provisions in regard to the debtor's future income? If she could later preserve her autonomy while paying off at least some of the old debts, should not this be the practice? And what about her property? Should part of it be exempted? Even if we agree on the need to protect a bankrupt's autonomy, there are several ways to achieve that aim.

PIECEMEAL OR ONE-OFF?

If my account of the moral nature of contractual obligations is accepted, we have a reason to make the discharge as prompt and total as possible. The debtor's autonomy is given a fatal blow when she loses everything she has owned. She can no longer be held morally responsible for her word because she has been deprived of the fundamental precondition for that responsibility. Since the moral obligation no longer exists, there is no ethical reason for society to enforce the contract spelling out the promise. Accordingly, the legal obligation to pay should be extinguished.

It could be said that the obligation returns when it no longer poses a threat to the autonomy of the debtor. But how could it rise from the ashes? Obligations do not have lives independent of their constitutive subjects – autonomous human beings. The revival of the extinct obligation is possible only if the agent, after regaining her autonomy, chooses to re-establish the limits over her future scope of options. What vanished when the agent became insolvent does not return by itself.

This point could be criticized because it gives moral duties a temporary nature only. Our duties, one might argue, like the duty not to inflict physical harm upon others, cannot be subject to the contingencies of life. We have to observe them always. If we lose our autonomy for some time, say as a consequence of imprisonment or insanity, we are, nevertheless, supposed to respect a number of duties. My reply is that in examples like this the duties are immediate and enforceable because they depend on the necessary conditions for conciliating the existence of autonomous human beings within the limited spatio-temporal environment of the earth.

Individuals are, by the very nature of their autonomous existence, entitled to certain inalienable rights, including the right not to be physically violated. This right follows, ultimately, from the fact that freedom from physical violation, like some material rights, is a necessary precondition for the existence of a human being – and for her autonomy as well. Therefore, others may continuously enforce these rights against me – that is, force me to observe the corresponding duties – even if I have permanently or temporarily lost my autonomy. When my autonomy collapses, only the particular duties which were established by my promise go – those resting on the autonomy of others remain intact.

Thus, our moral rights and duties can be divided into two classes. The first, and more fundamental, class flows from the universal human rights shared by all people in virtue of their autonomous nature. This is the fundamental class because these rights and duties are contingent only on the general characteristic of the species: autonomy. An insolvent's right to discharge is a member of this privileged group. The second class is more contingent. In order to be valid, its members have to be called into service by a voluntary act of the agent under obligation and, simultaneously, they must not destroy the underlying characteristic, autonomy, which makes it possible for the agent to invoke such rights and duties.[1]

The moral duty to pay debts falls into the second category involving more contingency. The duty to pay is a consequence of a promise: it has been invoked by a particular act of my autonomous will. This act carries the moral commitment only insofar as my own autonomy exists. But why could we not say that the commitment returns when my once knocked-out autonomy is back? Do we have a kind of new person present in the restored autonomy, a person who is no longer responsible for the acts the suppressed autonomy once took?

My answer is, first, that the return of commitment would put us into a vicious circle: it was the overwhelming obligations which destroyed the autonomy, and if they were restored, they would again threaten autonomy. In order to revive the autonomy it is necessary, at least in some cases, to regard the old commitments as permanently ceased. Second, if something ceases to exist, it is gone once and for all. There is no realm where a moral obligation could go hiding on its own, and be handily invited back at the convenience of the creditors.

After autonomy collapses, promissory moral obligations are not simply suspended; they vanish because there is nothing to support their existence. No new person is created when the autonomy of an insolvent is restored, but her autonomy is, in the temporal sense, not a continuum of the earlier autonomy. Therefore, she is not bound by the voluntary restrictions undertaken in her earlier autonomous period. Loss of autonomy does not make us new persons, although it changes our status as moral persons.

This takes us to the alternative which would allow a useful way out of our obligations. If we consider ourselves as constituted by a succession of personalities, the promises made by our earlier selves would not bind the later ones. Derek Parfit has been the most prominent philosopher to speak for this view:

> We may regard some events within a person's life as, in certain ways, like birth or death. Not in all ways, for beyond these events the person has earlier or later selves. But it may be only one out of the series of selves which is the object of some of our emotions, and to which we apply some of our principles.[2]

This seems to solve the problem of discharge: the commitment to pay was made by an earlier self, and does not carry any moral force in regard to the later, insolvent, self.

I think this way out is too easy. The arguments for successive personalities are not convincing. I find myself to be a single person when I reflect upon my past. When I consider my future, I plan events which I think will happen to me. This, together with the fact that I locate my person inside my body, which is one physical substance extending over time, is for me a sufficient reason to consider myself as one and the same self yesterday, today and tomorrow. The continuing unity of myself is, like the starry heavens and the moral law, an immediate fact available to my consciousness.

Furthermore, the everyday practices of human beings support

the unity of our selves. To me and to my fellow humans I exist, as an individual living over a period of time, more through the expressions of my actively conscious mind than through expressions of my physical body. Expressions of both are needed, but if we look at what constitutes me as a living person, it is not primarily the appearance of organic activity in my cell mass, but appearance of activity related to my mind. Plenty of my cells may well continue their lives after my death but my mind cannot, in any rational sense, be active after I have passed away. This indicates that the more basic constitutive factor of personhood is mental activity. I am perceived as one person as long as my mind is active. It would be odd if I was considered as one person in everyday life but my morally relevant mental personality was treated as if it were a succession of separate selves. My personhood is an outcome of physical and mental activity continuing over my lifetime. It is the one and only me that is the result.

Having said this, I should recognize that I cannot point out any particular mental substance which would establish the temporal unity of my mind. However, there is no need for the perception of such a substance. We need it only for the purposes of moral theory, and for that purpose we can refer to our noumenal nature. There is, within ourselves, the 'thing in itself' which acts as the entity bearing the unity of personality through time. We do not know anything about it, and there is not any need to know either. Nevertheless, we are entitled to assume its existence since we behave and perceive ourselves as if the assumption were true. This is the Kantian answer to the problem of successive personalities. We do not die if some of our properties evolve, emerge or disappear. However, the changes in our properties may alter our relations to other human beings, including our rights and duties.[3]

Indeed, if I seriously start to think that I am Napoleon Bonaparte, this will not make me a new person in any meaningful sense. It is true that I would be relinquished from my moral obligations. However, this would happen, not because my new self was no longer bound by the commitments of my earlier self, but rather because I would be considered as having lost my reason. The obligations would disappear along with the mental capacities necessary for having any obligations at all.

When someone says that she has been transformed from one person to another within the life of a single physical body, what we have at hand is not a description of the birth of a new moral agent, but a symptom of a personality disorder. Parfit has said: 'We can indeed choose to *speak* of a new self, just as we can choose when to speak of the end of Medieval England.'[4] Yes, we can so choose, but the choice does not give any meaningful explanation of personhood for the purposes of a rational normative theory.

In the case of English history, a continuum of events gets a name when called, for example, Medieval England. In the case of our selves, the continuum of our existence is disrupted if it is divided into a successive series of separate selves. The disruption is as serious an escape from rationality as it would be to claim that Medieval England did not have any continuity with the later periods of English history. I do not think that Parfit's theory is helpful when we look for an explanation as to why the discharge should be total and perpetual. Luckily, its help is not needed because we already have established, from the deontological point of view, that the return of once languished contractual moral obligations would be detrimental to autonomy, and is in any event impossible.

This is not to say that we should never apply measures extending a debtor's obligations beyond the moment she becomes bankrupt. There are other ways than a straight discharge to increase the options of an individual. Social security is one of them. However, autonomy is certainly supported more by independent life than by wardship, therefore I would be inclined to see discharge as an institution which is morally superior to debt bondage alleviated by social security payments. As J.B. Schneewind, a Kant-scholar, has put it: 'If nothing is properly mine except what someone graciously gives me, I am forever dependent on how the donor feels toward me. My independence as an autonomous being is threatened.'[5]

Another alternative for reorganizing the options of an insolvent are the exempt rules, telling how much property a bankrupt may keep for her fresh start, or the income orders, which put the insolvent under obligation to contribute part of her income to her creditors for a certain period of time. I conclude that these measures are, as long as they remove the threat of debt bondage, a matter of judgement relative to the community standards.

A philosophical theory cannot determine in every detail the insolvents' route back to square one; local habitat and terrain have an impact on the itinerary. However, this research has revealed that there are no deontological obstacles to a straight discharge, but many moral and practical problems associated with the more arduous paths. Utilitarian lines of argument lead to similar conclusions. Most bankrupts are so poor that prolonged collecting efforts are just a waste of resources and a disincentive for the debtors to regain their financial independence: why look for work and income if it would only end up in the creditors' hands?

NON-CONTRACTUAL DEBTS

So far we have studied how an insolvent could be cleared of the moral obligation to pay debts initiated by her promises. This has covered the vast majority,[6] but not all, of the liabilities of bankrupts. There remain, for instance, the debts that are results of torts, fines and taxes. These liabilities are, in one form or another, imposed by the state. What could justify their discharge?

Generally speaking, the discharge of non-contractual debts can be defended on the same basis as that of contractual debts. Impossibility of performance, respect for autonomy and beneficial consequences – all speak in favour of easing the insolvent's burden regardless of the nature of the liability. Nevertheless, the picture is now more complicated. Two morally relevant features, used in the preceding chapter for the deontological justification of discharge, are not present now. First, a non-contractual debtor has not herself consented to perform, she has not made the initiative to conceive the duty. Second, her creditor has not voluntarily given the credit in order to make economic profit.

The absence of the debtor's consent means that her autonomy is not the source of the moral obligation to pay. The state has unilaterally imposed the legal obligation upon her. This may bring her under the general moral duty to respect the law. But if the debt is owed directly to the state, to the body which has the power to impose and enforce it, and subsequently the same body decides to abolish the legal liability, the debtor's moral liability goes too. In other words, if the state imposes dues upon us without our consent, the state has the authority to repeal them as well. There are no compelling moral reasons to keep alive an insolvent's non-contractual debts, such as fines and taxes, which are not owed to any particular individual or group. On the contrary, there are good reasons to clear them away. The state should be the jealous watchdog of the autonomy of its citizens; it should serve its mission by giving up the financial claims it may have against bankrupts.

Do some non-contractual debts carry moral weight regardless of the rulings of public authorities? This question takes us to the second, more problematic, peculiarity of non-contractual liabilities: the creditors have not become creditors by their own consent. The insolvent may have, for instance, inflicted harm upon them, which makes her liable for damages.

Intuitively it seems, at least in the light of deontological ethics, that the loss of autonomy does not help the insolvent to shrug off these kinds of moral obligations. They are able to resist exoneration since their moral force does not rest on the autonomy of the insolvent herself or on the authority of the state, but solely on the autonomy of the creditor. Going into the nature of these insolvency-resistant moral duties in any greater detail would take us too far from our subject, but I take it to be obvious that there are situations when an insolvent's plight does not displace her duty to compensate for non-contractual harm or dependence she has inflicted upon others.[7]

Autonomy can, nevertheless, accommodate the compensatory non-contractual obligations in the overall picture. It is the human property which, again, is the origin of the moral obligations involved: once we have put other people's autonomy in jeopardy without their consent, we are morally liable to rectify the situation. The value of rebuilding the insolvent's autonomy is now balanced against the moral weight of the other party's autonomy requiring redress, not against the moral weight of the insolvent's promise. The conflict is between universal human rights, not between universal human rights and specific contractual rights.

Debtors bear the consequences of their unilateral actions alone: if they go broke, their human rights lose out to the human rights of creditors-against-their-will. This means that non-contractual damages or compensations may survive discharge. A good example is child maintenance: in order to exist and develop, the child, who is receiving the allowance, needs the contribution. A discharge of liability toward her could so severely limit her future options that it would be morally unjust. An ethical explanation of the legal practice of exempting certain liabilities from discharge lies in the fact that sometimes the debtor's loss of autonomy has to be reconciled with the loss of autonomy of a creditor-against-her-will.

Here we might be tempted to ask, does the same reasoning apply to voluntary creditors? Should the discharge be refused if it bankrupts creditors and destroys their autonomy because the borrowers are cleared of debt? My answer is negative. The voluntary creditor has, like the debtor, deliberately limited her future options by entering into the credit contract. The contract has, out of many possible worlds, laid in front of her a future which includes the chance of financial ruin if the borrower does not perform. The creditor has decided to take the risk. It is her own action, not that of the debtor's, which has put her autonomy in jeopardy. Therefore, the creditor has no moral right to restitution. Instead, she has the right to restore her autonomy by filing for bankruptcy.

The last turn in the present discussion has already taken us to the arguments seeking to maintain the rights of creditors. It is time to boil down the results of Part III before going deeper into this new area. Once the contract has killed the autonomy of an insolvent promisor, the moral basis of creditors' contractual rights evaporates. Having lost everything, the debtor has cleared the playing field for her last defence to take over. She is shielded by human rights, which debtors possess 'simply as human beings with the capacity to make plans and give justice'.[8]

The loss of an insolvent's autonomy not only justifies discharge, but fortifies it to an ethically prerogative human right. Forgiveness, impossibility, utilitarianism and distributive justice provide it with additional support. A host of ethical verdicts point to similar practical principles in regard to debt and insolvency.

Part IV

In defence of dunning
A counterattack

The preceding chapters examined the moral basis of our contractual liability. They established that an insolvent does not commit a moral wrong if she does not fulfil her promise to pay a debt. This outcome may be challenged in various ways, drawing either on the circumstances surrounding the default, or on the harm associated with it. The focus now shifts from the acts of promising and non-performance to the behaviour that precedes these acts, or coincides with them, and to the effects of that behaviour on others.

On the deontological front the counterattack seeks to produce new evidence of wrongdoing by insolvents. Some moralists may try to wipe the dust off traditional and religious philosophies and claim that duties established by promises are absolute, while others rely on codes of conduct which the community takes to be reasonable in an objective sense and which have been violated by bankrupts. The shared feature of the deontological counterattack is that wrongness is due to the violation of moral standards which exist independently of the promisor's actions. The thesis that moral standards relevant to promising exist independently of the particular acts of promising would, if successful, impose bindingness on promises even after the autonomy of the promisor has collapsed.

As for the utilitarian argument, it has become conspicuous that the discharge of an insolvent's debts makes sense, yet doubt may be cast upon this conclusion by arguing that debtors who have been reckless, negligent or extravagant should not be let off that easily. Do these doubts entitle a utilitarian to impose reprisals on at least some bankrupts?

In this part, Chapter 9 answers new challenges focusing on contract, breach of trust and tort. If the discussion does not provide moral evidence of civil wrongdoing by insolvents, then criminal justice is the last resort with the potential of upholding their liabilities. That potential is charted in Chapter 10, which looks at the reasons for punishing bankrupts.

Chapter 9

Propping up civil liability
Contract, breach of trust and tort

LEGAL AND MORAL ABSOLUTISM

When I addressed the question 'Should debts be paid?', I set naturalist philosophies propounding absolute obligations aside rather
abruptly. However, there is an even more simplistic argument which
tries to base strict contractual compliance on positive law. We could
be told that contract is the law between the parties because it is
backed by the jurisdiction, and that it would be wrong to ruin the
legally binding web of obligations by letting debtors go without
paying.

The opening paragraph of Part II has already paid attention to
the obvious problems faced by this line of argument. It represents
an effort to conclude from existing laws what kind of laws there
should be. Moral obligations are merged with legal ones. However,
if we identify moral obligations with the dictates of positive laws,
any kind of positive law gains moral approval – to assume that
some laws are morally more obliging would require introduction of
criteria external to positive legislation determining the moral hierarchy among the laws. A positive law absolutist has to give the laws
granting a discharge the same moral standing as the laws
supporting contracts. Thus she could not use the law of contract to
brush aside the law of discharge.

In addition, regardless of the nature of bankruptcy laws, there
always remains a place for consideration when implementing
contracts.[1] It would be an unreal world in which every and any
contractual commitment were sanctioned. Impossibility, duress and
false representation are examples of situations where the fairness of
contracts is questioned before a decision is made regarding their
eventual enforcement.[2] Through consideration contract law gives

support to the idea that fallibility is one of the inherent characteristics of contracts. The opponents of discharge have to go beyond positive law in order to substantiate their criticism. They have to find a moral theory which offers persuasive reasons for absolute promissory obligations.

The past cornerstone of ethical absolutism, natural law theories, crumbled long ago. The theories depend more on uncritical belief and extra-sensory insight than is acceptable for a rational normative account. Their conclusion, the absolute nature of duties, is too much at odds with conditions of human life to enable them to explain and guide human conduct. Therefore, it is no wonder that contemporary philosophy prefers to approach contractual obligations from a more mundane point of view. Modern ethics focuses on human capacities: utilitarians focus on the satisfaction of interests, and deontologists on the moral choice made possible by autonomy. Absolutism is unfit to stave off the discharge, yet creditors may still have some moral ammunition left – more scattered but not void of power to defend their contractual claims.

WASTING OTHER PEOPLE'S MONEY

An argument with plenty of emotional appeal is that debtors have spent other people's money, and should be held accountable for the consequences. Clearing them amounts to giving them a licence to waste at their will the property of others. Douglas Baird has expressed the idea neatly: 'Allowing someone to gamble with someone else's money is always a bad idea'.[3]

In the United Kingdom law reform inquiry *Insolvency Law and Practice*, known as the Cork Report, the same point is used to justify restrictions that prevent a bankrupt from obtaining credit: 'He has by his financial failure lost the money represented by the credit extended to him, and it is not reasonable that he should be completely at liberty to lose more of other people's money.'[4] The intuitive appeal of the argument gets its strength from the idea that debtors have not had any authority to use the borrowed money in ways resulting in losses. It is clearly reprehensible if someone plunders something which belongs to somebody else. However, the argument obscures the nature of credit by equating it with other forms of property held by a creditor.

It is true that credit is an asset to the creditor. In this sense it is her property. But the very nature of that property is that it is credit, which means that the actual contents of the asset is not in the exclusive control of the proprietor. On the contrary, by her voluntary consent she has delivered its control to another party, the debtor. Normally the creditor has given her consent, and accepted the accompanying risk of default, in the expectation of economic profit.

Private property is not simply a matter of particular individuals having exclusive control over assets.[5] Property consists of complex clusters of rights: liens, encumbrances, legal restrictions and other types of qualifications are common. Credit is no exception. The creditor has herself handed to someone else the right to control the asset lent, and thus diminished her own rights to it. Aristotle was the first philosopher to draw a normative conclusion from this fact: 'men who have bargained on a basis of credit ought to accept the consequences'.[6]

The consequences are that both the creditor and the debtor are responsible for the credit losses. There is nothing warranting the view that the blame is the debtor's alone, that she has somehow exceeded her rights when she has wasted the money at her will. The truth is that she has wasted the money at a joint will, under the authority of the creditor who has voluntarily given her the proxy by granting the loan.

Creditors make a judgement on the risk, express it in the form of an interest rate, and pass the control of the asset to the debtor subject to the terms of the contract. As Merton H. Miller makes clear, those who stress finance as the art of gambling with other people's money overlook the creditors' power to determine the contents of the contract: 'Gambling with other people's money would indeed be an artistic way of making a living, if only one could find the other people to supply the bankroll at the riskless rate of interest. In general one can't.'[7]

In the United States, according to statistics, 92 per cent of credit to bankrupts has been voluntarily granted.[8] We have no reason to think that the figure is significantly lower elsewhere. This confirms that debtors usually gain control of borrowed assets as a result of business transactions. These must be assumed to be fully informed, conscientious decisions on the creditors' part. They are decisions of people who are able to reach deliberate judgements, and who should carry the responsibility for them. Granting some bad loans in order to maximize returns may be a rational decision.[9] This should cool the emotions stirred up by images of debtors indulging themselves at other people's expense.

Like creditors, debtors are rational agents who make deliberate judgements when they borrow money. As Adam Smith has emphasized, there is nothing irrational, or morally suspicious, in credit:

> In all countries where there is tolerable security, every man of common understanding will endeavour to employ whatever stock he can command, in procuring either present enjoyment or future profit. . . . A man must be perfectly crazy who, where there is tolerable security, does not employ all the stock which he commands, whether it be his own or borrowed of other people.[10]

Smith sees credit as rational because it boosts trade and production, which in turn provides for consumption, the satisfaction of human wants.[11] His confidence has recently gained empirical support from a study which assessed the impacts of deregulated money markets, and which indicated that credit aggregates provided useful leading information about GDP and have unambiguously led investment since deregulation.[12] Contrary to common belief among economists, the paper suggests that supply of credit may indeed spur investment and growth – the most sought after economic goals. This should not come as a great surprise: with easier credit the given level of capital is higher, which fosters production to a higher level too.

Thus, granting or taking a loan is a useful and perfectly normal form of human activity. It involves risk, as most human life does. The difference between credit and some other risks imposed upon us is that in the case of credit we can decide whether to accept the risk or not. If we grant a loan, we alienate the lent asset from our immediate control. We cannot avoid accepting, concurrently, the chance that the borrower may lose the asset, because that chance is always present.

If she actually loses it, she does not waste other people's property. A look at her balance sheet, real or hypothetical, at the time she initially put the subsequently lost wealth at risk would have told us that the wealth was an asset to her. She jeopardized something over which she had control and therefore the complete right to waste. It is another matter that she also had a liability in her books, a commitment to pay the loan back. This, as a legal commitment, is subject to the laws that may involve discharge, and when the commitment is understood in the moral sense, it has to be accommodated with other moral considerations – which may well turn out to justify discharge.

The terms of the joint venture between a creditor and her debtor culminate in the price of the credit. The agreed interest rate reflects the risk involved: if a deal turns sour, profits from other risky lending should cover it to the creditor. When a creditor's business performs worse than expected as a result of bad debts, she has failed in her judgement. A creditor's bad judgement is not made by the insolvent debtor, even less is it the insolvent's moral fault.

The terms of credit provide more security for the creditor than for the debtor because the debtor's obligations are not normally dependent on profits, and because debts are preferred to equity in the event of insolvency. These are not unfair terms. They are jointly and voluntarily agreed upon and strike a balance between risk and yield; what is wasted under their authority is scrupulous wasting.

The claim that an insolvent has wasted other people's money is false, and thus cannot justify the conclusion that she should not be granted discharge. A legal procedure which clears an insolvent of her promise does not licence the wasteful use; the licence was given much earlier by the creditor herself. Creditors are not outsiders who have to absorb the losses of insolvents, and a debtor does not, in general, have a fiduciary duty which would require her to exercise particular care, caution and consideration of her creditor's interests.

BREACH OF TRUST

In the moral sense, intentional breach of the trust expressed in a relation of dependency is wrong. As this principle is also behind the legal concept of fiduciary duty, which is well debated and defined, I shall now turn to jurisprudence. A recent consultation paper by the Law Commission of the United Kingdom[13] places holders of fiduciary duties into two categories: status-based fiduciaries and fact-based fiduciaries. The established and more common category is that of status-based fiduciaries, who 'by virtue of their involvement in certain relationships are considered, without further inquiry, to be fiduciaries. Such relationships include those between trustee-beneficiary, solicitor-client, agent-principal, director-company, and partner-partner.'[14]

Sometimes a relationship may be a fiduciary one although it does not fit the description given in the above quotation. Then the fiduciary duties are incurred because of the factual situation of a particular relationship. The Law Commission examined cases in which courts have considered such a factual situation to exist:

> The factors included an undertaking by the fiduciary to act on behalf of or for the benefit of another person, a discretion or power which affects the interests of that other person, and the peculiar vulnerability of that other person to the fiduciary. This vulnerability can be shown by factors such as dependence upon information and advice, the existence of a relationship of confidence and the significance of a particular transaction for the parties. This test is based on discretion, power to act and vulnerability.[15]

After defining the status-based and fact-based fiduciaries, the Law Commission draws the following conclusion as to fiduciary duties in the financial services area: 'In applying the status-based and fact-based tests to the financial services area it is evident that in general a firm advising a customer or making purchases on a customer's behalf will be acting in a fiduciary capacity.'[16]

In the debtor–creditor relationship, the debtor does not undertake to act on behalf and for the benefit of the creditor, although the debtor exercises a discretion which affects the interests of the creditor. More importantly, the creditor is not in a particularly vulnerable situation when she grants the loan. Thus, a credit contract does not establish a fiduciary relationship.

However, banks and other financial institutions accepting deposits and advising clients may form an exception. Their depositors may have been led to understand that the deposits are secure investments, and the depositors as the receivers of this information may have been in a vulnerable position. If a depositor has lost her money as a result of a bank's risk exposure, she might have a valid claim that the bank has breached its fiduciary duties.

In the ethical sense the bank's breach of fiduciary duty can be seen as a form of breach of promise: if there has been a tacit or explicit assurance of the risk-free nature of the deposit, the borrowing institution has in effect promised not to put the funds at risk. When the institution fails it is quite obvious that it has broken not only its promise to pay the deposit back, but also the promise not to risk it. The latter promise is broken when the institution was solvent and accepted the fatal risks, and there is a moral wrong involved. The promise not to risk the depositor's borrowings is a specific covenant which may make a borrower liable to a fact-based fiduciary duty. Credit contracts not constrained by such covenants imply only that the debtor has to make a sincere effort to pay the debt. They do not tell her to follow whatever course of action is in the best interest of the creditor.

TORT

So far we have successfully repelled legal and moral absolutism and emotions stirred up by the idea that insolvents have wasted something which belongs to others. We have also found that debtors hold fiduciary duties only under specific circumstances. The release of bankrupts looking imminent, could a pledge to tortious liability maintain their burden? Should the insolvents not compensate for the losses they incur? These questions shift the focus to principles of tort. According to Salmond, they are capable of introducing liability even in the absence of fault:

> We may accordingly define a tort as *a civil wrong for which the remedy is a common law action for unliquidated damages, and which is not exclusively the breach of a contract or the breach of a trust or other merely equitable obligation.* . . .
>
> In general, a tort consists in some act done by the defendant whereby he has without just cause or excuse caused some form of harm to the plaintiff.[17]

Tortious liability is different from contractual liability. For our purposes the most significant distinction is that a breach of contract is not a tort: 'Summing the matter up, we have seen that there are four classes of wrongs which stand outside the sphere of tort: . . . (3) Civil wrongs which are exclusively breaches of contract.'[18] Thus, it is well established that a contractual default is not, as such, a tort – although it may be a tort. It is true that a creditor experiences a loss as a result of non-payment due to insolvency. Is that loss a tort for which the insolvent should be held liable?

There is a morally relevant lack of causal proximity between a debtor's insolvency and the harm suffered by her creditors. A voluntary creditor exposes herself to the harms of insolvency in the pursuit of economic gain, just as a debtor exposes herself to those harms when she takes a loan. The creditor's decision to extend credit, not the unforeseen contingency of insolvency, establishes the intentional, and therefore morally relevant, causality between the creditor and her subsequent harm.

Since insolvency is not the morally relevant cause of harm experienced by creditors, their losses should not impose liability in tort
upon bankrupts. In the absence of the causal proximity we do not
have to go into a detailed debate on the negligence of bankrupts in
order to assess their tortious liability. However, what will be said
about recklessness and negligence in the next chapter has pertinence
to tort in credit, in the sense that the two concepts turn out to be, by
and large, out of place in the context of business lending.

My claim above has been that if a person suffers harm after
intentionally exposing herself to it she is the cause of that harm in
any morally meaningful sense. This is not at odds with judicial evaluation of causal relations:

> Granted that each member of a set is essential to produce an
> occurrence, one must next consider, when there is only one set
> present, whether one condition can be selected from the complex
> as 'the cause'. There is no precise legal rule, but common sense
> and law unite in looking for the abnormal or the deliberate
> human act, and regarding that as 'the cause'.[19]

In general, insolvency is neither an abnormal, nor a deliberate
occurrence. It is a necessary condition of credit and economic
progress, but it is not a sought after outcome of these phenomena.

Even if, for the sake of argument, we accept that a relation which
prevails between insolvency and credit losses is enough to incur
liability for damages, it remains questionable whether that liability
should be allowed to survive discharge. If contractual liabilities
were also provable as tortious liabilities against the trustee of an
insolvent's estate, the creditors would be able to claim both the original debts and the damages. Assuming that the damages were not
written off at the end of the proceedings, the institution of
bankruptcy would make no sense: what is left of the original debts
after distribution of assets would be discharged, and exactly the
same debts would still be enforced against the nominally discharged
bankrupt as tortious liabilities. The creditors would be pursuing
twice the amount of their original receivables without increasing
their odds for getting a better settlement.

From the practical point of view, liability in tort that survived
discharge would only add pain and cost to the insolvency proceedings without any beneficial effects. This would be an anomaly. It
explains why law in the United Kingdom, for example, does not give
a bankrupt's tortious liabilities any special treatment:

Section 382 of the Insolvency Act 1986 provides that in respect of torts committed before the bankruptcy that liability is a bankruptcy debt and provable against the trustee in bankruptcy. . . . In respect of torts subsequently committed the bankrupt remains personally liable but may not be worth suing![20]

Thus, the principle that harm deserves remedy fails to support creditors' action for recourse.

Loss distribution is an alternative way to see liability in tort:

The traditional approach of the law of torts has been merely to ask whether a loss which B has suffered should be shifted to A. If A were at fault the answer would usually be to shift that loss from innocent B to wrongdoer A. . . .

There is, however, another view: by spreading the loss from an individual victim to many who benefit from an activity that has caused it, the loss is more easily borne.[21]

If we adopt the first paragraph's interpretation of the principle of loss distribution, the difficulty is to point out the wrongdoer. It has been established that an insolvent is not a wrongdoer in the moral sense, and the argument to this end will be further qualified in the next chapter. On the other hand, the discussion in Chapters 6 and 7 has shown that distributive justice strongly favours the release of insolvents. Thus, if the principle of loss distribution is understood in the second paragraph's sense, insolvents are among the victims whose lot should be eased by spreading the losses. We may conclude that principles of tort are not capable of reviving collapsed contractual liabilities. Criminal justice is the only avenue open for those who want to keep the heat on insolvents.

Chapter 10

Punishment

The centuries-old idea that bankruptcy is something criminal is still alive and kicking. It continues to tarnish insolvents despite the spirit of reform which has, for most of the time, had the upper hand in the legislative process.[1] Since it is evident that criminals ought to be punished, and relieving a debtor from her burden does not exactly sound like a punishment, the heritage of incrimination makes discharge look doubtful. Should we have harsh bankruptcy practices in order to teach the insolvents a lesson in pecuniary decency? The search for an answer will start from general theories of punishment. It will then proceed to examine whether insolvency-related fraud, recklessness, negligence and bad judgement should carry penalties. In the end the deterrent effect of punitive bankruptcy laws will be assessed.

Generally speaking, there are two major, rival ways to explain and justify punishment: retributivism and utilitarianism. They have been expressed in various forms, including attempts to accommodate both within a single theory, but their main point can be put quite briefly. I shall borrow from C.L. Ten for the definitions. A retributivist is not interested in the consequences, but considers punishment as appropriate only if it is inflicted upon someone guilty of wrongdoing:

> Retributivists regard the offender's wrongdoing as deserving of punishment, and the amount of punishment should be proportionate to the extent of the wrongdoing. The offender's desert, and not the beneficial consequences of punishment, is what justifies punishment.[2]

On the other hand, to a utilitarian only the consequences of the punishment count:

The utilitarian theory justifies punishment solely in terms of its beneficial effects or consequences. . . .

So for the utilitarian, since punishment is itself an unpleasant experience for the offender who is punished, the infliction of punishment can only be justified if it prevents greater suffering. It is never right to punish if the good consequences of punishment are less than the suffering caused by punishment.[3]

The retributivist uses the notion of wrongdoing in a moral sense: only those committing morally reprehensible acts ought to be punished. This is in stark contrast to the utilitarian view, which always sees punishing as appropriate when the overall consequences are beneficial. Do these theories encourage us to take punitive measures against bankrupts?

RETRIBUTIVISM

Let us put the retributivist's case under scrutiny first. The mere fact of insolvency does not offer many hints of moral wrongdoing, which means that a discharge is hardly a violation of justice. In our inquiry, non-contractual debts constitute, so far, the only instance in which a retributivist has solid grounds to speak of punishment. We found that some non-contractual debts compensate for the harm or dependency for which debtors are solely responsible. If a retributive theory of punishment is correct, then these non-contractual liabilities should survive a bankruptcy in order to prevent punishments and compensations from becoming meaningless.

But discharge of the vast majority of liabilities, contractual commitments and public levies, cannot be objected to on retributive grounds. On the contrary, retributivism is closely related to deontological ethics. Both assume that there are independent moral standards which are the measure of our actions and our institutions. A viable retributive theory cannot rely, ultimately, on a philosophical foundation – a picture of the world, of human beings, and of values defining relations between them – that is very different from that of a viable deontological normative theory.

If we are to punish people because they have violated moral principles, then we must assume that moral principles exist. Furthermore, we have to hold that we can rationally determine that some of these principles are the right ones. Of course, a retributivist can allow for a wide scope of benchmarks for wrongdoing, but some deontological elements are always included: a retributivist can punish those breaking utilitarian principles, but the punishment itself has to rest on a non-utilitarian basis. If it does not, then the theory becomes a utilitarian one.

So, every retributive theory has at least some deontological elements. These elements should represent rationally established moral values. An anything-goes retributivist, one who accepts any principles as moral, would shoot herself in the foot: if any principle could identify wrongdoing, any action could be wrong and punishable. There would no longer be any measure to tell what actions morally deserve punishment because every action would be morally wrong according to some principles, while, at the same time, being morally right according to other principles with equal moral strength.

Therefore, in order to keep her theory afloat, a retributivist must impose a limit as to the nature of the principles whose breaking can constitute moral wrongdoing. This she may achieve only by respecting rational argumentation for non-consequentialist moral values, which tend to put the emphasis on autonomy. It follows that a retributivist should not only refrain from punishing the bankrupt in the absence of moral wrongdoing, but be inclined to feel sympathy for preserving the bankrupt's autonomy. In our inquiry, insolvents have appeared, by and large, as innocent and in need of protection of their autonomy. In a retributivist's scales this should weigh in favour of a discharge. However, the case is not yet exhausted.

It might be argued that any theory, including any retributive theory, must allow, at least in some instances, for punishing the innocent. Extreme circumstances may arise, in which innocents may have to be sacrificed for some greater good.[4] This idea raises two objections. First, it cannot be used to justify an institution systematically punishing those who have done nothing wrong. Such an institution would definitely be contrary to the basic idea of retributivism. Therefore, the necessity of sacrifices does not provide a retributive justification for an institution which is built on the systematic punishment of innocents.

The second objection concerns exceptional circumstances. Should at least some bankrupts be punished as warning examples in order to scare people from taking extravagant risks? The few random punishments would yield great benefits in keeping moral standards high. But now the argument starts to get a distinctively utilitarian tone. I shall return to this problem a little later in the discussion of high-flyers, who make a particularly appealing example of a deterrent against risk-taking. Here I contend that, as long as we remain within the confines of retributivism, it is confusing to talk of purposely punishing the innocent. Since the concept of punishment involves wrongdoing, and 'innocent' stands for a person who has not done anything wrong, it does not make retributive sense to talk of punishing an innocent. There are certainly situations when, all things considered, even a retributivist could, because of some great good, end up sacrificing an innocent by imposing a legal punishment upon her. But this would, indeed, be a sacrifice. It is not something an innocent has deserved.

Sacrifices may be accommodated within a retributive framework, but it would be a contradictory use of the language of the theory to say that punishing innocents could have a place there too. I shall soon argue that the language of strict utilitarianism is so much at odds with our everyday intuitions that the theory is seriously flawed. The same conclusion does not apply to retributivism. It can accommodate our intuitions and, nevertheless, allow for an explanation as to why in exceptional situations we may have to punish the innocent: some other moral considerations may outweigh the immunity the innocent normally enjoys. The moral justification for the reprisal does not stem from wrongdoing, but from some other ends. This makes 'sacrifice' the morally appropriate notion for the act, although in legal language it may be called a punishment because of the nature of the social institutions used to implement the sacrifice. Furthermore, the nature of the penalizing institutions is determined by the standards they apply as a rule. If these are retributive standards, the sacrifices remain exceptions.

UTILITARIANISM

The utilitarian is free from constraints imposed by innocence. But this freedom can yield, as critics of utilitarianism are keen to point out, results that are strikingly counter-intuitive. Crucifying a few just for the pleasure of many would be an outrageous practice, no matter how great the overall benefits. The theory can be made to look less harsh if it is modified so that only those who have inflicted harm upon others should be punished. Whether this still represents utilitarianism, or presupposes an independent principle making any causing of harm wrong, may be debatable. However, for the sake of argument, I do not mind accommodating the revision within the utilitarian doctrine. The harm-inflicted side condition makes the utilitarian theory of punishment more appealing, as it now appears to be less prone to hurting the innocent.

Hence we have two sorts of utilitarianism which may justify punishing bankrupts. The strict version allows such punishment whenever the consequences are beneficial, and harm-inflicted utilitarianism whenever the insolvent has caused harm to others and the consequences of the punishment are beneficial. The analysis which follows will concentrate on harm-inflicted utilitarianism. As a moral theory, strict utilitarianism is too counter-intuitive to be of interest. Punishing the innocent is a concept loaded with meaning; we immediately understand what stands behind it, and the idea causes revulsion in us.

Another, and in the present context more important, reason for focusing on harm-inflicted utilitarianism is that if this more moderate theory turns out to favour restraint in punishing insolvents, the same conclusion should apply to strict utilitarianism as well. If punishing bankrupts who have inflicted harm upon others does not turn out to be a beneficial practice, how could good consequences flow from punishing bankrupts who have not caused any harm?

To start the analysis, we have to admit that bankrupts normally cause harm to others, not least to their creditors. But causing harm is only a necessary condition of punishment for a harm-inflicted utilitarian – it has to be supplemented by utilitarian calculations. I can think of two sorts of positive consequences of punishing bankrupts: increases in returns to creditors, and deterrence against financial recklessness.

In examining the utilitarian justification for discharge we noticed that empirical studies have shown that the vast majority of bankrupts have no hope of paying back their debts. Thus, the eventual positive outcome of punitive perpetual enforcement of debts – increased return to creditors – would only be a very marginal one. On the other hand, as we also pointed out, the cost of perpetual enforcement to the society and to the bankrupts would be detrimental. Therefore, a utilitarian should not be inclined to punish bankrupts by denying them access to discharge. This conclusion is not yet a final one. A utilitarian may find penalties beneficial as deterrents guiding the behaviour of the overall population, although their effect is detrimental to the parties directly involved. I shall soon examine this aspect more closely.

It starts to look as though retributivism and utilitarianism, the two major theories of punishment, do not encourage us to use the denial of discharge as a penalty. However, before we decide to set bankrupts free, an important qualification should be added. An assumption underlying the argument has been that debtors have not intended to cause harm to others. I have not, above, spelt out this condition of good faith since I have taken it to be implicit in the notion of promising.

When good faith is not present, the promising loses its role as the constituent of the relevant moral obligations. If the promisor's intention in committing herself is not to keep the promise, but to gain unilateral profit by breaking it, the morally meaningful concept describing the act is fraud. Then the liabilities of the promisor do not flow from the promise alone, but also from the fraudulent nature of her act within the context of a promise.

FRAUD

In the utilitarian sense, fraud is harmful to the parties cheated, and to society as a whole. It undermines the useful institutions that rest on the practice of promising. Hence, a utilitarian would penalize a person for insincerity, including punishing fraudulent bankrupts. The retributivist would agree. It would be hard to find an ethical theory saying that it is right to cheat. Those who cheat do wrong and they deserve to be punished.

What constitutes a fraud? The distinctive attribute is the intention to cause damage.[5] This intention should be understood in a wide sense, including false pretences and other ways of seeking improvement in one's own position by misleading lenders. Thus, an insolvent is guilty of fraud if she, intentionally, does not employ her means to meet her liabilities. As the promisor, she is at liberty to deliver on her promise but decides not to.

In the language of my theory of promissory autonomy, a fraudulent promisor pretends that she narrows the scope of her future options without actually doing so – she chooses not to pay in spite of having excluded this choice. Thereby she deceives others. Ethics can tolerate deceitful behaviour as little as it can tolerate the abandoning of one's contractual commitments at one's will: if accepted, both would make moral conduct obsolete. Making moral conduct obsolete is implausible, because the capacity for moral conduct is the distinctive, inherent capacity of the human species. Therefore, if we are to have any morally meaningful interaction with other people, we are entitled to consider deceitful behaviour punishable, including the fraud by bankrupts.

When does a bankrupt's behaviour constitute a fraud? Do we have any less abstract terms than 'intention to cause harm' to define their crime? I suggest a simple criterion: fraud is involved if a person seeks bankruptcy in order to improve her expectations to the extent that insolvency appears a more rewarding alternative than solvent life. A fraudulent debtor tries to exploit, at the expense of her creditors and after she is aware of her actual or impending insolvency, the protection bankruptcy offers by preserving more options than would be open to her if she sought to satisfy her creditors. She may transfer borrowed property out of the reach of the trustee, or spend it for her immediate benefit.

The common, morally reprehensible denominator of fraudulent bankruptcies is that insolvents, knowing that they are broke or will go broke, continue to use the property in their control to advance their interests, although the full control of the property ought to have returned to the creditors already by virtue of the insolvency. The debtors' moral right to control the borrowed property was based on the loan contract, and the right exists only insofar as they are capable of delivering their part of the contract. If the debtor does not deliver, the contract is broken, and the moral basis of the right to control crumbles. Insolvency brings to an end not only the duties a contract imposes, but also the right to control the borrowed property.

Fraud deserves punishment, and so does a bankrupt's fraud. The punishment may exclude her from discharge, because it is part of the nature of punishments that they may violate the offender's autonomy. Hence, we have good moral reasons to oppose discharge when it is misused to profit bankrupts instead of relieving them from a desperate situation. Indeed, most bankruptcy laws make intentional exploitation of bankruptcy a criminal offence.

It is worth noting that, in some sense, all bankrupts profit from the discharge of debts. But the morally meaningful distinction which defines a fraud is the intention to turn the financial damage to the insolvent's benefit. The damage can benefit the insolvent only through dishonesty, when creditors are not given something which is due to them and which the debtor has the power to give to them.

Discharge is different: it does not turn to the debtor's advantage anything which was borrowed by her. To an honest debtor, the only profit from discharge is that she is treated, again, as an autonomous person: she is made free to start building a normal life. This gives her recourse to what she is as a human being, not recourse to anything of her creditors' own.

RECKLESSNESS

It may be claimed that even honest debtors who have not intended to cause harm have contributed to harmful events by taking inappropriate risks. Can we find characteristics which would render some fiscal risk morally inappropriate, thereby giving reasons for retribution? We shall now move to examine cases where the insolvent, while not seeking bankruptcy for her own benefit, has not done everything she could have done to avoid it.

There are circumstances when it seems appropriate to say that we are morally responsible for the harm we inflict upon others, even if we have not intended to cause it. I shall focus first on the retributive view and, again, quote C.L. Ten for the definitions:

> Let us begin by distinguishing between recklessness and negligence. When a person causes harm recklessly, he or she does not intend to cause the harm, but foresees that the course of action taken runs a significant or substantial risk of causing harm, and chooses to proceed with the action without a social justification, and without taking reasonable precautions to avoid the harm. On the other hand, when someone causes harm negligently, he or she does not intend to cause the harm, is unaware that the action runs the risk of causing harm, but the harm results from a failure to observe a reasonable standard of care. In both recklessness and negligence there is failure to observe certain standards of care. We expect people to take precautions when they engage in activities which run the risk of causing harm to others. The standards of care required are those which a reasonable person would have taken in the circumstances. But in the case of recklessness, a subjective element is also present in that the reckless person foresees the risk of harm.[6]

The distinctive characteristic of recklessness is the deliberate acceptance of an excessive risk of harm. It is undeniable that all debtors deliberately accept the risk of harm. Are they all reckless? Have insolvent debtors been too adventurous? Is there an objective standard of caution which should be followed by creditors and debtors in their subjective risk assessment? With the privilege of hindsight, the answer might seem to be that all insolvents have been reckless, in breach of an adequate standard of caution. A reasonable person does not borrow more than she can pay back. This would seem to impose some moral guilt upon insolvents, and justify a punishment.

On the other hand, we could say that there is a social justification for their acceptance of risk. If loans were taken only when there were foolproof guarantees, economic progress would be hard to achieve. In addition, the creditors have voluntarily given the credit. Should not their voluntary consent be taken as evidence that precautions to avoid the harm were considered? The creditors gave away something which was in their full control, and had they feared for the recovery of the lent asset, they would hardly have parted with it in the first place.

Hindsight is not the appropriate measure of the caution of the parties in voluntary contracts. Debts always involve risk of harm. It is up to the parties to the contract to estimate the risk, determine the terms of contract, and decide whether it is prudent to accept the risk with the given terms. The parties establish the objective standard of caution together. In a market economy the markets are the mechanism which facilitates this ongoing process. The outcome of the process, a web of contractual relations, is a useful and rightful expression of rational deliberations of autonomous agents which involves, occasionally, some of the parties going broke as the risks are realized.

The fact that the parties were more willing to assume future risks than are average citizens, and the subsequent fact that the risks eventuated, cannot establish moral wrongdoing. Autonomous persons are at liberty to risk their property in contractual relationships, both in the capacity of a borrower and in the capacity of a lender. We have no obligation to follow the average conceptions of propriety when our actions fall within the limits of our rights as autonomous individuals.

It is impossible to find objective premonitory criteria to draw the line between excessive and acceptable financial risk: none of us has an infallible crystal ball. Therefore, the best judgement as to the acceptable amount of future chance is the subjective valuation of the parties most affected: the creditor and the debtor. Against this background, inclination to risk gives no reason to impose punishment on those who make a mistake in their valuation and go broke.

What about the debtor's determination to take risks after she has borrowed the asset? Can we raise our eyebrows here? Under the heading *Wasting other people's money* in Chapter 9 we have already found the answer. If the debtor has, in accepting the risks, acted within the covenants of the credit contract, she has only exercised her rights to control the borrowed asset. Exercising one's rights cannot be a cause for moral blame. However, the situation is different if the debtor has had motives for her risk decisions other than that of seeking the best return on her capital. If she has sought a greater risk because it may bring her some material or emotional benefits, even if the loan is not repaid, we may have a reason to reprove her. This reason is provided by the intentional element present in the acceptance of the risk: in order to improve her personal life prospects, the debtor ignores the promise to pay the debt.

An irrational, reckless debtor – irrational in the sense that she prefers less wealth to more – seeks greater risk only because it pleases her, and she may get satisfaction out of her failure. More common would be rational fiscal recklessness where the borrower seeks to construct her finances so that she can only win while the creditor bears all the risk of loss. An example of such action could be a leveraged equity deal.

Let us assume, to better illustrate the point, that a debtor borrows money to buy listed stocks; she owns nothing except the stocks bought, and the creditor does not require security in addition to those stocks. These are unlikely terms of credit in the tough 1990s, but not altogether imaginary. Now, the debtor may use a trust, whose beneficiary she is, to sell out-of-money call options against the stocks purchased with the loan. As the beneficiary of the trust she gets the premiums to her benefit in all cases, whereas the creditors stand to lose if the value of the shares plummets.

In case the share price goes up and the options turn in-the-money, the debtor keeps the premiums and can use the equity for delivery on the exercise day. The exercise price she gets will pay off her debt. If the stock goes down, the debtor keeps the premiums in the trust, the options expire worthless, and the lender is exposed to a loss because the market price of the collateral has dropped. By operating through a trust the debtor has made sure that she gains no matter what happens.

In the real world the financial engineering required to achieve the outcome depicted in this example may be much more complex, but the morality remains the same: risk is acceptable as long as it is assumed in the hope of profit, and as long as the assumer also carries her share of the risk. In our example, if the debtor had forfeited the premiums to the lender collecting the loan, everything would have been all right. The lender might still have suffered a loss, but this time it would have been because of her own bad lending decision, not because canny structuring increased the creditor's chance of loss and secured the debtor's chance of profit.

Such financial engineering is different from gambling. It is tempting to think, following the laws of many countries, that a gambler who goes broke is fraudulent. However, a gambler may have a firm intention to pay her debts from the winnings, but may genuinely lose all she has. For the reasons which I will detail in Chapter 11 we should refrain from making gambling an outright offence if it leads to insolvency. I am content here to note that my definition does not necessarily make an insolvent gambler guilty of fraud, not even of recklessness. The definition has to allow for intentional risk taking, otherwise it would brand all insolvent debtors reckless because all debt involves risk.

Of course, if a high amount of risk is never, as such, an indication of recklessness, then the creditors should be more wary. For instance, if they do not want to lend for gambling, they should make their position known to their debtors. Having done this, they could avoid borrowers who declare that they will gamble, and accuse of fraud debtors who punt in breach of their credit contract. Creditors have the keys to make gambling with borrowed money impossible or immoral. It would be naive to assume that they always want this: enter a casino and you are offered banking facilities to draw money on your credit card. If creditors are willing to lend for gambling, losing a borrowed fortune should not be treated as inappropriate recklessness.

There is nothing morally suspicious about seeking high returns from risky ventures, but if the returns are more secure than the chance that the debt will be paid, we have evidence that the debtor intentionally misrepresents a risk. In so doing she crosses the line between acceptable commercial risk and recklessness. Whether she deserves punishment is another matter. In those societies where discretionary trusts are a legally recognized means to protect wealth from creditors, it would be a little odd to punish bankrupts who have been far-sighted enough to use the service. Rather, the example of call options sold through a trust points out the need for legislators and creditors to trim the statutory and contractual limits that constrain debtors, so that they are not left with legal artefacts capable of covering them from the risks associated with their leveraged undertakings.

Moral considerations also enter the picture if the debtor does not conduct her affairs in the ways she let the creditor believe. For instance, a debtor may have a firm intention to pay back, but nevertheless approves much greater risks than she indicated when she induced the creditor to extend finance. Dishonest disclosure of intentions provides a reason to claim that an insolvent has been reckless and deserves to be punished. Here the evil nature of recklessness is a consequence of a breach of promise which takes place during solvency: the debtor may not have wanted to cause the harm, but has intentionally sought the increased chance of harm in spite of having promised not to do so.

Excessive risk may be enough to warrant moral blame for recklessness, but only if the debtor in taking the risk has broken the standards of caution agreed upon, tacitly or explicitly, in the contractual context, or if she has intentionally misrepresented the risk by reducing the likelihood of her credit performance below the likelihood of her being better off. This means that when the damage from risk-prone economic decisions has been unintentional it is, once again, difficult to draw ethically meaningful distinctions between reasonable and reckless credit.[7]

NEGLIGENCE

With negligence the case is less straightforward. I shall start to unravel the complexities by looking again at the initial credit decision where both the creditor and the debtor are involved. The parties to the contract have been negligent if they have not seen the possibility of risk whilst, according to some objective standard of care, they ought to have seen it. But do the parties who fail in their risk analysis breach any morally meaningful standard of care? They enter an agreement, do their best to ensure it is a successful one, but are not astute enough to foresee all the pitfalls lying ahead. It is hard to see how moral blame could arise if they simply are not competent enough and their imprudence imposes the harm upon themselves. Should that not be their business?

The harmful effects of high-risk failures may, of course, flow to third parties: society, the depositors, the shareholders, the employees. But the harms flow through a contractual network in which everyone has, at some stage, deliberately accepted her risks – or at least should have accepted them deliberately. The acceptance of risk means that undesirable consequences are accepted too.

One cannot blame others for something which one has got involved in voluntarily. However, if the harm done to third parties is genuine non-contractual harm, we have seen that it could sustain liability. Even then the unintentional nature of the insolvents' harmful actions, and the overall usefulness of risk-prone behaviour in business, should be taken into account, and may provide good reasons for leniency.

Actually, the most secure way to exclude outsiders from harm related to bankruptcies is to encourage insolvents to go broke. Bankruptcy confines the damage to the parties who have dealt with the insolvent. Complete outsiders suffer only when the losses are covered from the public purse. We should remember that bankruptcies do not cause recessions, they open the way for new enterprise. If subsidies or regulations prevent the institution from doing its job, pain is only added to the damage caused by bad business.

Bankruptcy brings the pain to an end, and confines it to those who have sought exposure to it. A failure to see risks that a reasonable person should have seen in setting out a credit contract is not an instance of morally blameworthy negligence. If the institution of bankruptcy is allowed its proper role in a market economy, the contracting parties impose harm only upon themselves, which they have every right to do.

What about events that take place later in the life of the contract? This is a concern in the case of the debtor only, since the creditor's judgements have little importance after she has surrendered control of the asset. The question is now whether the debtor's risk assessment should be subjected to some objective standard, or whether it is enough that she works out the chances as well as she can?

BAD JUDGEMENTS AND DOING ONE'S BEST

In negligence, according to the definition on p. 109, there is no intention to cause the harm and no knowledge of the impending harm, but rather a failure to observe a reasonable standard of care.

Accordingly, we shall now examine what the reasonable standard of care in economic judgement should be, or the strength of the prognosticating powers that may be required of a debtor. Thus it should be borne in mind that the following discussion is about failure in the assessment of risk, not about failure in the actual payment.

My claim is that all bad judgements do not deserve moral blame. Business judgements are morally bad only when it is reasonable to say that we had the power to do better. If I use, as a debtor and in order to meet my commitments, my skills to a lesser extent than I am able to, and the consequence is harm to others, it is an intuitively appealing idea to say I have done moral wrong because I have been slack or lazy. But if I intend to do the best I can, and make a genuine effort to that end, it is futile to declare that I did a moral wrong when I did not fare well.

Lack of intention to do a first-class risk evaluation is the criterion for negligence which sets the moral standard for punishing negligent bankrupts. It is a subjective criterion which holds that if an insolvent has not used all her talents to meet her commitments, she deserves moral blame. She has not, like a fraudulent debtor, withheld wealth from her creditors, but she has failed to exploit skills and intelligence which could have been turned into wealth.

Before starting to punish bankrupts who seem to do worse than they should have been able to, a few words of warning are necessary. First, we have to limit the eventual punishment to the cases where failure to do one's best causes the damage. If the debtor had arrived at the perilous decisions even after her best efforts had made her aware of the greater amount of risk, the case is one of recklessness. She would still, in her full capacity, have been willing to take the chance, and there would not have been anything morally wrong in her doing so as it would only have been an exercise of her rights – provided that she acted within the authority granted by the credit contract, and that her intentions were sincere in the sense specified above in our discussion of recklessness.

Only if the debtor, by committing herself totally, had drawn a different, more successful conclusion leading to more successful consequences, could the damage caused by her bad judgement be assigned to her negligence, which then could be subjected to moral blame. But it is always an extremely difficult, if not impossible, matter to evaluate what a person's conclusion would have been had the factual situation – the degree of engagement of skills – not been what it actually was. Therefore, it is best not to convict a person morally on the basis of speculation as to what she might have done in a hypothetical situation.

Now the second word of warning. Lack of intention to do one's best is a subjective state of mind, and relative to the bankrupt's skills. There are certain dangers in attaching to credit an objective standard of care, falling short of which exposes one to moral censure. We are now dealing with the ethics of bankruptcy of natural persons, which means that the theory covers all individuals who can go broke, that is, all individuals who have financial liabilities. We are talking about everybody and anybody.

In the case of negligence in traffic, the licence examination and the Traffic Code present the objective standards of care required. In the case of bankruptcy, the Bankruptcy Code may attempt to do so. But for the purposes of an ethics of bankruptcy we do not have a universal code of care, setting the standard for approved risk behaviour in financial affairs. All we have is the idea that everyone should take as good care as she can, and make as good judgement of the risk as her skills allow. A moral theory can argue that contracts should be honoured, unless certain excusing conditions are present, but it cannot determine how, within that general framework, every single business or household should run its finances. There is no ethically correct minimum of prognostic prudence all individuals must possess. For instance, a standard of care based on average talents would automatically victimize those whose skills fall below the average; they would find it impossible to observe a benchmark which is beyond their capacities.

Every person who is not in custody has to deal with finance in the modern world. It would be wrong to postulate a standard of care which would, automatically, make some person's dealings immoral. We have to leave it up to the persons themselves to decide on the level of care. These decisions are made every day in the context of monetary transactions and the matter is settled in the marketplace. This makes the idea of negligence in business different from negligence associated with activities such as driving.

I cannot choose with whom I shall share the road and the risks of driving – a fact which makes it appropriate to enforce a public standard upon those who use the road. The standard is one that all are capable of observing: it is reasonable to expect that everyone driving in traffic can do what the rules require. In the case of credit, it is my decision who the other parties are. In the world of credit, an objective standard of care is not needed to stave off unwanted risks.

COMMERCIAL RISK CALLS FOR COMMERCIAL JUDGEMENT

Financial activities take place in contractual frameworks. In a free market voluntary contracts remove the protection we normally enjoy from harm caused by others. A loan contract exposes the parties to perils as well as to benefits. Standards and rules which increase predictability and risk-avoidance should not dominate commercial activities because seeking benefits by accepting risks is the essence of business. At the present stage of technological development traffic cannot exist without risk, but its functions are improved if individual risk-taking is discouraged. Business cannot exist without risk, but its success is enhanced if individual risk-taking is encouraged.

It is true that contracts may lead to risks that are undesirable from society's viewpoint because of the economic consequences of a failure. These are the cases when we would say that the risks involved have been excessive. Nevertheless, if voluntary contracts were controlled by rules defining the approved levels of commercial risk, the consequences would be far more damaging than occasional insolvencies caused by excesses.

Risk, and the ensuing reward for successful risk-taking, are the movers of the economy, which is a process of constant weighing of risk involved against the reward offered. Some people want more risk and more reward, others are happy with less. All projects deemed reasonable find funding, while unreasonable ones do not find it because no creditor is willing to part from her wealth against her perceived interests. The success of market economies is a fact which proves that the self-interested rationality of market participants is the unsurpassed guarantee of efficient and balanced allocation of risks, far superior to any standard or rule imposed upon the process from outside.

A competitive market where autonomous agents make informed voluntary decisions yields the optimal output, and failures are its inevitable dross. The practical justification, both for the procedure and for the dross, is that they facilitate a better overall result. As one of Australia's most eminent economists, Max Corden, has put it:

> One should assume that private savings and investment decisions are optimal unless there are particular reasons to believe to the contrary. There is no reason to presume that governments or

outsiders know better how much private agents should invest or save than these agents themselves.[8]

A more philosophical justification to the same end is that both markets and failures manifest autonomy. A market economy allows an individual to build her economic life upon choices. It reflects her nature as an autonomous agent better than any central planning could ever do. Market is the morally superior economic system because it pays greater respect to the most fundamental moral characteristic of human beings. It is no miracle that it has proved to be the most successful system too: like any living organisms, humans flourish in an environment which takes into account what kind of beings they are.

Market forces guarantee that, in general, creditors are successful in evaluating risks and pricing credit: those who are not will lose their money and can no longer extend loans! This explains why voluntary contracting beats any bureaucratic effort to regulate entrepreneurial risk-taking. While insolvencies are the killer cells of an economic body, quick, efficient and unstigmatizing bankruptcy proceedings finalize the healing process without causing disturbing complications. When insolvents' autonomy is restored without extra fuss they can contribute to the economy instead of draining judicial and welfare resources. The institution of bankruptcy can be harnessed to do its bit for the prosperity of society.

It may be noted that some legal standards punish reckless or negligent behaviour by insolvents, or by representatives of insolvents. For now, I want to pay attention to the distinction between the moral and legal use of the concepts. I have, previously, used the terms in a strictly moral sense, and sought to prove that moral guilt is associated with reckless or negligent financial behaviour only if a guilty mind, *mens rea*, is present as an attribute of the debtor's intentions.

My argument is actually supported by the legal use of the terms: in law insolvents are not examined in regard to the amount of risk they have accepted. Rather, judicial standards of care relate to how well they have been aware of matters of fact: it is required that the borrowing agent makes her decisions from the position of a fully informed reasonable person. The law does not punish risk-taking during solvency, but it may punish ignorance after the risks have brought about losses because it assumes that a person ought to be aware of her state if she is insolvent.[9] Thus, the legal association of recklessness and negligence with insolvency offences does not indicate that engaging in risky ventures is a morally dubious activity in itself.

The effort to find an objective way to draw a distinction between morally reprehensible financial negligence on the one hand, and bad judgement on the other, runs into insurmountable difficulties. The same applies to recklessness. We cannot avoid the principle that moral reprimands for reckless or negligent investments should be triggered only by irrational or fraudulent intentions. Therefore, bankrupts deserve punishment for recklessness only when they have assumed risks for irrational pleasure or misrepresented risk in order to gain personal benefit, and for negligence only when they have not been serious in their efforts to assess the risks.

However, it becomes more a matter of terminology than substance whether these moral wrongs should actually be included in the concept of fraud. So far the discussion supports the doctrine that sincere acceptance of high risk is not morally wrong, but these results were mostly reached in a retributivist context. A utilitarian might still insist that when risk-prone financial behaviour causes harm, it is reckless or negligent in the evil sense without qualifications. She may want to discourage damaging failures, and penalties are a good deterrent.

DETERRENCE

It is a popular assertion that bankruptcy should be a harsh institution in order to deter people from adventurous, extravagant or fraudulent living. I shall call this the deterrence thesis. The harshness can be brought about in varying degrees. Even in its most lenient form, the US Bankruptcy Code being the best example, bankruptcy is something people rather seek to avoid. The reason for this is simple: a bankrupt loses her assets, and has to live through a stigmatizing period of life when the trustee distributes her estate. No one, except an insolvent, sees this as an attractive idea.

Many countries have tougher laws in order to ensure that the deterrent works. Conditions may be attached to the discharge to increase the pain. Typically, they interfere with the civil rights of the bankrupt by limiting her powers to look after her affairs or participate in communal life. The pain can be made even greater by prolonging the time a bankrupt is deprived by these disabilities. Such measures have played an important role in common law countries.

The highest level of harshness dispels the notion of discharge altogether. In continental Europe and Latin America, where discharge has been virtually unheard of, the deterrent has been regarded as effective only if the debtor has no means, except perhaps death, to part her from her debts. These jurisdictions reduce bankruptcy to an instrument of debt enforcement and collection, without consideration for the rights and well-being of the insolvent.

As became evident in the section examining the history of the institution, bankrupts have in the past been subjected to even more intimidating ill-treatment. Violence, slavery and imprisonment have only in the twentieth century given way to more humane deterrents. The basic argument behind these now outdated extremes was the same deterrence thesis which is used to justify the quasi-penal nature of some contemporary laws. Thus we have reason to ask whether the thesis can support the current deterrents any more than it could excuse the practice of cutting insolvents into pieces.

In looking for the answer I shall draw a distinction between deterring hardship as a behaviour-guiding levy on the one hand, and as a punishment on the other. The former hardship would be acceptable to a retributivist even when no moral wrongdoing is evident, the latter would not. I shall also examine the utilitarian aspect: do punitive deterrents actually bring beneficial consequences?

DEBTOR'S CHARACTER AND SKILLS

There are two assumptions underlying the deterrence thesis. First, insolvency is seen as something which is the debtor's fault – either in the moral sense or in the sense of deficient skills. Were it not the debtor's fault, it would not be something her deliberations – and deterrence seeks to guide her deliberations – could affect. Second, it is believed that deterrents cause more benefits than harm.

The first assumption tells us that insolvents lack integrity, prudence or both.[10] They have a dubious character, therefore it is not desirable that they get involved with credit. On the contrary, they should be discouraged from it by being told how nasty the consequences of eventual insolvency are. It is assumed that there is some inherent inadequacy in the insolvents' personality which contributes to the insolvency. Bankruptcy rules are a social measure compelling people to identify their inadequacies and to act within the limits of their talents.

The argument which seeks to justify deterrence by focusing on the character and skills of the debtor obscures the line between punishment and social control. Both a retributivist and a utilitarian would take it as fully acceptable for a society, at least for a democratic one, to guide human behaviour by making some actions attractive, and some repellent. Taxes on luxury items, or on polluting activities, are an example. Let us put pollution under closer scrutiny. This is an activity which has negative effects for society. By the same token, it is related to practices – production of goods and services – which are beneficial. Therefore, an extra levy is put on the unwanted element – pollution – while the activity itself is not outlawed. It might be suggested that harsh bankruptcy practices represent a similar behaviour-guiding levy on the negative side-product – insolvency – of a beneficial practice, which is credit.

However, the analogy is mistaken. In the case of disincentives created through taxation everyone involved in the beneficial activity gets their share of the charge. This is not the case in harsh bankruptcy proceedings. Only those who actually turn insolvent get to taste the hardships. This makes the calamity more like punishment than social engineering. It does not help to reply that all those going insolvent get what is their due. Credit, not insolvency, is the relevant generally beneficial activity. Behaviour can be guided only if it is in the control of the agent. When the debt was taken, the insolvent did not know she would go broke. Her decision to borrow was not a decision to become insolvent, neither was it the outcome the lender intended.

Insolvency is a sign of things gone out of control. Therefore, for behaviour-guiding purposes the relevant activity has to be credit. Encumbering the insolvents alone would be just a punishment for the unintended course the events subsequently take. If a number of people get involved in a generally beneficial activity which, occasionally and unexpectedly, may cause harm, and only those people who can be identified as the direct cause of the harm are targeted for reprisals, then the people targeted are not paying a levy for the purposes of social control, they are being punished.

If bankrupts are exposed to deterring hardships, the correct analogy to pollution taxes would be that only those polluters whose activity could be shown to cause immediate environmental damage, such as destruction of surrounding forest or responsibility for deterioration of nearby water, would pay. Then again, it would be more natural to call the payment for pollution a fine, a punishment for doing harm, rather than a levy.

So, from a retributive viewpoint, penalizing bankruptcy laws cannot be justified as behaviour-guiding levies because insolvencies do not happen at the discretion of the impecunious. Honest debtors may want to initiate bankruptcy proceedings which relieve them of their agony, but they never want to go broke while they are solvent. This remains valid as long as we presume that rational beings prefer more wealth to less wealth.

Next, we shall leave the debtors' subjective intentions aside. Is there some objective standard which, if observed, could help them to avoid the unfortunate failures? If we could accept that bankrupts should have known that they would end up losers, then the events leading to insolvency would still be within their discretionary capacity, and it would not be irrational as social engineering to make them pay the price for their false optimism.

In the case of recklessness and negligence, the moral problem was the willingness to accept risks and the failure to evaluate the amount of risk. We found that exposure to commercial risk is desirable, which, in the present context, implies that a deterrent should only seek to discourage risk-taking which actually leads to a failure. Thus, in the case of deterrence, the focus is on the capacity to know that a risk will eventuate, that it is actually a 100 per cent certainty.

Our angle is now a more utilitarian one than in our discussion of recklessness and negligence: can damages be prevented by a higher level of talent if ineptitude attracts extra pain? However, an affirmative answer to this question carries retributive significance too. It would indicate that insolvencies are a consequence of a want of proficiency rather than of unexpected circumstances. If the decision-making could be improved by painful deterrents, the added pain could be described as a levy and be all right to a retributivist.

Is it reasonable to assume that the debtors' fitness for borrowing would be increased by extra pain when going broke? This is an empirical rather than a philosophical question. Research suggests strongly that debtors' characters and skills play only limited roles as causes of defaults. Most studies conclude that macroeconomic changes are a major factor behind bankruptcies.[11]

Another important reason is unpredictable changes in personal circumstances. On the basis of a literature review, Ryan found that debt default cannot be attributed to the fault of either the debtor or the creditor, but rather is due to illness and unemployment:

'research findings indicate that debt defaults tend to be a multi-faceted phenomenon, which cannot be clearly attributed to either being solely the fault of the debtor or the fault of the creditor'.[12]

The message of empirical research is that insolvency is not, primarily, dependent on the personal characteristics of the debtor. Thus, it is hardly something whose odds the debtor could have estimated any better in the light of more draconian bankruptcy rules, which tried to induce her to weigh more carefully her chances of survival. Suppressing the civil rights of insolvents would not bring debtors any new information on pending changes in interest rates, employment or health.

As a rational agent who does not want to go broke, a debtor plans her actions as well as she can on the basis of what she knows. This takes us back to the assumption that a debtor can only be held accountable for her subjective intentions. They, necessarily, lead a rational person to the best judgement she can make. If the intentions are sincere, the best judgement will be best ethically too, as it has been reached after paying respect to the promise made to the creditor. On top of that, there is no objective truth about the survival skills required in future, which could or should be observed by the debtors. Insolvency is not an activity on which a social charge or levy could be imposed because the increase in harm inflicted cannot help those deterred to better performance.

BENEFITS FROM DETERRENCE

We are now led to the second, markedly utilitarian, claim underlying the deterrence thesis: the less appealing the institution is made, the less bankruptcies – and consequently less harm – there will be. After the conclusions reached above, it should not be a surprise that empirical evidence proves this claim false. In the United States the advantage of bankruptcy varies from one state to another, since the states have the power to legislate on the amount of exempt property (i.e. property not distributable to the creditors). Experience has shown that larger exemptions do not increase the susceptibility to bankruptcy.[13] Another finding is that when personal bankruptcy rates are high the creditors' losses do not rise in the same proportion.[14]

These facts reiterate the conclusion, drawn in the examination of the utilitarian argument for discharge,[15] that bankruptcy is the last resort for the poor, not a safe haven for fortune seekers. People do not find it easier to commit bankruptcy if it leaves them with a few thousand more, nor do forced-down bankruptcy numbers guarantee fewer losses to the creditors.

Empirical evidence suggests that hardships imposed upon honest debtors do not bring any additional benefits. Could benefits be obtained if austerity scared crooks? The tradition associating bankruptcy with crime has always been a boost to the deterrence thesis. If bankrupts are crooks, there is no reason to save them from tough times. On the contrary, potential criminals should be deterred by sinister laws.

However, the identification of bankruptcy with crime is a delusion. In Canada a maximum of 2.4 per cent of business bankruptcies may have involved fraud,[16] in the US the figure is of the same magnitude.[17] Likewise, in personal bankruptcies dishonesty is found to be a very small factor.[18] The suggestion that harsh laws are justified because they may reduce fraud falls short of the mark because bankruptcy is not exploited by profiteers and crooks to any significant extent. Fraud deserves a punishment, but this does not justify deterrents punishing all bankrupts collectively.

Institutional hardships would cause extra harm without bringing additional benefits. The fact that an insolvent loses everything she has is a gloomy enough scenario to ensure that people do what they can to keep their noses above the water. As Adam Smith has said, 'Bankruptcy is perhaps the greatest and most humiliating calamity which can befal an innocent man.'[19]

Actually, some research findings hint that draconian laws may encourage crime related to bankruptcies. A recent study has found that in Sweden and Finland there may be criminal offences behind more than one in five business bankruptcies.[20] In comparison with American and Australian findings, this figure is very high. One reason for it could be that in Nordic countries discharge has not been available to personal bankrupts.

It is common in small business everywhere that owners are personally liable for the debts of their enterprise. When a business fails, the liabilities overwhelm the owner-guarantor. If she cannot get a discharge, the penalties for fraud that secures her a nest egg may well appear more attractive than bankruptcy law's mandatory sentence of life in servitude. Deterrents have adverse effects if they make honesty look like a less appealing alternative.

The fall of deterrence thesis marks the end of the moral armoury mobilized to break up the insolvents' rights. When the battlefield is cleared we are left with the conclusion that the justification for discharge, set out in Part III, has fended off the attacks focusing on the contractual, fiduciary, tortious and criminal liability of honest debtors who have not wanted to cause harm.

Ethical and empirical evidence join hands to point out that insolvents should be relieved of their misery efficiently and promptly without punitive conditions. The benefits of debtor protection are not achieved at the cost of a collapse of commercial standards, but are fully compatible with the general duty that debts should be paid, and with the general fact that debts will be paid.

Part V

Applying the principles
A current affair

I shall finish the excursion into the bankruptcy of natural persons by applying the results so far obtained to some topical issues within contemporary legal, social and political debate. My purpose is to decide whether existing institutions meet the ethical standards we have found appropriate, whether some recent suggestions for institutional reform are based on an adequate and consistent ethical insight, and whether the so-called 'excessive 1980s' exposed any new phenomena which should be accounted for in an ethics of bankruptcy.

Chapter 11

Bankruptcy law reform
An ethical perspective

LAW REFORM INQUIRIES IN THE UNITED KINGDOM AND AUSTRALIA

In the 1980s two thorough and influential committee reports examining insolvency were published. These are *Insolvency Law and Practice* (Cork Report) in the United Kingdom, and *General Insolvency Inquiry* (Harmer Report) by the Australian Law Reform Commission. My commentary on legislative reform will concentrate on the Cork and Harmer Reports. They represent the freshest and most inclusive approach to insolvency. In particular, the Harmer Report is topical since a comprehensive legislative reform on the basis of its findings has yet to be implemented in Australia. The two inquiries have wider relevance in spite of their Anglo-Australian framework because they seek to clarify the philosophical problems of bankruptcy as well.

My criticism seeks to point out that the philosophy propounded by the committees relies to a higher degree than is acceptable on bias instead of argument and analysis. The outcome is that some of the concrete proposals the reports put forward are inconsistent with the aims they set out as the principles for reform. The use of bankruptcy proceedings as a civil law punishment or deterrent lies at the heart of these inconsistencies. They reflect the vigour of prejudices that keep the deterrence thesis alive.

In revising insolvency laws it has been customary, for a long time, to pay attention to the unethical and undesirable nature of complicated bankruptcy proceedings. For example, in the United Kingdom the Greene Committee commented in 1925 on the harshness of proposed measures against alleged misconduct in insolvent companies:

Many of the suggestions made to us show that the idea that fraud and lesser malpractices can be stopped by the simple expedient of a prohibition in an Act of Parliament, dies hard. Other witnesses with a view to making such malpractices impossible have advocated the imposition of statutory regulations and prohibitions calculated, not merely to put a stop to the activities of the wrongdoer, but to place quite intolerable fetters upon honest business. . . .

It appears to us, as a matter of general principle, most undesirable, in order to defeat an occasional wrongdoer, to impose restrictions which would seriously hamper the activities of honest men and would inevitably react upon the commerce and prosperity of the country.[1]

In north America the spirit of expediency and efficiency has dominated legislative work on insolvency. This is best expressed by the concept of straight discharge, which means an institution clearing debts after the shortest possible time required for the administration of the estate. The views adopted by the United States Bankruptcy Commission in 1973, and by the Canadian Study Committee on Bankruptcy and Insolvency Legislation in 1970, have been summarized in the following manner:

Both the United States Commission and the Canadian Committee gave considerable thought to matters of policy including the philosophy of bankruptcy. Neither saw its recommendations as constituting a denial of the principle that debts properly incurred should be paid. For each body, that principle was an important one. Nonetheless, it had to be balanced against other social interests and set against the benefits which might be obtained from a system in which discharge from both one's debts and from the status of bankruptcy might be more readily achieved.[2]

Both the Cork and Harmer inquests open by giving explicit recognition to the ideal which inspired their American and Canadian counterparts. The Cork Report states that it is important

to devise a system of law to deal compassionately with the honest though unfortunate debtor who is often no more than a bewildered, ill-informed and overstretched consumer. The system must enable the insolvent to extricate himself from a situation of hopeless debt as quickly and as cheaply and with as little fuss as possible.[3]

The Harmer Report is even more straightforward:

> On a more abstract level insolvency law is viewed by some as the guardian of values that seem appropriate in the conduct of the credit economy. It is sometimes perceived as the vehicle for regulating the credit economy by imposing sanctions, often penal in nature, upon those who misuse or abuse the credit facilities that are made available to them. However, it does not seem appropriate to the Commission for a law, the prime function of which is to provide an ordered legal process, to be the vehicle for such a regulatory role.[4]

CONDITIONAL DISCHARGE

Immediately after the passage quoted above, the Harmer Report allows for two exceptions: regulatory sanctions are appropriate in regard to directors of companies engaged in insolvent trading, and in regard to individual bankrupts 'whose behaviour should be circumscribed through the mechanism of discharge from bankruptcy'.[5] After leaving the gate open for attaching penalizing conditions to discharge, the Harmer Report misses no opportunity to emphasize the regulatory role discharge should play: '*Recommendation.* The Commission agrees that protection of the community and deterrence of commercially unacceptable conduct are considerations which should feature prominently in determining the appropriate discharge policy.'[6]

These considerations lead the Harmer Report to reject the concept of straight discharge. Thus, in the end, the Commission is not at odds with the common law tradition of conditional discharge, or with the Cork Report which never renounces the regulatory and deterrence functions of bankruptcy as its Australian counterpart at first appears to do. Unlike the Australian reformers, the Cork Report lists the maintenance of commercial morality as a basic objective of insolvency law:

> It is a basic objective of the law to support commercial morality and encourage the fulfilment of financial obligations. Insolvency must not be an easy solution for those who can bear

with equanimity the stigma of their own failure or their responsibility for the failure of a company under their management.[7]

This well expresses the hard-line philosophy which in common law countries, in spite of attempts to recognize more liberal principles, upholds the punitive order of conditional discharge. The core idea is that tough bankruptcy laws are justified because they deter debtors from defaulting. It is an erroneous philosophy because deterrents are unnecessary in encouraging potential insolvents to respect moral standards.

RETROSPECTIVE INCRIMINATION

In discussing offences related to insolvency, the Harmer Report drafts a major principle which should guide the development of modern law: 'It is not appropriate to frame bankruptcy offences in such a way that the conduct referred to is only an offence because bankruptcy occurs.'[8]

The justification for the principle is easy to understand: it prevents retrospective incrimination. Nonetheless, the Cork Report recommends that gambling should be treated as an offence if the punter later becomes insolvent.[9] The Harmer Report – although recognizing the discrepancy between retrospective punishments and the current philosophy of bankruptcy – falls short of recommending the revision of the Australian bankruptcy law[10] which makes gambling an offence if bankruptcy follows.[11]

I shall here examine gambling as an example of retrospective incrimination of bankrupts. Although it is an intuitively appealing idea to discourage the betting of potential bankrupts, the incrimination lacks ethical sense. If punters have no intention of becoming bankrupt, and could not have foreseen the bankruptcy, they have not committed any moral wrong, and have not been in a position to adjust their behaviour in the fear of penalties. A threat of punishment does not increase their odds, or their knowledge of their odds.

Losing a legally placed bet should not be punished any more than winning a legally placed bet should be rewarded – in addition to what the rules of the game stipulate. In particular, gambling can hardly be seen as harmful or immoral in societies which encourage it as a major means of collecting public revenue. A good example is the state of Victoria in Australia, where a ministerial comment expressed official pleasure after news that newly introduced poker machines had reached the highest average per machine turnover in the world: 'It's very pleasing Victorians have taken to gaming machines in the way they have.'[12] It would be ludicruous if the legislators, who praise gambling and build public services on the wheel of fortune, were willing to incriminate those who happen to turn insolvent after answering the state's call to turn the wheel.

DISABILITIES

Similar anomalies are evident in the reports' handling of non-criminal penalties. Apart from conditional discharge, infringements of the civil rights of bankrupts have been advocated as a deterrent. The two reports, anxious to present a modern outlook, scorn punishing insolvents who have not committed any offence. The Cork Report explicitly states that: 'Bankruptcy is not, in itself, a crime and never has been. The bankrupt is not a criminal.'[13]

Nonetheless, both inquiries insist on severe disabilities to be imposed upon bankrupts for long periods of time. Summarily, these may include one or more of the following: surrender of passport and restrictions on travel; exclusion from the common law privilege against self-incrimination; restrictions upon obtaining credit; prohibition against acting as a director, liquidator or trustee; redirection of mail; disqualification from public offices; and presumptions of liability (reversed burden of proof).

Some of these disabilities are necessary to facilitate the administration of the estate, but their overall extent and the time during which they limit the rights of insolvents clearly carry, like the conditions attached to discharge, the nature of punishment. As the Harmer Report puts it: 'In relation to bankruptcy, the laws covering discharge may be an alternative way of "punishing" bankrupts without resorting to the criminal law.'[14] Or the Cork Report: 'It is this aspect which has in the past largely contributed to the view that bankruptcy is of a quasi-penal nature.'[15]

The aspect of punitive disabilities, of which the Cork Report prefers to speak in the past tense, is still very much alive. However, it has to be recognized that both inquiries, especially the Cork Report, seek to alleviate the situation for most insolvents by suggesting alternative methods, which subject debtors to fewer rigours, when dealing with less grave or suspicious bankruptcies. These alternatives, debt arrangements and liquidation orders, would serve exactly the same ends which the Americans achieve by straight discharge.

Nonetheless, we may question what advantage can be gained from punitive bankruptcy, even when its application is limited to a few complex insolvencies.

The reason for suspicion is that a prejudiced and inconsistent philosophy still blurs the outcome. If bankruptcy, as such, is not a crime, and it is accepted as a general philosophical principle that punishments should be imposed only upon those committing offences, bankrupts do not deserve penalties by virtue of their insolvency alone – no matter how spectacular their downfall has been. This basic ethical conclusion cannot be by-passed by transferring penalties to civil law. To an ethical theory, a penalty is a penalty, no matter what category of law imposes it. Therefore, bankruptcy laws of a penal nature remain an anomaly – even if the group of people who come to suffer from the anomaly is more restricted.

Bankrupts guilty of fraud and misconduct should be punished. Even severe punishments may be justified but they should not be imposed through collective and discriminatory civil law quasi-penalties. The law contains provisions for offences committed by insolvents. More resources may be put to investigation and prosecution in order to make the wrongdoers liable for their deeds. All this is compatible with the ethics of bankruptcy. But obscuring the line between crime and insolvency is not. It is immoral to obscure the line because innocents get punished, and it is not beneficial because it does not work well as a deterrent.

The two insolvency reports have proposed some general guidelines as to behaviour which may justify harshness in applying bankruptcy proceedings.[16] The guidelines are rather ambiguous, and as such leave the decision on the nature and length of the procedure largely to the discretion of the court, with the requirement that the interpretation should lean heavily towards the opinion of the trustee and the creditors. This makes the situation even worse from the ethical point of view.

The punishment, which follows automatically from a decision to employ bankruptcy proceedings, is left largely in the hands of those who have suffered harm from the acts under consideration. In theory, the role of creditors, and the trustee representing their collective interests, allows the creditors to use punitive bankruptcy proceedings as a form of revenge against the insolvent. Conditional and disabling bankruptcy laws are not only punitive in a discriminatory and collective sense, they presume guilt and leave the sentencing largely to the victims. This is not ethically defensible. If punishments are imposed, they should be imposed upon those found to be wrongdoers after a fair and impartial trial.

The fundamental philosophical reason for advocating punitive bankruptcy laws is exposed in the following quotation from the Cork Report: 'The foundation of the whole credit world and the maintenance of respect for the legal structure surrounding it, rests upon a belief in the sanctity of contract.'[17] Nevertheless, our philosophical analysis has not supported the idea that the 'sanctity of contract', understood as the moral principle whereby parties to an agreement are under a moral obligation to carry out the agreement, justifies punitive bankruptcy proceedings. The sanctity of contract does not depend on how insolvents are handled, nor does an insolvent commit a moral wrong by breaking a contract. Commercial morality which recognizes the morally obligatory nature of a commercial debt rests, primarily, upon the debtor's autonomy, that is, her nature as a moral agent who is vested with moral duties and rights and who has voluntarily promised to pay the debt.

The moral obligation to keep one's promise is not established by the legal enforcement of contracts, although enforcement is needed to sanction immoral breaches of contractual promises. This means that there is no philosophical obstacle to discharge which achieves the aims of American bankruptcy laws: expediency and effectiveness without jeopardizing the moral principle that debts should be paid.

THE CONSISTENCY OF CREDITORS' SUBMISSIONS

When stating its vision, the Harmer Report explicitly details the modern approach to insolvency law. However, in the Report's recommendations the hard-line philosophy gets the upper hand. In the next quotation the Harmer Report concedes the defeat of its original aim:

> Guided by the consistently adverse reaction in submissions to its proposals to reduce the period before which discharge would be 'automatic', the Commission acknowledges that the prevailing perception in the community appears to be that a period of at least three years of bankruptcy is appropriate to sanction commercially unacceptable conduct.[18]

It was the submissions by creditors which persuaded the committee to give up its principles. Let us have a look at the rationality of the creditors' views. In the study by Martin Ryan, creditors' attitudes towards bankrupts were examined, and an interesting dichotomy was found to prevail: 'Despite credit-providers' often strong rhetoric against bankrupts, when queried about specifics, all credit-providers, bar one, thought there were circumstances where debtors should petition for bankruptcy and all said that they would lend to a discharged bankrupt.'[19]

The same logic moves financiers who warn of the perils of a liberal law reform. On the one hand they demand hardships for failing debtors who they see as dishonest and fraudulent, but on the other hand they are glad to grant them loans. The equivocality of creditors is understandable as their business philosophy, but fails as an argument for the purposes of the ethics of bankruptcy.

Creditors' submissions are driven by what J.K. Galbraith calls the Puritan ethos,[20] while their business is driven by their debtors. One of the flaws in the committees' work has been that creditors' opinions have enjoyed a dominant role. Only few debtors' representatives, if any, have been heard. Their views, and those of social workers and researchers, do not get enough attention because the inquiries are biased in favour of lenders. The obvious reason for the bias lies in the erroneous philosophy which puts the moral blame for the failure on the debtor.

The re-emergence of tough attitudes in the recent law reform debate may be a sign of the times. This is suggested by the fact that, in the Australian case, the 1977 Law Reform Commission proposed far more liberal legislation than its successor eleven years later. In its report *Insolvency: The Regular Payment of Debts* the 1977 Commission presented statistics pointing out that no real gains can be achieved by complicated, lengthy and penalizing bankruptcy proceedings. Accordingly, the Commission wanted to bring the legislation closer to the idea of straight discharge. When the Harmer Report was completed in 1988 the first omens of the late 1980s big bust were visible and prompted calls for reprisals.

Social historians have called the now denounced practice of imprisonment for debt a senseless system, and have seen fear of fraud as the force which kept the senselessness alive for centuries.[21] They have also pointed out that fraud had little to do with insolvency. Bankrupts were, in fact, punished for being poor, not for wrongdoing.[22] The same truth applies today. Penalizing conditions and disabilities are advocated from fear of fraud, yet fraud is a rare cause of insolvency.

The aftermath of the 1980s boosted the fear. However, an unfounded fear is nothing but a prejudice which should not replace reason in the process of legislative reform. Before we allow the excesses of the 1980s to lead us to a tougher philosophy of bankruptcy, we should find evidence that these excesses increased the amount of wrongdoing which calls for restitution, not just the intensity of our phobias fomented by a news media anxious to gormandize on famous carcasses.

CROSS-BORDER INSOLVENCY

Modern money is fast money. The electronic ability to transfer capital across the world, together with the relaxation of regulatory impediments on foreign exchange, mean that in a split second fortunes may move from one country and currency to another. The trading of goods and commodities is getting ever more international too. These developments mean that potential insolvents have their property spread around the world. When the insolvency eventuates, the creditors and trustees want to take the property under their control, but run into difficulties. Money knows no borders, but bankruptcy laws do.

Only a few international conventions are available to facilitate the recovery of property in cross-border insolvencies.[23] Otherwise the creditors and trustees have to avail themselves of national legislation in each of the countries involved. This is not only costly but the contents of the law, that is, the rights and duties allocated to each of the parties, vary considerably and may even stand in contradiction to each other. It is no wonder that the situation has been found unsatisfactory.

For instance, the Cork Report made the following observation concerning the extra-territorial aspects of British insolvency law:

> The statutory provisions governing this branch of United Kingdom law were largely devised in the Victorian era during the heydey of Imperial supremacy. They have never been reviewed or overhauled in the light of modern constitutional developments and as a result make a totally inadequate contribution to the structure of international commercial life in the context of insolvency.[24]

Similar reasoning led the Australian Law Reform Commission to the conclusion that 'Australian insolvency legislation should provide for the event of cross-frontier insolvency and, subject to certain limitations and considerations, enable an ancillary administration to be conducted in Australia as expeditiously and efficiently as possible.'[25]

National efforts to tackle the cross-border aspects of insolvency have been supported at the multinational level. In particular, European countries have sought to establish a treaty to regulate bankruptcies beyond national frontiers. Although bankruptcies are an exemption to the General Jurisdiction Convention of the European Community, which provides that civil and commercial rulings of a court in one member state are recognized and enforced in all other member states, the Community had a Draft Convention on Bankruptcy seeking to introduce a single and universal bankruptcy covering the EC. The idea of the Draft Convention is expressed in the following quotation from the House of Lord's Select Committee Report: 'The purpose of this draft Bankruptcy Convention is not to make any extensive change in the substantive law, but to ensure that a bankruptcy order made in a Member State will have effect in any other Member State.[26]

So far the EC's Convention has remained a draft. However, the Council of Europe, which by no means has the same power to bind its members as the EC had, and the European Union now has, has succeeded in going further. In 1990 the Council of Europe concluded the European Convention on Certain International Aspects of Bankruptcy (Istanbul Convention).[27] I shall not go into the details of either convention. For the purposes of an ethical study their relevant point is the same as that which the Australian Law Reform Commission made: insolvency administrations which have originated in one country should be recognized and enforced in other countries.

This doctrine is often called universal insolvency principle. Where do the ethical problems enter the picture? Ethical principles are universal by their very nature. Therefore, there should be nothing opposed to their universal application. The ethics of bankruptcy is compatible with the principle that debts should be paid. If the debtor becomes insolvent, her property should be handed over to the creditors. The accidental fact that some of the property may lie in another country should not hamper the liquidation. So far things look fine for the universal insolvency principle.

The problems start when we realize that the distribution of a debtor's property is all that the principle, as understood by the legislators and international draftsmen, implies. The Draft Convention of the EC, the Istanbul Convention of the Council of Europe, the Cork Report and the Australian Law Reform Commission completely ignore the debtors' interests. In the international context bankruptcy is still seen in a medieval light: its only function is taken to be debt collection.

The ethics of bankruptcy reveals the discharge of debts as the ethical core of any institution dealing with insolvency. Accordingly, debtors' interests have to be accounted for when the institutions are established. This has been recognized, at least to some extent, by the laws of the English-speaking world for more than a century. It should be recognized by international treaties too, and by the amendments to national laws giving recognition to foreign insolvency proceedings. However, in the two European conventions the interests of debtors, let alone the concept of discharge, have not been worth a single clause. To be exact, the Istanbul Convention contains the word 'discharge', but only in the sense that the debtors of an insolvent may get a 'discharge' from their liability once they make a payment to the liquidator of a cross-border estate.[28]

The interests of insolvents culminate in how and when they are exonerated from debts. The indifference international treaties show to this core issue of bankruptcy has ethical bearing because in most countries of the world insolvency laws do not have a provision for discharge. Debtors are enslaved for the rest of their lives by their overwhelming burdens. This is ethically unacceptable, and when proposals for regulating cross-border bankruptcies seek universally to enforce that unacceptable practice they fall short of appropriate standards.

In addition, we should remember that bankruptcy always impedes the civil rights of the debtor in a serious manner. These rights have a strong moral dimension, and should not be tampered with lightly. Unless we can be certain that legislation in other countries pays adequate respect to civil rights, we should not expose citizens to foreign laws which may strip them of their rights.

Lack of discharge in much legislation is not the only cause of worry from the debtor's point of view. The current efforts towards universal bankruptcy laws have not sought to ensure that national laws have similar definitions of the acts that may lead to personal liability. For instance, in France company directors are presumed responsible for an insolvent company's debts once a case under the relevant statutes of French law is heard against them.[29] An

Australian director of a French company could, on the basis of this kind of presumption, become bankrupt in France. If the French bankruptcy was automatically enforced in Australia, the director would lose her Australian property for a liability which might not be recognized under Australian law.

Luckily, indifference to debtors' interests has not been the only relevant flaw in the drafts for international conventions. They have been unclear and inconsistent with respect to creditors' rights too. The equal treatment of creditors has always been the cornerstone of bankruptcy proceedings. However, the classification and treatment of different groups of creditors varies from one country to another. The drafts have not been able to settle this problem properly. While neglect of the interests of debtors has not raised a critical response from learned insolvency specialists, the vague manner with which creditors have been dealt has led to strong objections. To use Ian Fletcher's expression, the 'cynical inconsistencies' in the treatment of creditors in the EC Draft Convention have been a major factor in slowing down the emergence of international treaties controlling cross-border insolvencies.[30]

It is only desirable that the slowdown, both on the level of treaties and on the level of amendments to national laws, continues until the cynical indifference to debtors' interests is corrected too. Otherwise the countries recognizing discharge may put the rights of their citizens in jeopardy by exposing them to unethical foreign laws enforcing perpetual debt bondage. The legislative principle of universal insolvency poses no ethical problems if it deals with the rights of debtors and creditors in an ethically accountable manner. Recent attempts to regulate cross-border bankruptcies have failed in this sense.

Chapter 12

Gearing up, crashing loud
Should high-flyers be punished for insolvency?

The average insolvent may be poor, in ill health and unemployed. However, some who become impecunious have led a completely different life, and may succeed in preserving their lifestyle even after a financial failure. Although only few in number, the high-flyers, as the riches-to-not-necessarily-rags bankrupts are commonly called, carry great importance in shaping the institution of bankruptcy. The publicity they attract, and the envy mixed with disgust their activities raise, contribute to the image of bankrupts as crooks. This, in turn, creates an outcry for harsh and punitive proceedings, so that the crooks will get what they deserve. Is the public image of high-flying entrepreneurs based on ethically sound judgement? Do high-flyers deserve to be punished for gearing up and crashing loud?

Let us first define 'high-flyer'. Stephen Aris has given two characteristics of high-flyers: they are engaged in a high level of debt, and their lifestyle is extravagant.[1] Paul Barry's biography of the famous Australian wheeler-dealer Alan Bond helps us to add more flesh to Aris's definition. It points out that the cruising altitude gets elevated if excesses and extravagance are associated with ostentatious display and casual treatment of luxuries.[2] Hence, we can conclude that high-flyers are people who are unashamed to indulge openly in luxuries, and who use borrowed money more than is customary to finance their business or lifestyle, or both.

RETRIBUTION FOR SOLVENT HIGH-FLYING

It became evident in the preceding chapters that we have to look at punishments from the retributive as well as from the utilitarian angle. First, to repeat the retributive standpoint, if high-flyers have committed a moral wrong, they should be punished. Does the fact that they have been keen borrowers call for retribution?

Ever since Adam Smith published *Wealth of Nations* it should have been clear that there is nothing morally suspicious in credit as such. Our inquiry has gone a step further: even a debtor's default is not enough to constitute moral wrongdoing. This conclusion should not be affected by the absolute amount of credit used, or by the gearing ratio. As a social and economic phenomenon, credit is a useful form of human activity, which rests on the right of autonomous people to engage in voluntary transactions of wealth.

What about the casual treatment of luxuries? There are plenty of moral theories under which, to mention only a couple of possible moral evils, the inequalities and environmental damage associated with grandiose spending are blameworthy. I have no intention of taking sides in regard to these theories. Whether their arguments succeed or fail does not matter for present purposes. What matters is that there is no theory which could establish that a luxurious life is morally wrong only when the indulgent subsequently turns insolvent. The moral problems of insolvency relate to the debtor–creditor relationship, and to the wider impacts it may have. As Thomas Jackson has pointed out, insolvency cannot determine the rights and wrongs of solvent living.[3]

The ethics of bankruptcy has laid down the principle that an insolvent should not be punished if her efforts to pay her debts back have been genuine. Now, in the case of high-flyers it could be claimed that the money they have wasted on luxuries is a proof that their effort to pay back has not been a genuine one – the money could have been directed to the repayment of debts. I agree that this argument may have some force had the cost of luxury been such that it would have made the difference between going broke and keeping one's nose above the water, but then the pending failure should also have been obvious to the insolvent. Since she chose to spend on herself, she intentionally left her obligations unfulfilled. Intentional forfeiture of funds from creditors in the face of insolvency amounts to fraud which deserves punishment.

However, high-flying insolvents hardly come across this situation. Their insolvencies, typically, follow from business failures. In order to get a high level of gearing the entrepreneurs are required to personally guarantee the loans of their companies – if they manage to avoid this, the chance that they will turn penniless is decimated. The immense liabilities to which high-flying bankrupts personally commit themselves in the course of their businesses are in no proportion to their private wealth. Therefore, their spending, although extravagant, usually has no relevance to the eventual insolvency.

It can be argued, of course, that any insolvent has committed a moral wrong if she has not paid off her debts with every cent disposable after she has ensured the barest minimum for the survival of herself and her family. However, this rigorous principle is at odds with the modern concept of credit. The credit contract is based upon an agreement that an individual pays back the credit, and interest accrued on it, according to a certain schedule. It does not presume that the debtor stretches her means to the extreme – although this may actually often be the case – to pay the loan off as quickly as possible.

Therefore, an ordinary mortgagee has not broken the contract if she has had a holiday in Queensland, instead of using the two grand to pay off the mortgage, six months before she is made redundant and goes belly up. Since she has not broken her promise while solvent, in spite of the little luxury she had, she has not committed a moral wrong. Nor has a high-flyer broken her promise when she goes bankrupt as the guarantor of the borrowings of her companies. She has promised nobody that she would use, prior to the bank calling for the guarantee, every penny available to her to improve the financial position of the companies. Her extravagant spending, in relation to the liabilities she has undertaken to guarantee, is as insignificant as the holidays or children's school fees of an ordinary mortgagee.

It is also worth noticing that, according to the definition, the excesses of the high-flyers have been manifest. Therefore they have been known by the creditors, who have not undertaken to curb the personal spending of their clients, but accepted the risk fully informed. The public nature of excesses is further evidence that the lifestyle of solvent high-flyers does not constitute a breach of promise. Hence, it may be morally wrong that people are rich, or that they spend money on luxuries, but the fact of eventual insolvency alone is insufficient to make these modes of living evil. As long as it is not a moral offence to be ostentatiously rich, people should not be punished for it – no matter how poor they later become. On the other hand, if extravagant living is a punishable wrong the recriminations should hit the solvent rich as well! This is the retributive verdict in regard to punishing crash-landing high-flyers.

RETURNS FROM PENALTIES

Let us shift the focus to the utilitarian argument. Here the punishment imposed upon high-flyers would seem to serve some useful ends. The targets are relatively few in number, so the harm imposed upon them, although personally great, would be rather limited. On the other hand, large benefits could be achieved by deterring people from excessive lifestyles while in debt. Whether this point is correct depends, first, on whether we accept the utilitarian view of punishing innocents, and second, whether the belief about the beneficial effects is true. Even if we found it unproblematic to punish innocents, the truth of the belief is a vexed question. It rests on the more general view that curbing credit by means of deterrent sanctions is useful.[4]

In particular, the deterrent is seen as useful because it discourages entrepreneurs. However, in the recession of the early 1990s, the factors often seen as most desperately in need of a boost have been risk-taking entrepreneurship and business borrowing.[5] Who has demonstrated more stature in the excellences of innovation, risk-taking and borrowing, which are suddenly wanted in order to do away with the recession, than the despicable high-flyers? Their tragedy is that had they just been happy to accumulate their personal wealth, greedy in the most egoistic sense of the word, they would have gone broke in far fewer numbers. But expanding their businesses rather than their private wealth was their obsession. They did not hesitate to put their personal life at risk in order to keep their enterprises on the move. A good Australian example is Alan Bond, who repeatedly pledged his massive private wealth to pay wages in his faltering companies[6] – and in the end fell victim to his commitment.

After all that has happened, it is sad irony that had people such as Bond concentrated less on safeguarding their businesses and more on their lifestyle, they would never have gone personally broke. It may be that their commitment and contribution is not so completely negative as it has become customary to assume in the immediate aftermath of their failures. Nor should we forget that, in the case of listed companies, their personal guarantees worked in favour of other shareholders as well. All got the upside potential from the gearing, while only the entrepreneurs put the total of their private wealth at stake.

The innovators and entrepreneurs put all that they have behind their efforts. It is necessary that many of them fail. Nonetheless, even the failures are needed to get an economy ahead.[7] This may sound foolish, but when we recall that the majority of new businesses fail[8] it becomes more understandable: business is not much different from any other process of development in that it is guided by trial and error.

The fiascos that resulted from leveraged corporate raiding in the late 1980s did cause damage, but they are far from constituting crystal clear utilitarian evidence of the perils of credit. It is all too common to add up all the losses of both the failed entrepreneurs' companies and their financiers, and cry: 'here's the legacy of their blunders'. For instance, a headline in *The Age*, a leading Australian daily paper, tells us that 'Tycoons leave a $30 billion legacy'. The story goes on to unveil the sin-bin: 'Australian companies lost more than $30 billion in shareholders' and depositors' funds during the frenzied "boom-and-bust" buying spree that gripped corporate Australia in the late 1980s.'[9] The grim picture is a real one in the sense that it puts all the suffering together. However, it is also a manifestly distorting way of calculating the total disappearance of wealth. *The Age* listed the ten biggest loss-makers of the 1980s, and added up their losses to get the '$30 billion' figure. This way of counting multiplies the effect of the entrepreneurs' mistakes.

Let us suppose that financier A lends to company B one billion for a venture C. Subsequently C fails, and the one billion invested in it is lost. As a consequence B goes bankrupt, and A does not get back the money it has lent. Now A has in its books a bad debt of one billion, B a one billion dollar worthless investment and C a loss of one billion from its operations. All the companies involved include a loss of one billion in their annual statement of profit and loss. Adding them up makes it look like the legacy of the failure was three billion. Nevertheless, it remains a fact that the money lost in Venture C was one billion, not three billions. The real amount of loss is distorted if the loss figures of all the companies associated with a business failure are compounded.

Exactly the same happens when exorbitant figures are presented as the legacy of the failed entrepreneurs. In the same article in *The Age*, the ten biggest loss makers are listed. The sum of their losses is allegedly $30 billion. But six of the losers are financiers, whose total losses amount to $14.1 billion, and four represent highly geared borrowers with losses up to $15.3 billion. Even a quick look at the numbers suggests that the total of $30 billion is a figure swollen by reiterating the results of bad business. The same rotten eggs are included in many different accounts, and in counting the overall harm this should be remembered.

However, it remains a fact that the tycoons did economic harm. But, for a utilitarian, the essential thing is to balance the harms against the benefits. This should be done on a global level, because the interests of all individuals should be taken as equal. Here the utilitarian gets into real difficulty if she wants to show that excessive debt is harmful. We have to keep in mind that for each bad deal, and for each wasted dollar recorded in red print in an annual report, there is someone who has benefited. The wealth invested in failed projects has not vanished from the surface of the earth. There have been wages paid for unproductive work, or prices paid for buildings worth only a fraction of the value of the deal, or maybe even grants to centres doing research in business ethics. Someone has always been on the receiving side. If the unit of harm and benefit is money, and if the point of view is global, the harms and benefits of entrepreneurial adventures are even. The wasted dollars have been pocketed by someone, either as the hard-earned reward for work done or as windfalls.

The credit expansion in the 1980s, and the subsequent assets inflation, were economic disturbances, but it is important to notice how the market mechanism was able to deal with them. It was the market, not any legislation or police operation, that brought down the harm-inflicting debt-barons. Harm was done, but the direct appeal which the collapses may lend to the utilitarians who want reprisals is deceptive. A utilitarian cannot justify the benefits of punishing the high-flying bankrupts simply by pointing to the losses they incurred in their businesses.

I shall not pursue the issue of the overall usefulness of high-flyers any further here. It is a matter of empirical research rather than philosophy. For my purposes it is enough that the utilitarian argument demanding punishment for high-flyers seems suspect when we are reminded that in the real world of bread and butter the returns from credit aversion, even the returns from aversion to high-risk credit associated with luxury lifestyles, are far from self-evident. Let us recall what Adam Smith took to be the purpose of an economy: 'Consumption is the sole end and purpose of all production.'[10]

If anything, the high-flying entrepreneurs, fuelled by credit expansion, boosted consumption – including spending in the lower air-space reserved for more modest mortals. What entrepreneurs did was merely a tribute to capitalism. Therefore their deeds cannot add impetus to a moral curse within the terms of reference of that particular economic system.

Deterrence could effectively reduce the number of bankruptcies only if it brought down the overall exposure to credit and risk, an outcome which is not welcome as it would hamper economic activity. Thus, the role of deterring penalties should be restricted to discouraging crime – the intentional misuse of bankruptcy for profiteering. Punishing innocents is not needed to scare conmen. Sentencing the offenders is enough to ensure that crime does not pay.

INSOLVENT EXTRAVAGANCE

So far we have concentrated on the pre-bankruptcy excesses of insolvent high-flyers. But what makes moral indignation especially tempting is that their lifestyle seems miraculously to survive bankruptcy. The luxuries in their lives may be reduced a little after the insolvency, but in comparison to the average standard of living most of them continue to be remarkably well off. How can this be explained? Here are three clues: fraud, relatives and legal means to set property out of the reach of creditors. I shall concentrate on the two latter alternatives as they pose more philosophical problems. Fraud, that is, concealing property from the creditors, is an already exhausted case: it deserves punishment.

Many bankrupts who fall from riches may continue lavish living at the expense of their relatives. Should this be prevented? Should the families be made to pay for the debts? I start the answer by claiming that if one person wants to donate money to another person, this should be within her powers. I cannot see any ethical reason to restrict a solvent person's right to give away something she is fully entitled to control. It is another matter that as soon as a bankrupt gains control of the wealth donated to her it may be considered as her income, and she may be liable to pass all or part of her income to the trustee.

Even if one is happy to accept that income orders may be enforced to satisfy the creditors, it should be borne in mind that honest debtors, those who sincerely have sought to pay their debts, have not committed a moral wrong deserving a punishment, nor would it be beneficial to punish them. The justification of income orders can come only from the monetary gain to the estate.

Preventing a bankrupt from driving someone else's car, or from staying in someone else's apartment, does not bring a penny to the creditors' coffers, not even if the cars and apartments are luxury ones. Interference in the bankrupt's enjoyment of luxuries owned by other people would only serve as a punishment, and would therefore be unjustified.

How about making the relatives pay the debts? They are normally the people who support the ex-entrepreneur, and they have often gained their wealth from her leveraged business undertakings. Let us first see if blood or marital ties should make us liable for other people's debts. Here it is quite evident that the answer is no. Every modern ethical outlook takes us as individuals. We are, as autonomous moral agents, responsible for our actions, but not for those of other autonomous agents. In a community we have moral responsibilities in regard to other people, but not in regard to single voluntary acts of individuals not in our custody. A credit contract is an example of such a single voluntary act which cannot impose liability upon anyone else except the individual undertaking the contract. If we were made to pay other people's debts, we would have moral responsibility imposed by something over which we have had no control; that is, other people's promises. This is not a sustainable ethical principle, regardless of the possible family relationship to the promisor.

We can counter by adding that family members may have been given, prior to bankruptcy, undeserved profits, salaries or gifts. First, a look at profits and salaries collected by relatives. Undeserved is an important qualification here, since if they have worked for the money, or sold something at fair value, they, in the light of the argument above, should have the same right to the profits they have obtained as anyone else who had received her share of pre-bankruptcy monies.

So the crucial question is what constitutes an undeserved profit? This is extremely difficult to define in general terms. The money they have made cannot be undeserved simply because the future turned sour. If profiting from a deal that later turns sour for the other party, or getting wages for a negligible employee contribution, were the criteria that determined when people have to share the liabilities of bankrupts, then a huge array of pre-bankruptcy beneficiaries would be exposed. Employees who have not been productive enough, vendors who have sold goods and properties to the failing businesses – all should take their part of the burden. This is not a viable idea. These are third parties, so they are not parties to the credit contract establishing the promise to pay back. Therefore, they have no moral obligation to participate in the paying.

Nobody commits a moral wrong by profiting from a contractual relation with a business or an individual who later goes broke. Since blood and marital ties have no relevance in allocating moral responsibility for the voluntary fiscal actions of consenting adults, relatives' pre-bankruptcy profiting is no more wrong than anyone else's. Nevertheless, there remains the possibility that their profits have been intentionally exaggerated in order to improve the post-bankruptcy prospects of the bankrupt or the beneficiaries. If so, the conduct is fraudulent. Judging when it is actually so, is not a matter for an ethical theory, but an empirical matter to be dealt with by appropriate authorities.

In the case of gifts, we have to deal with more complications. It is most appealing to think that entrepreneurs are generous, especially to their relatives, in order to secure benefits for themselves in case of eventual future bankruptcy. This line of thought goes on to the conclusion that it should be within the powers of the creditors to reclaim the donated wealth. When I examine the plausibility of this view I assume that the donor is solvent when the donation is made.

When a solvent debtor gives away something she owns the chance is always present that she may later go broke. However, since she is solvent she has a full right to control her possessions – unless some contractual covenants apply – and accordingly it is in her discretion to give away some of those possessions. This is true as long as the give-aways do not threaten her solvency. A solvent debtor's right to be benevolent is not altered if her intention in making the gift is to increase her expectations of receiving favours as a potential future insolvent, that is, if she presents her gifts 'just in case', hoping that the recipient will return gratuity should the donor fall victim to misfortune.

Since benevolence, using funds which the donor fully controls, is generally allowed we cannot say that benevolence associated with some assumed subjective state of the donor's mind is not permitted. It would make the line between permissible and prohibited actions too blurred. Also, we would have to assess the solvent donor's subjective intentions after she has actually gone broke. However, it is practically impossible to decide retrospectively whether some particular gift was given 'just in case', or out of genuine love and affection.

When we draw the line between permitted gifts and unethical hiding of property from the creditors we cannot rely on guesses as to the donor's subjective intentions. We have to stick to the facts. The first, and most important, fact is the financial status of the donor: was she insolvent, or should she have been aware of the pending insolvency, at the moment the gift was made? If she was insolvent when she acted generously, the moral right to control her property was already in her creditors' hands. She gave away her creditors' funds. A gift made by a solvent person is different. A solvent mentor spoils others with something which is genuinely her own.

There is another fact which is ethically relevant to solvent debtors' donations, no matter what their intentions are. The intentions of the donor are a fact relative to her, not to the recipient of the donation. The recipient has a right to equal consideration with everyone else, including a right to control her property. Her rights should not be diminished because her benefactor later turns insolvent and has, allegedly, had some unexpressed ulterior motives, or because she happens to be a family member. A creditor's right to get her money back from her debtor cannot be stronger than, for instance, a spouse's right to private property. Matrimonial liabilities would seriously degrade a spouse's status as an individual and as a citizen.

Whether a gift is something which violates the moral rights of creditors does not depend on the family relationship between the donor and the recipient. The crucial fact determining whether a gift should be forfeited is the financial status of the donor at the time of benefaction. Solvent donors are entitled to alienate their wealth, and recipients of those gifts are entitled to control what they own. Because creditors' rights are not broken in this chain of events, they have no right of recourse. The relation back doctrines common in bankruptcy laws impose time limits that seek to ensure that creditors have access to funds debtors have alienated pending the insolvency. The limits are ethically appropriate as long as beneficiaries are treated equally and recovery is not extended into transactions carried out during genuine solvency.

To avoid misunderstanding I wish to end the discussion on gifts by emphasizing that if they involve reciprocity they should be treated as any other kind of property. Hence, if the donor has some agreement or stipulation which gives her access to the donated funds should she turn bankrupt, they are an asset to her. As such, she should list them as her property when she files for bankruptcy and hands her assets to the trustee. What I have wanted to advocate above is that mutual love and affection is not a distributable asset. It may have been a source of wealth for a solvent debtor's family and friends, and it may be a source of wealth for an insolvent debtor. However, it is not possible to distribute love and affection to the creditors. The gifts a bankrupt has made in her solvent past should stand because the parties were morally entitled to perform the transaction. The gifts made to an insolvent should stand when they have no value to the creditors.

It seems that we have few ethically viable means to prevent bankrupts from a comfortable living at the discretion of their relatives or friends. In addition, the law has, in many countries, left potential bankrupts some legally approved means to safeguard their property. Trusts, in particular discretionary trusts, are the most notable of such vehicles. When property is transferred to a trust where it remains nominally wholly at the trustee's discretion, but in practice at the discretion of the person initiating the arrangement and providing for the trust's capital, a new legal entity is created. This entity is considered as separate from the bankrupt's person to the extent that the property vested in the trust is not available to the creditors. After the discharge there is nothing to prevent the bankrupt from availing herself of the property, which the trustee will generously pass to her upon her request.

It is interesting to note that the legislative reformers, who otherwise have recently advocated harsh measures to defend the commercial morality and creditors' interests, have chosen not to propose legislation which would require the trustee of a discretionary trust to apply in favour of a bankrupt's estate.[11] In the moral sense it seems dubious that a legal technicality can be created between property and a person who is factually in a position to benefit from that property with the effect that the creditors of an insolvent are prevented from taking the position of the factual beneficiary.

ETHICS AND SELF-INTEREST

Insolvent high-flyers are not crooks, unless they have done crooked things. Going broke is not a crooked thing if the bankrupt's intentions to pay her debts have been sincere. Whether a life loaded with debt and luxuries is crooked, may be debated. However, to me it seems unreasonable to say that people are not entitled to use what-ever purchasing power a democratic society has considered appropriate for them to have to any legal purpose they wish. It should not matter if the spending takes place in the limelight, or if there is borrowed money involved.

Basking in luxuries does not prove good character. It is no cause for grace and admiration, let alone moral praise. Rather, it reveals self-interested hedonism and ignorance of the pain and want that controls the lives of the majority of humans and animals on the earth. What it reveals is human nature in its average wretchedness. But to do a moral wrong we have to be worse than self-interested. We have to break the moral principles regulating the co-existence of self-interested creatures. These principles may, as Rawls[12] has brilliantly pointed out, emphasize the needs of those who are worse off – but only after self-interestedness has been accommodated in the picture.

Ethics cannot require us to do more than we can achieve in virtue of our natural properties. It is an empirical fact that our rationality is guided by self-interestedness. A quick look at the world as it is tells this to our common sense, and the observation is confirmed by what the more scientific faculties, like economics and psychology, assume to be the motives of human behaviour. This is not to say that glorious instances of benevolence and sacrifice never take place. On the contrary, their presence is constant evidence of the human capacity to give consideration to fellow human beings. However, praiseworthy unselfishness does not rule on the earth – if it did, ethics would be redundant.

If ethics ignores the fact that human rationality is guided by self-interestedness, it may be virtuous but can hardly be rational. We can make the point even stronger: the requirement that only altruistic deeds are ethical is without foundation because ethics stems from ourselves. There is no higher power, external to ourselves, which could make it ethically irrelevant that our own interests dominate our thinking – including ethical thinking. Now comes the final blow to the attempts to define ethical good in purely altruistic terms: it is a logical necessity that our voluntary actions are guided by our interests. Even an altruistic person performs her acts of benevolence because she wants to do so. Her interest just happens to be the fulfilment of other people's interests.

When we combine the empirical fact of self-interested rationality as the prevailing mode of human behaviour with the philosophical presumption that ethics arises out of ourselves, and with the logical necessity that our voluntary actions are guided by our interests, we cannot avoid the conclusion that what matters in ethics is our interests. They have to be the starting point of moral inquiry. By the same token, we know the necessity of accommodating our interests with those of other similar agents: ethics has to give equal consideration to everyone's self-interested standpoint. A moral theory has to explain why and when our duty is to look after the interests of others even at the expense of our own pursuits, as well as why and when it is our right to expect that others pay similar respect to our interests.

As a result of these considerations there emerges a framework within which it is acceptable for an individual to satisfy her own wishes. As long as she observes the given limits she commits no moral wrong if she chooses to promote her own well-being. Applied to high-flyers this means that if they have, in a democratic society, chosen their flight path in conformity with the rules that define the framework allowed for self-interested aspirations, they have not committed an offence and do not deserve moral blame just because they occupied the upper layers of the financial atmosphere.

DEBT AND DISTRIBUTIVE JUSTICE

Robert Nozick has drawn a distinction between historical and end-result theories of distributive justice.[13] According to historical theories, to use Nozick's words, the justice of a distribution 'depends upon how it came about'. Any distribution of wealth is just if it is a result of first acquisition, and consequent voluntary transfers of title. The high-flyer's share of wealth clearly satisfies the historical criterion as properly as any non-leveraged accumulation of wealth would do. Use of credit does not break the chain of voluntary transactions. The end-result theories, in contrast, hold 'that the justice of a distribution is determined by how things are distributed (who has what)'. Moral principles, like Rawls' two principles of justice,[14] are applied to determine each person's just share in a society. The outcome may or may not justify the high-fliers' riches, but it cannot depend on the fact that their wealth is visible, nor on the subsequent incidence of insolvency.

No matter what perspective on distributive justice we adopt, the ways a debtor has spent her money are not ethically relevant to the debtor–creditor relationship as long as the spending has taken place within the confines of the contractual framework. At the end of the day, lavishness remains morally irrelevant to the blameworthiness of insolvency. Whether the bankrupt's passion has been charity or pink convertibles makes no difference. High-flyers who go broke have zoomed around in fast flashy planes on lease, and have had a good time aboard, but these facts do not cause the ethical radar to indicate that their crashlanding is a sign of crossing the limits of the authorized airspace. Since this conclusion may sound counter-intuitive to many of us, let's see what could be said of hard work and parsimony, virtues that are often taken to be a more acceptable source of wealth.

PARSIMONY VS LEVERAGE

Living an ostentatiously luxurious life and using a high level of debt is contrary to commonly held values. So is going bust. The repugnance we associate with high-flyers is bolstered by the ideals of hard work and parsimony. The Puritan ethos reserves the privilege of enjoying worldly goods to those who have earned their wealth through the sweat of their brow, and have sparingly put aside the fruits of their labour.

Although commonly held, these ideals do not represent any ethically defensible justification for the distribution of wealth. A coherent ethical theory may argue, as John Locke did, and Robert Nozick is compelled tacitly to assume, that mixing one's labour with unowned objects, together with subsequent voluntary exchange, gives an entitlement to private property.[15] However, a high-flyer may work up as much sweat on her brow in closing leveraged equity deals as the owner of a small business sweat-shop does in supervising her employees.

The personal effort of both may be the same, no matter whether we measure it by the amount of their perspiration or by the kilojoules they burn. Both of them use voluntary contracts with other people to maximize their reward for the sweat. There is nothing in the labour theory of property which could make one or another's effort better ethically. If the point is that hard work in a universe of voluntary contracting gives entitlement, we are bound to accept the outcome – regardless of whether it is associated with parsimony or with extravagance and credit.

From Adam Smith to Karl Marx, economists have emphasized the role of capital as a means of production: it satisfies human needs, it is good rather than bad. The productive function of capital is vastly improved by the introduction of credit which transfers capital into the hands of those who believe they can get the most out of it, and who also most often succeed in their effort: 'Credit is essentially the creation of purchasing power for the purpose of transferring it to the entrepreneur'.[16]

Capital being a necessity for the satisfaction of needs, and credit being a voluntary expression of the will of autonomous agents, which leads to a greater satisfaction from capital, we have every reason to regard credit too as a blessing. It is the mover of economic development:

> Thus, there has been an inexplicable but very real retreat from the Puritan canon that required an individual to save first and enjoy later. . . .
>
> The process of persuading people to incur debt, and the arrangements for them to do so, are as much a part of modern production as the making of goods and the nurturing of wants.[17]

As I have appealed to Adam Smith, I should recognize that he might have raised some doubts about the blessings attached to high-flying entrepreneurs. He would, most probably, have taken them as prodigal – a term he reserved for persons who consumed in excess of their productive output.[18] Smith considered frugality, or spending which leaves part of a person's production untouched as savings, to be sustainable and useful consumerism.

However, Smith's view that only manufacturing, 'productive hands', increase national production is mistaken. So is his apparent assumption that if an idle person spends a dollar, that dollar disappears from the surface of the earth. In reality, production of services brings about wealth, and prodigal spending disperses it to those who get paid for their labour and in whose hands the money recreates demand, then production and supply, and in the end consumption and satisfaction of their wants. It is obvious that the Puritan ethos of the noxiousness of credit led Smith to denounce prodigal life in spite of the fact that he otherwise recognized the trickle-down effect of spending.[19]

Parsimony may be a justifiable social norm in the face of environmental destruction, global poverty and growing population. However, smuggling it in as an associate of a labour theory of justice does not work. The hard work and parsimony ideology is just an attempt to reserve the privilege of wealth to those who already control it, or whose personal skills happen to make them unable to boost their earnings by the use of leverage. Credit is shunned because it is the great egalitarian vehicle of the market economy. It provides people with opportunities to reshuffle the pack, and by doing this it kicks the economy into motion. The kicks may cause less efficient capital to diminish in value, which is the fundamental fear of those who despise borrowers.

The Puritan ethos is advocated by conservative wealth, and by those who assimilate their interests with established and stagnant capital, with the purpose of making the rest of us believe that life should be miserable: the conservatives believe that if we do not already have the capital to pursue our aims, we should not be given the opportunity through borrowing either. Our ethical analysis points in the opposite direction: the system of free enterprise embeds freedom to get into debt as well as freedom to fail.

The effects of high interest rates, imposed in the early 1990s as a counter-measure to the excessive 1980s, are an empirical confirmation of the ethical conclusion that hard work and parsimony are not good reasons to denounce the use of credit. Parsimony was rewarded as the number one virtue when real-term interest rates were brought to historically unforeseen heights in much of the industrialized world. When the yield on risk-free deposits exceeded the long-term average return on equity in risk ventures, it became irrational to take any financial risk. It no longer made sense to take a loan for investment purposes because there was hardly any hope of enough return to pay the interest. This meant that it became irrational to invest in anything which relates to production, be it property, equipment or people.

While the assets inflation of the booming 1980s distorted economic activity, the interest-rate surge in the early 1990s killed it. High-flyers made ordinary people painfully aware of their relative poverty. The counter-measure, praising hard work and parsimony, made the pain real by introducing mass unemployment and impoverishment in absolute terms. As a matter of fact, parsimony does not create any new wealth, except perhaps interest earned on savings. However, the interest is earned by the debtors, who pay it to their creditors. The lesson of the start of the 1990s was that untenable ethical ideals proved to be untenable economic guidelines too. Or, to be more exact, they succeeded in forcing parsimony upon those who became unemployed, but only at the expense of hard work.

Credit and insolvency are just two examples of social practices which may be found offensive, but are not intrinsically evil. To recall Adam Smith: a person who does not employ whatever stock she can command, whether it be her own or borrowed, in procuring either present enjoyment or future profit, is completely crazy. Smith's declaration tells us that the use of credit is as little irrational as it is unethical.

In the 1980s, when credit was readily available and asset prices soared much faster than interest accumulated, it would have been simply foolish to focus business on anything other than leveraged asset deals. This reflects an unhealthy direction for the economy, but it does not make the business people involved in the deals bad business people. They just picked up the dollar where returns were the best. Those who were not astute or quick enough to see the turning point went broke, but they did not make the decisions that allowed the economy to put assets before production. The irrational decisions were made on the macroeconomic level when credit expansion was set loose, not on the micro level where individuals sought to profit from the distorted climate. Punishments for irrational courses of action may have some utilitarian benefits as a deterrent but punishing high-flyers for insolvency cannot, since their rationality worked as it is supposed to work. They merely erred in matters of fact and timing.

It is appropriate to end the discussion about high-flyers by recalling that they are by no means children of recent times. Since the birth of capitalism there have been cyclical fluctuations of the economy, booms followed by busts. Famous examples are the South Sea Bubble in England after the expansion of colonial trade in the early eighteenth century,[20] and the railroad collapses in the US after the nineteenth-century expansion to the west.[21] As certainly as booms gave way to busts, moral censure put the blame for the turn of the tide on credit and excessive luxuries.

In the last few years, we have witnessed this happening once again in recent law reform debate and in the media. However, we should keep in mind that high-flyers are a renewable resource, and as such do not pose any particularly new ethical problems for the institution of bankruptcy. The institution should be built upon sound ethical judgement and economic analysis, not on emotions stirred up by a few narcissistic individuals who have failed.

If high-flyers have done no wrong warranting punishment, the ethics of bankruptcy favours the discharge of their debts. Before the law and ethics, all deserve equal consideration. This means that a lifestyle associated with debt and luxuries is no more a reason to punish ex-entrepreneurs than it may be a reason to punish those able to pay their debts, and that a high-flyer should be presumed honest unless proven fraudulent.

Part VI

The corporate veil
Chador or gauze?

The two chapters of this final section take up the challenge of the impersonation of responsibility, thrown down on us by corporate capitalism. The corporate veil, woven by the limited personal liability that usually accompanies corporate structures, is an integral part of the outfit of a market economy. It is a major vehicle in the material progress of consumer capitalism, which has overshadowed the productive efforts of other economic systems.

The creation of the corporation as an economic, legal, social and even political entity, separate from the individuals who cause its existence and actions, has unleashed new human potentials. Limited liability has multiplied the opportunities for risk-taking and accumulation of capital, as well as increased the sophistication of these processes immensely. It has allowed private property to flourish in all its modern conceptual richness – a tribute to the moral character of proprietal relationships dependent on human consent and contracting.

We are now living the latest and most advanced phase of capitalism. Its hallmark is the intangibilization of property. Physical objects of ownership – land, buildings and plants – are securitized, securities give birth to derivatives, new derivatives sprout from existing ones. All the time previously unforeseen aspects of property rights are defined, standardized and traded. These conceptual commercial products witness to the superiority of the philosophy of private property as bundles of rights that rest ultimately upon a normative basis over the classical notion of property as absolute or exclusive possession.

Incorporation has opened up to the human initiative the true moral complexities of our social relationships and helped us to use them as ostensible tools of our everyday economic interaction. The success of the market economy verifies that incorporation captures and institutionalizes some central characteristics of human nature. Institutions which were contrary to the interests and potentials of people would not be able to bring about an outcome which best satisfies people's interests and realizes their potentials.

Granted the superiority of the market economy garbed in the corporate veil, plenty of ethical dilemmas remain. How thick is the veil? Is an individual acting on behalf of a corporation free from all liability? Intuitively, it is obvious that she is not. Philosophically, business ethics tries to detect the answer. Group responsibility, whistle-blowing, corporate virtues, directors' and managers' duties, and corporate citizenship are examples of its syllabus.

Over the last twenty years research in business ethics has really taken off. The ever-ethical do-gooders have picked up that the macro-level fight against capitalism is in vain. Capitalism seems to thrive in democracy, and vice versa. This empirical fact makes such an appealing combination that only the most die-hard theorists are persuaded to favour the grim totalitarian alternatives that still continue their meagre existence in some parts of the world.

Alas, the attention of those who know better has shifted to the micro-level: if the system cannot be forced to conform with noble theoretical models, the actors within the system should be submitted instead. The corporation should be a Good Citizen doing Good Business: it ought to promote the interests of the wide community, save the environment, pay taxes and contribute to charity. Depending on the individual zeal of the advocate of Good Business, corporations ought to promote moral virtues at the expense of their profits, or in addition to making them.

It is no surprise that many corporate executives feel sympathy to the do-gooders' pursuits. The success of a corporation depends on its success in satisfying the customers' interests. If potential customers are amenable to environmentally friendly, charitable corporations, it pays off for a corporation to adopt those characteristics. So far so good, but the problems start when it is claimed that corporations have a moral duty to do Good even when it is against their long term economic interest, i.e. at the expense of their profits.

When business ethics has tackled these normative problems it has traditionally restrained its scope to descriptive ethics. Examples have been given of corporate behaviour; they have been reflected against the attitudes that prevail in business and in the community, and a discussion has sought to draw practical conclusions. Usually the conclusions underline that it does not make much sense for business to challenge a society's established ethical convictions.[1]

More recently, virtue ethics has started to play a role in business ethics. Rather than seeking to justify ethical principles through arguments, it assumes that caring for fellow beings is the fundamental ethical disposition which corporations and individuals should demonstrate alike in order to be Good Citizens. Thus, virtue ethics takes unselfish caring to be the ethical essence of the corporation, supreme to the motive of profit-making.

The problem with virtue ethics is the lack of argument in it. For instance, Robert Solomon and Kristine Hanson reply 'Of course!' to Milton Friedman's question whether corporations have social responsibilities over and above those to their stockholders.[2] But 'Of course!' gives no reason to those minds who only think about profits. The real challenge for philosophical ethics lies in finding the persuasive arguments which justify ethical rules to people who otherwise could not care less, in finding the arguments which are strong enough to justify even the enforcement of rules upon those who do not believe in suasion. This is not to say that virtue ethics is redundant. It may have an important role in developing our moral psychology towards a more altruistic direction. But it does not solve the fundamental normative problem: what should we be allowed to do, what not, and when are we entitled to force others to do something?

One major criticism from virtue ethicists towards rule-based ethics has been their fear that rules may lead to tyranny. A simple counterclaim is that ethically correct rules do not lead to tyranny – they support autonomy. It is not the 'ruleness' that is the dangerous property imposing tyranny, it is the unethical behaviour that uses rules as tools for oppression. Besides, the same dangers lurk in virtue ethics.

Joseph Des Jardins is an example of a business ethicist favouring virtues. He defines virtuous excellence in business as 'the pursuit of goods and services that contribute and advance the social good'.[3] The definition of 'social good' he leaves up to a political decision, but a political decision may imply anything. Thus, according to Des Jardin's virtue ethics, if a society firmly believes that tyranny and persecution of minorities is virtuous, that is what we should strive for! In my opinion, it is far more perilous to leave ethics at the mercy of what happens to be the current perception of virtues than to systematic arguments seeking rules and principles constrained by rationality and knowledge.

Descriptive and virtue ethics aside, we are left with the prescriptive approach to moral problems. Efforts to prescribe normative principles for business tend to rely heavily on intuition and casuistic examples. At best they take for granted some fundamental principle which is then applied to the particular problem at hand. Utilitarian principles are the most popular ones. There is nothing wrong with this approach. Business ethics is applied ethics, it cannot solve all the dilemmas of philosophical ethics. However, a better understanding of concepts like 'corporation', 'agent', and 'responsibility' may help to define the ethical environment for business. This leaves room for 'pure' philosophical analysis, but we shall also see that analysis may lead us astray if made from a too isolated perspective.[4]

Insolvency is among the areas where those who call for Good Business have raised their alarm. Good Businesses do not go broke, it happens to cowboys only. They are morally bad, and should not be left hiding behind the corporate veil. In Parts II and III we discredited the claim that insolvency as such is morally bad. Now the inquiry will go further and examine company debt and bankruptcy. What is the justification for the limited liability corporation? Is a corporation morally liable for its debts? What is the moral liability of the directors and owners of an insolvent corporation? Does a bankrupt corporation have a right to reorganize? Do we have a moral duty to pay our corporate creditors? These questions will be answered as we penetrate to the pattern of the corporate veil.

The ethics of bankruptcy has so far obtained most of its normative power from a modest Kantian notion of autonomy, and from utilitarian reasoning. I shall try to preserve the holistic approach of the theory in this section. Hence, in Chapter 13 I shall use the results unearthed in earlier chapters to assay contemporary theories of corporate moral personhood, which is the crucial determinant in the allocation of moral responsibility, rights and duties to corporations, their constituents and those affected by their actions. The discussion culminates in a new philosophy of the corporation, which draws together my account of corporate moral agency.

After Chapter 13 has characterized the moral soul of the corporate body, Chapter 14 will endeavour to solve the normative puzzles of corporate insolvency. We have already set limits to an individual's economic liability. These last chapters will reveal whether it is ethical to replace those limits by much more liberal provisions of incorporation. The analysis and justification of limited corporation is the final building block which completes the construction of the ethics of bankruptcy.

Chapter 13

Corporate moral personhood

Milton Friedman's 'The social responsibility of business is to increase its profits' is a classic piece of business ethics which opens the discussion about corporate personhood in many textbooks.[1] It is usually followed by articles which then refute Friedman's thesis, often by arguing that the corporation is more than a mere aggregate of individuals or an agent of stockholders. Friedman's critics give different reasons why the agency[2] or aggregate view he represents is mistaken, but their common credo is that the corporation has a distinct personality of its own which has responsibilities and rights similar to those we attach to natural persons. I shall begin with Friedman's paper. Then I will proceed to the strengths and weaknesses of the main rival theories, combine that material with some results of the earlier parts of this study, and finally, present a new philosophy about the kind of personality corporations have.

MILTON FRIEDMAN: NO CORPORATE PERSONHOOD

> in his capacity as a corporate executive, the manager is the agent of the individuals who own the corporation or establish the eleemosynary institution, and his primary responsibility is to them.[3]

According to Friedman, the corporation has no morally relevant personality as such but is only a technical medium to further the interests of the aggregate of individuals who own it. It can have no moral responsibility apart from the purpose for which it has been set up, that purpose usually being profit-making. If the managers who decide on behalf of the corporation assume roles which do not support the profit motive, they are actually imposing taxes without a warrant from the owners. They surpass the area of their legitimate governance by introducing some of the functions of government to the running of business. This is contrary to the interests of those whose agents they are. It is also subversive, as it extends the scope of the political mechanism to an area where it does not belong.

It should be noted that Friedman is not advocating ruthless, unlimited profiteering without regard to any rules. He is not saying that the corporation should try to maximize its profits by breaching the law or contractual obligations. Friedman's view is distorted when it is claimed that he leaves the ethical guidance of business completely to economics.[4]

What Friedman is propounding is that the framework of rules that governs business activity, as well as other human activities, should be left up to the political process to decide, and that individuals should be free to pursue profit within the field a democratic government has marked off for business. This division of powers preserves a lot of room for ethical thought, both in regard to the nature of rules which are politically decided, and in regard to the manner in which profit ought to be pursued under these rules. It is another matter that Friedman's work as an economist tells us that he would favour a fairly loose framework of control, but this is not a necessary consequence of his normative argument in his paper on corporate social responsibility.

The corporation as an agent for an aggregate of owner-individuals is the core of Friedman's normative argument. This conception of the corporation enjoyed wide acceptance among legal theorists[5] and economists[6] when he wrote his article. However, new ideas have taken over legal and economic theory since the 1970s. I shall draw on them later when I develop my own proposal for corporate moral personhood.

Law and economics apart, there are also philosophical objections to Friedman's position. They point out that corporations and their actions cannot always be reduced to individuals and their conduct. Peter French was the pioneer in applying the tools of analytical philosophy into business ethics. The results of his analysis are diametrically opposed to Friedman's views.

PETER FRENCH: FULL-FLEDGED CORPORATE PERSONHOOD

> In short, corporations can be full-fledged moral persons and have whatever privileges, rights and duties as are, in the normal course of affairs, accorded to moral persons.[7]

French starts from the fact, evident in language, that corporations have intentions. He then focuses on corporate decision-making processes, which he calls CID-structures, and says that they introduce permanence into the corporate entity, thus making it able to stand on its own regardless of changes in its constituency (owners, managers, creditors, etc.). To French, corporate nature is non-eliminatable, irreducible to an aggregate of individuals. A corporation has intentions and rights of its own, and is a moral person and a moral agent.[8]

The definition French uses for agency is a Davidsonian one. The following quotation from French, in which he refers to Daniel Dennett, sums up which entities are entitled to a Davidsonian agency:

> For an entity to be treated as a Davidsonian agent it must be the case that some of the things that happen (some events) are describable in a way that makes certain sentences true, sentences that say that some of the things the entity does were intended by the entity itself.[9]

French's argument goes smoothly. It is no wonder that it has received wide recognition. Nevertheless, it has also been subjected to crushing criticism.[10]

The critics underline that while corporate actions can be described as intentional, it is always natural individuals' minds which possess the intentions. The corporation is an eliminatable subject, not a moral person. As we will see, these philosophers do not necessarily exclude corporate social responsibility, but their broadside against French should be enough to sink the idea of full-fledged corporate moral personhood.

French was led astray by his over-reliance on the narrow definition of personhood he borrows from his peers. He commits a fallacy when he first grants full ontological, and subsequently all-encompassing moral, existence to every entity which we describe as intentional. We may *ascribe* properties to entities without assuming that the ascribed properties exist in those entities in any ontological sense. We ascribe the properties of a car to a toy without transforming the toy into a car, we ascribe God's will to empirical events without changing the causal order of nature, and we ascribe intentions to corporations without altering their existence as legal fiats.

True sentences that ascribe intentions to corporations may be enough to make them Davidsonian agents, but those sentences are insufficient to make corporations into full-fledged persons or moral agents. The nucleus of moral agency is autonomy, which is the capacity to produce and possess not only intentions but also moral judgements. Without the help of agency vested in natural persons, corporations could never perform their intentional and autonomous functions; this is why intentions and agency can be ascribed to them but can never be possessed by them. People acting on behalf of corporations exist and are persons regardless of definitions, but corporations exist and have traits of personhood only because we as persons find it convenient to describe them in a certain manner. Through our ascriptions we define the corporation into existence and confer on it a personality.

French claims that he has provided grounds 'for holding corporations *per se* to account for what they do, for treating them as metaphysical persons *qua* moral persons'.[11] Unfortunately, his philosophical vision of the corporation is taken from the ivory tower of analytical philosophy. Sometimes that tradition has a notorious tendency to prefer obscure definitions to perception and common sense, with the effect that philosophy suddenly starts blowing life into weird entities. Time-travel, reincarnating persons, ontologically real possible worlds, and swampmen are well-debated examples of weirdos artificially inseminated by contemporary analytical philosophy. French conceives them a new next of kin: the corporation as a full-fledged moral person.

His fundamental mistake is his adherence to orthodox conceptual analysis, which forgets the role that Kantian agency plays in the constitution of the world and moral judgement. The orthodox analysis of the concepts denoting objects ignores the constitutive interplay between the perceiving subject and the sensibilia. As a consequence, mysterious entities without any empirical reference gain reality only because they have linguistic plausibility, which is seen to warrant them as potential targets of perception. The orthodox analysis of normative concepts ignores the constitutive interplay between the moral agent and the moral judgement and, as a consequence, real corporations are obscured into mysterious personhood.

THOMAS DONALDSON AND KENNETH GOODPASTER: STAKEHOLDER THEORY

Failure to establish the corporation as a full-fledged moral person does not mean that it is a mere aggregate of its constituents. The proposition that social responsibility arises from social power is simple but strong. Corporate actions affect us. They cannot always be reduced to any particular natural person's actions, and their impact may be felt by persons who are not constituents of the corporation. Because corporations affect persons, they have moral obligations to the persons affected.[12]

We have accepted that intentions are ascribed to corporations and that their actions affect persons. Therefore, it would be difficult to deny that moral obligations could be attached to them over and beyond the obligation to maximize profits. But this does not take us very far. What is the nature of corporate morality? Is it captured by a negative stipulation that self-interested pursuits should not cause unjustified harm, or does it amount to positive duties which require the pursuit of profits to be constrained by more noble causes? More philosophical analysis and argument is needed to specify how much morality corporations can be loaded with.

Stakeholder theories are a recent attempt to explain the source of corporate moral obligations and to define their extent and contents. These theories understand the corporation as a broad concern for all who have a stake in corporate policy. In addition to shareholders, the interests of consumers, employees and the community at large count.[13] Two distinguished philosophers arguing for this view are Thomas Donaldson and Kenneth Goodpaster. I shall put Donaldson's work under scrutiny first.

Donaldson uses a hypothetical social contract to illustrate the answer to the question 'Why should corporations exist?'. His point is that corporations are productive organizations which enhance the welfare of society through the satisfaction of consumer and worker interests. This is the moral foundation of the corporation. It is enforced by all stakeholders' hypothetical approval, and therefore the corporation has a moral obligation to take their interests into account.[14]

Donaldson's explanation for obligations towards stakeholders has charm, but it stumbles into serious theoretical difficulties. Their source is the hypothetical nature of the social contract sanctioning business:

> The distinctive basis of the 'social contract theory' is that under such a theory obligations arise only if they have been voluntarily assumed, and Donaldson has no reason to believe that corporations have assumed voluntary obligations. The doctrine of tacit consent cannot help Donaldson.[15]

Following this passage, Paul Hodapp details the reasons why business persons cannot plausibly be said to have given the tacit consent required by the social contract theory. I leave this discussion aside. I think it is clear that a hypothetical social contract cannot play the same normative role for corporations as it may play for natural persons.

If the spirit of Rawlsian contractualism[16] is followed, hypothetical arrangements do not decide the moral nature of individual agents. On the contrary, their moral nature controls the outcome of the contractual set-up, the outcome being general moral principles whose application is left to actual contractual arrangements. In the case of natural persons, a Rawlsian social contract acts as a philosophical tool which reflects the contractors' moral personality, thereby exposing the moral principles that ought to prevail between them. This is achievable because the contractors are autonomous agents whose agency furnishes the hypothesis with enough material to bring forth substantive normative conclusions.

In the case of the corporation, the same model is implausible. A hypothetical contract cannot tell us what sort of corporations we ought to have because a corporation does not exist until we have actually contracted it into existence. Our moral agency may be the source of our right to create corporations, but it can never be the source of a corporation's right to exist in its own right. Because corporations lack moral agency of their own, they lack the moral personality necessary for having moral responsibility allocated to them through hypothetical contracts.

Thus, Donaldson is right that the moral foundation of the corporation is a contract, but he errs in focusing on the hypothetical contract. The moral foundation of each and every existing corporation is always an actual contract: 'corporateness simply coincides with the qualities of a separate legal entity'.[17] The coincidence is no accident. Corporations lack inherent moral potentials, therefore actual contractual and legal arrangements are the material used to determine their moral obligations. Hypothetical procedures cannot illustrate moral potentials that do not exist without actual contracting first taking place.

Donaldson is also right in assigning moral weight to the interests of all stakeholders of the corporation, but these interests do not necessitate a hypothetical contract. They are well served if the actual contractual undertakings of the corporation are given appropriate attention. Donaldson has helped us by raising contract as the main component of corporate moral essence, and by pointing out the importance of all stakeholders, but he has fallen short of providing an adequate theoretical explanation of these characteristics.

Kenneth Goodpaster presents an alternative theory that seeks to establish the corporation's moral responsibility to stakeholders in general.[18] He does not assign full personhood to the corporation, but uses an analogy to relate it to the individual person. This leads him to the following conclusions:

> Organizational agents such as corporations should be no more and no less morally responsible (rational, self-interested, altruistic) than ordinary persons.
>
> We take this position because we think an analogy holds between the individual and the corporation. If we analyze the concept of moral responsibility as it applies to persons, we find that projecting it to corporations as agents in society is possible.[19]

The crux of Goodpaster's argument is the finding that we may project moral responsibility to corporations. We may indeed do so, as our common language, and legal, social and economic practices evidence. Goodpaster is careful not to claim that this makes the corporation a person in a literal sense, yet he claims that it 'should be no more and no less morally responsible'. Where is the difference then?

Goodpaster's analogy holds because it is true that we project, attribute and ascribe moral responsibility to the corporation. His conclusion that the corporation is 'no more and no less' morally responsible than a human individual does not hold for exactly the same reason. When we project moral responsibility upon an entity which is not, as such, a moral agent, a plethora of problems emerge.

Do we create new responsibility by projecting, or does it transfer some of our existing burden to others? What if the amount of responsibility projected by us differs from that projected by others? Can we project away all our personal moral constraints? Once projected, do the responsibilities vested in the non-personal entity change somehow, for instance by the effect that many individuals unknown to each other and unaware of each others' actions participate in the projection? Questions like these are not answered simply by assuming that the corporation's responsibilities are the same as the individual's. The two agents clearly differ in kind; why should the contents of their responsibilities not differ?

The merit of Goodpaster's analogy is that it captures the source of corporate moral agency, that is, projection of responsibilities. Its flaw is that it fails to show how the moral obligation to pay respect to stakeholders' interests springs from that source. Even if we are capable of projecting moral properties to corporations, why should we do so? In particular, why should our projections indicate moral concern for stakeholders' interests?

PATRICIA WERHANE: SECONDARY AGENCY

> a corporation functions as a unit, dependent upon, but distinct from, its constituents. Because a corporation is capable of secondary action, it is a secondary moral agent but is not morally autonomous.[20]

Patricia Werhane's book *Persons, Rights, & Corporations* is a careful study which contains detailed criticism of the major theories of corporate personhood, and a constructive corporate ontology. Werhane refutes French by pointing out the difference 'between ascribing goals *to* an organization and determining what are the intentions and goals *of* an organization'.[21] The descriptions of corporate actions in terms of intentions do not make the corporation a moral person.

On the other hand, Werhane denies that the corporation is merely a fiction standing for an aggregate of individuals. Corporations have an impact on the world, and our language refers to them as the cause of that impact. In corporate decision-making the causal role of an individual is distinct from corporate action. The aggregate theory fails to explain this. Having rejected the two extremist views, Werhane moves towards stakeholder theories. She explicitly underwrites Donaldson's idea of social contract[22] and, although she criticizes Goodpaster for assigning too much moral character to the corporation, she adopts a position very similar to his analogy examined above: 'Corporations *function*, then, as if they were real, autonomous, individual entities.'[23]

Werhane adds to these familiar ideas an ontological analysis exploiting her distinction between primary actions of natural persons and secondary actions of corporations. The latter are '*secondary collectives*, whose actions are ontologically reducible to, but not identical with, actions of individuals performing on behalf of the corporation'.[24] Although this is not enough to blow life into corporate personhood, it entitles us to ascribe moral agency to corporations in order to ascribe moral responsibility to them. The crucial difference between corporations and persons is that corporations 'lack the autonomy necessary to perform primary actions'.[25] Nevertheless, since they are capable of secondary actions, we may ascribe responsibility to them, and that includes moral responsibility.

Werhane's analysis is illuminating in many respects. She exposes the weaknesses of rival theories, makes their tenable concepts work together, and complements the picture by introducing new concepts. The resulting secondary moral agency explains how corporations can be held morally responsible without procreating new unnatural moral persons.

Can the success of Werhane's corporate ontology give wings to normative conclusions? She speaks of ethics in the language of rights, and says that the rights of corporations 'are derived from, dependent upon, and secondary to, individual rights, although they are not identical to them'.[26] Her normative view relies heavily on a Goodpasterian analogy. She claims that just as human beings possess moral rights because they 'are capable of independent (primary) action', corporations possess secondary moral rights 'that they derive from their capacity to "perform" secondary actions'.[27]

Werhane finalizes her normative steps by saying that all moral rights are equal, and thus secondary moral rights are equal rights as well, though she makes the concession that their nature is 'somewhat different from individual or primary rights'.[28] One of the implications of the equal standing of secondary rights is that they, like their primary counterparts, impose duties upon their holders: 'If corporations have rights, they have obligations to respect the equal rights of persons as well as other corporations.'[29] Hence, corporations have moral obligations to all stakeholders, not just to their owners.

Here Werhane's ontological results do not support her normative claims. She sets aside too bluntly the complications caused by the fact that the morally relevant qualities of primary agents and secondary agents are significantly different. The former are autonomous, which may be used to justify the normative conclusion that they are entitled to some inalienable moral rights, but the latter are not autonomous. Why should the rights of non-autonomous agents be equal to the rights of autonomous agents? Why should secondary agents have any rights at all?

The analogy between natural persons and secondary agents is not enough to remove doubts raised by the moral difference between the two. Their unlikeness is manifest in autonomy – the source of a natural person's moral agency, rights and obligations. This is recognized even by Werhane, who, in spite of her call for equality of rights, admits that secondary rights are 'somewhat different'. She takes heed of the difference when she specifies two peculiarities of corporate rights: they can never 'exceed any individual's entitlement to a right', and they are 'collective rather than aggregate rights'.[30] But this means that secondary rights clearly have inferior powers. Why is their equal standing now forgotten?

Werhane sorts out well the differences between primary and secondary moral agency, and between the rights peculiar to each kind of agency, yet her normative argument is built upon the equality of rights. The weak point of her reasoning is that she does not have an adequate justification for that equality, nor do her normative conclusions conform with it.

Werhane's shift from ontological analysis to normative discourse falters at a crucial step. This does not necessarily invalidate the applied ethics that follow in her book, but hinders the exploitation of the full potential of her otherwise penetrating analysis. I shall now make an attempt to further refine corporate ontology with the purpose of better explaining its connection to corporate ethics.

A NEW PHILOSOPHY OF THE CORPORATION

The outcome of the foregoing debate over corporate moral personhood is that the corporation is neither a mere aggregate of its owners, nor a full-fledged moral person. The language we use and the social and legal customs we have adopted bear witness to the fact that the moral responsibility for corporate actions cannot always be reduced to individual responsibility. Together with the fact that corporate actions cause impact on others this is enough to shoot down the aggregate theory. On the other hand, we have found that attempts to make corporate bodies the source of their intentions run into difficulties. Most importantly, the corporation lacks autonomy, which is the central precondition of moral personhood. These flaws in corporate character render it ineligible for the status of a full-fledged moral person.

On a positive note, we have been offered good reasons to focus on contracts in explaining the corporation. We have seen that the impact of corporate actions in society brings stakeholders' interests to the forefront. The moral responsibility for these actions has been given a plausible explanation in terms of being 'ascribed' to or 'projected' to corporate agents. The analogy between the individual and the corporation seems to hold to some extent, but significant differences also remain between the two, justifying the characterization of the corporation as a secondary moral agent. The ensuing proposal for a new philosophy of the corporation is an attempt to increase the cohesion of these positive results in order to extract normative principles out of them.

Consider the following quotations from Eugene F. Fama and David Millon respectively:

> More recently the literature has moved toward theories that reject the classical model of the firm but assume classical forms of economic behavior on the part of agents within the firm. The firm is viewed as a set of contracts among factors of production, with each factor motivated by its self-interest.[31]

> Since around 1980, legal academics have developed a new theory of the corporation explicitly grounded on neoclassical economics. This theory conceives of the corporation as a 'nexus of contracts'.[32]

The view of the corporation as a nexus of contracts dominates economic and legal theory. Our philosophical analysis points in the same direction.

The corporation is a nexus of contracts. For what is it that makes it feasible for us to ascribe and project responsibility and obligations to secondary agents? It is the actual contractual arrangements, either explicit or implicit, that bring corporations into existence. Most often, in a modern society, the contractual arrangements creating secondary moral agents are explicit documents in a prescribed form – the articles, memorandum or charter of a corporation – but there is no necessity for them to be thus formalized.

For a secondary agent to exist, moral and legal attributes have to be attached to it. These attributes can, theoretically, be attached whenever natural persons reach a consensus that they act together for some particular aim. If they have so agreed, there is a conceptual entity on which actions, and responsibility for them, may be projected. If they have not so agreed, the projection of responsibility to a joint venture distinct from the acting individuals would target an entity which does not exist to the acting persons, and therefore the projection itself would be arbitrary.

It is a matter for an empirical judgement whether actual contractual arrangements creating the corporate entities capable of being the targets of projections do exist, and it is a matter for an ethical judgement what kind of contractual arrangements creating these entities are acceptable. We have faculties to settle both matters rationally. This study seeks to arrive at a rational ethical judgement as to the acceptable limits to the corporation.

A set of contracts is the ontological originator of the corporation. Because corporations lack autonomy, the moral categories applying to them have to be generated by actual rather than hypothetical contracts. Actual contracts embody a corporation's undertakings, place it in a social context and define its relations to other agents – both primary and secondary.

Just as the actions of natural persons may fall within the limits of law or step outside of them, so too may corporate actions. The actions of natural persons may be moral or immoral regardless of their lawfulness, so too may corporate actions. Is there any difference between the two? Yes, there is, because the nature of their moral agency is different.

The rights of a corporation are always ascribed to it, and so are its duties. If no natural person ever ascribes any rights or obligations to a corporation, a moral wrong is not committed. In fact, that particular corporation would be a moral vacuum which could hardly be said to exist. But a human being may exist even if everybody neglects her moral status as a person, and if that neglect leads to the termination of her existence, a moral wrong has been done.

The moral limits of a natural person's actions are set by human rights and contractual commitments. Human rights are at the top of the moral hierarchy. An individual is protected by these fundamental trumps, as well as bound to pay respect to others' similar trumps, by virtue of her potential for autonomy alone. On the other hand, a corporation cannot claim any human rights. Corporate actions are limited by human rights and contractual obligations too, but the actor is protected only by the moral bearing of the contracts effectuating it.

However, the interpretation of contractual rights, duties and obligations should not be, and never has been, confined to mere reading of the explicit text. In law, implications and unexpected circumstances call for judicial judgement. Part of the judicial judgement consists of moral judgement, as sources as diverse as common law and Ronald Dworkin's philosophy[33] show. More generally in life, the impact of corporate actions upon people leads us to moral ascriptions which may go beyond the law.

The new legal and economic theories of the corporation have carried the ballast of classical economics; their vision has been locked at the stockholder interest as the contractual core of the corporation. But there is more than one model of contract, as W.W. Bratton points out: 'Theories more relational than that employed by the neoclassical new theorists offer values protective of individuals who invest their labor and energies in business enterprises, including firms.'[34]

The new philosophy takes heed of the relational abundance of the corporation. It builds on three major hypotheses. First, an analysis which accounts for all the relations that seam together the contractual web. Second, an explanation of secondary moral agency. And third, a justification of values which protect all of the parties to the web: individuals, corporations and society. The justification of values will be detailed in the next chapter. When this is done the new philosophy of the corporation will provide stakeholder interests with an improved ethical foundation.

The composition of corporate ontology is now accomplished. The new philosophy appreciates the corporation both as a legal fiat and as a morally responsible agent. The outcome shows how secondary agency emerges as a result of our ascribing, projecting, or assigning moral properties. It owes a lot to stakeholder theories and Patricia Werhane's observations on secondary agency, yet it is a new theory in the sense that it accommodates the findings of these philosophers into one explanatory framework, which is compatible with contemporary mainstream economics and jurisprudence, and is capable of contributing to the normative discourse.

Much of the debate on the corporation revolves round the

distinctions public/private and aggregate/collective. The new philosophy reveals that these distinctions are not sharp and exclusive. Being based on contracts, the corporation always has public exposure, but it cannot exist without private actions behind it. As for the distinction aggregate/collective, we have found that corporate actions are constituted by individual actions, yet may not be reducible to them.

The legal and moral connotations of the corporation exist by virtue of our autonomy, which has the potential to construct contractual entities. We are furnished with means to exempt some of our intentional actions from the rigours of responsibility, yet that exercise is subject to constraints authorized by the nature of that potential itself. The following chapter will specify why our power to transcribe responsibility to artefacts cannot override moral notions that emerge straight from autonomy, or, as Patricia Werhane put it, why corporate rights cannot 'exceed any individual's entitlement to a right'.[35] The inquiry into corporate moral personhood has now made us ready to dwell upon ascriptions of responsibility for corporate debt and insolvency.

Chapter 14

Moral responsibility for corporate debts

The opening of Part VI has already spelt out a utilitarian justification for limited liability. Now we have begun to suggest another angle, that limited liability corporation is a contractual vehicle for autonomous persons to exercise their potential for moral judgement and conceptual thinking. It is a vehicle for bringing about more sophisticated rights and obligations. Just as derivative contracts commodify certain aspects of rights of ownership of tangible objects, so too the limited corporation refines and splits promissory obligations into packages which are more suitable for the purposes of modern trade and production.

Incorporation adds subtlety to promises. It emanates from autonomy, just like ordinary, unveiled commitments. Therefore the same moral constraints apply: incorporation cannot annul the moral property that brings it about. The ethical dress-code allows the corporate veil to cover individuals for moral liability because autonomous agents have the right to design their society in such a manner that they can commit themselves by promising to a limited degree only. However, before we can use this idea to solve the particular problems of company insolvency we have to define the moral territory declared available for hiding behind the veil more closely.

A MORAL PATTERN FOR THE CORPORATE VEIL

What kind of corporations should we have? What moral responsibilities are we justified in ascribing to them? Who are the rightful persons to do the ascribing? In the light of corporate ontology the answer should start from the fact that the corporation is a nexus of contracts. It is not an autonomous agent, but it is created by autonomous agents for some specific purposes. Thus, corporations

are means to achieve ends regarded as valuable: they are instrumental by their nature. The instrumental value we attach to them
may as well be moral value: as long as it makes instrumental sense
to treat companies as morally responsible it is rational to do so.

Natural persons may assume two roles of agency with regard to
corporate actions. They may be the persons behind the corporate
action, or they may be the persons who assign moral properties to a
corporation. These two roles may even be assumed by a single
natural person. Whenever an individual takes either role she
remains a natural person who enjoys the protection of human
rights, and is obliged to pay respect to them. No veil is thick enough
to wholly cover a natural person's agency, therefore we are always
liable to the moral requirements that stem from our potential as
agents alone.

On the other hand, covenants, including a corporate veil limiting
the personal liability of the individual performing the act of
promising, may be attached to promises in order to make them
more suitable for the purposes they serve. In a contractual context it
is only required that all parties accept the covenants and that they
do not violate autonomy. Instrumental aspirations that transcribe
liability for our actions to secondary agents cannot override the
intrinsic decrees of morality represented by human rights.

Detailing the contents of these supreme moral commands is
unnecessary here. The classical masterpieces of political philosophy
are not, however, much at odds about what human rights entail. For
example, Kant speaks of autonomy, Mill of liberty,[1] and Rawls of
political rights sanctioned by his first principle of justice. At least
theorists who take the source of morality to lie within human
reason take a person's intentions as inherently valuable as long as
they do not deny outright the value of other persons' intentions.

The approach of these philosophers leads to a liberal list of
human rights, good concrete examples of which are freedom from
bodily violation, freedom of contract and freedom of expression. A
number of corresponding obligations, such as the duty to keep
promises, arguably accompanies them. The accurate mapping of
their contents belongs to the process of reflective equilibrium. For
the purposes of our inquiry it is important that autonomy enables
and entitles us to project responsibility for our actions to artificial
entities created through contracting, but also that it stops us from
expanding these projections to an extent that would compromise the
autonomy of others.

This conclusion leads to ethical principles that mark out the moral territory allowed for corporate action, and the no-go zone where individuals always remain responsible. They tell us what sort of corporations we ought to have, and what moral properties it is ethical to ascribe to them. The public basis of the ethical pattern for the corporate veil rests on human rights conducive to human existence, and on social ordinance conducive to corporate existence. Obedience to human rights is necessary to ensure secondary agents' general compatibility with primary agents' intrinsic morality, and obedience to social ordinance is necessary for any particular secondary agent to exist.

Public constraints on corporate action

Mandatory morality

Rests on human rights that bind all natural persons regardless of the laws of the society.

Mandatory expediency

Rests on legal processes that bring the corporation into existence, and on a legal and social framework that makes its continuous existence possible.

The public constraints on corporate action are provided by the principles of public compliance.

The principles of public compliance

1   **Principle of public morality**   An individual acting in the name of the corporation, and therefore the corporation itself, is always bound to pay respect to human rights because she cannot veil her agency, or the agency of others, behind projections of responsibility.

2   **Principle of public expediency**   A corporation, and therefore an individual acting in its name, is always bound to pay respect to its incorporation and to the legal and social framework in which it operates, because its existence is dependent on them.

In addition to the necessary public constraints stipulated by human rights and incorporation procedures, a corporation may be constrained by its own contingent undertakings.

Private constraints on corporate action

Contingent morality

Rests on corporate decisions to promote genuinely altruistic causes.

Contingent expediency

Rests on corporate decisions to promote any other causes for the well-being of the corporation or its beneficiaries.

The private constraints of corporate action are provided by the principles of private compliance.

The principles of private compliance

3   **Principle of private morality**   A corporation may adopt non-profit obligations which are morally praiseworthy. They become binding only after their adoption.

4   **Principle of private expediency**   A corporation may adopt whatever obligations it sees as expedient, including the obligation to maximize profits.

The four principles listed above are clearly hierarchical. The supreme moral principle is the respect for human rights. No contractual or legal arrangement that overrides it should gain ethical legitimacy. When the supreme principle is observed, the corporate or legal charter may impose additional requirements which have public moral relevance, although only in an instrumental sense. The moral relevance of this latter case has a Humean flavour: it is a consequence of the fact that respect for rules is in the general interest and enhances the flourishing of the corporate enterprise.

Once the corporation satisfies the publicly established moral requirements, it is free to set its own private aims. These may include non-profit pursuits, but will most often concentrate on profit-making. However, even a business venture for profit has to account for more interests than those of shareholders alone. The contractual web constituting the corporation makes all the constituents relevant: shareholders, creditors, consumers, employees, society. The stakeholder theory is right in rejecting a narrow focus on shareholders' interests alone.

We have made explicit how projecting moral responsibility from individuals to corporations is subject to the moral constraints set, in hierarchical order, by human rights, law and corporate constitution, and corporate decisions and undertakings. Apart from the principles of public morality, the hierarchy seems to appreciate instrumentality and expediency. However, these are still vague guidelines. Who is to decide on their application? Who is the right arbiter to ascribe moral properties to the corporation? What quantity of moral contents can we ascribe to obligations arising from constraints which are expedient or contingent?

The answer to these questions is twofold. On the one hand, public constraints emanate from society as a whole. We are all entitled to participate in the debate about our human rights, and we are all entitled to participate in the political process which sets the legal framework for business activities. Also, we are all entitled to participate in the process of incorporation, although participation in any particular process of incorporation requires the acceptance of other participants. Public constraints represent the public side of the corporation; they involve moral judgements in which everyone may participate.

On the other hand, private constraints reflect the private side of corporate nature. They set the goals specific to each particular enterprise, and they are, therefore, a matter for those who make up the enterprise to decide. This includes owners, directors, managers and employees – each in their specific contractually defined role. As long as these agents for a corporation do not breach the public constraints or the corporation's earlier contingent undertakings, they only exercise their freedom of contract when they act from behind the veil which protects them from personal liability. Since their actions are within their authority, outside intervention would be morally wrong.

This means that there is no moral necessity to externally prescribe altruistic ethical obligations to a corporation. It is arguable that autonomous individuals have altruistic obligations, but the claim that they are bound to project those obligations on corporations, which they create as instrumental devices for productive purposes, hangs in the air.

In a democratic society laws recognizing limited corporation are a firm indication that an agreement of the general appropriateness of easing personal liability has been reached, and company constitutions may actualize the relief for particular purposes. Thus, the way is clear to ascribe responsibility for contingent corporate actions solely to the acting corporation. Whether these ascriptions are purely instrumental, or involve some moral aspects, will come under closer scrutiny in the next subsection on corporate debt.

THE CORPORATION'S MORAL RESPONSIBILITY FOR DEBT

Part II established that a natural person cannot unilaterally overthrow or manipulate her promissory obligations without jeopardizing her autonomy. The corporation is not an autonomous moral person, therefore it is not capable of imposing morally binding obligations upon itself. When a corporation promises to pay a debt its promise does not bring into existence a moral duty. Does this leave corporations morally free to fiddle their promises?

A corporate promise to pay a debt does not take place in a moral vacuum. Individuals who act in the name of the corporation, as well as other parties to the debt contract, may ascribe moral obligations to the borrower, to themselves, and to anyone involved – within the limits given in the four principles above. They are free to ascribe, but are they under an obligation to do so and are the ascriptions able to generate moral liability?

It seems that when a corporation promises to pay a debt the individual who physically extends that promise does not contradict her autonomy if she does not induce liability upon herself or ascribe a moral obligation to the borrowing nexus of contracts. The borrower's character as a corporation is made public: it is known to all of the parties, and they have agreed to proceed with the deal. Therefore, they have all voluntarily accepted that the individual acting for the borrower has made her person distinct from the borrower's secondary moral agency. The borrowing corporation's agency is represented through the individual's actions, but her moral personhood does not owe its existence to them.

This separation of identities leaves room for the manipulation of the legal and moral obligations of the parties. In fact, it is the reason why we want the separation to take place. The autonomous natural persons acting for the corporate parties of a debt contract – indeed, the autonomous natural persons acting as the members of a society allowing for free enterprise – have deliberately decided to open avenues to diminish their liability through incorporation. This decision affects moral liability too. It makes it acceptable for individuals to act in the capacity of a corporation. In this capacity they can extend promises which are not their own, but a corporation's, undertakings.

Nevertheless, moral aspects are not completely redundant in corporate borrowing. Although the individual executing the corporate will is set free from personal liability, and the corporation lacks the autonomy necessary for primary moral responsibility, ascription of moral responsibility to a corporate borrower is most likely to be a useful practice. It enhances the probability of payment, it is in harmony with our emotions, and it increases social cohesion and trust, thus increasing the funding available. The foundation for deontological duties seems to be missing, but the whole weight of Humean theories of promising beckons us to project moral responsibility on corporations for their debts. Hence, a corporate borrower may be held morally liable for its promises, but that liability looks, so far, more instrumental than is the case with the promises of natural persons.

What about the moral rights of a corporation? Are they instrumental too? The cornerstone of the ethics of bankruptcy of natural persons was the protection of their autonomy. It justified squaring off the insolvents' debts. Corporations cannot claim autonomy, yet under many legislations their debts may be squared off too. What are the ethical problems involved?

In the liquidation of an insolvent corporate body the problem of discharge does not arise. The proceedings end in the termination of the nexus of contracts after assets have been distributed to the creditors. Sometimes this means closure of viable businesses. A division of an insolvent corporation, and maybe even the whole enterprise, could perhaps survive if excess debt from past mistakes was not dragging the bottom line into the red.

Straight liquidation has been seen to induce added social costs because of its tendency to cash in assets. The remedy to this adverse effect is corporate reorganization, its most famous example being Chapter 11 of the US Bankruptcy Code. The following passages summarize what happens when a firm is reorganized:

In general, a firm that is considering Chapter 11 is facing a situation in which it cannot meet its short term debt obligations and it is not able to borrow further to do so. There is, however, no insolvency requirement for filing a voluntary Chapter 11 petition. . . .

A Chapter 11 petition is a petition to reorganize the firm. The object of the reorganization plan is to correct or eliminate the factors that caused the firm to enter bankruptcy. Voluntary proceedings can be initiated by the stockholders of a firm or by the directors of the firm with or without stockholder consent.[2]

What usually happens to the capital structure of the firm under reorganization is that the creditors exchange their debt claims for some combination of cash, stock and new debt in the reorganized firm. The old creditors become shareholders of the new firm. It is also possible that the old shareholders receive a share in the reorganized firm. Theoretically, unless the firm is equity insolvent, shareholders should not receive any value from the reorganization. In practice, this is not always the case. Once the plan is accepted it must be confirmed by the court.[3]

After the court confirmation all allowable debts are discharged. Can this be given an ethical justification?

The economic rationality of corporate reorganization has been widely debated from the perspective of stockholders, creditors, managers and other stakeholders. Especially, the potential controversy between creditor interests and management, who may use Chapter 11 to further their private interest to retain their jobs at the creditors' expense, has received attention. Another well-highlighted dispute is that between stockholders and creditors, the former allegedly extracting positive value from companies which have consumed all their equity. I shall not devote much energy to these issues as they are already well documented and relate more to economic and legal theory than ethics.

On the more philosophical note, Donald Korobkin's article 'Rehabilitating values'[4] is an interesting effort to argue for the corporation's right to reorganize. Korobkin relies on the assumption that a corporation has personality,[5] in virtue of which it deserves a chance to be rehabilitated when in financial distress.[6] The response is corporate reorganization which attends not only to the financial trouble, but also to the moral, social and political problems. Korobkin declares bankruptcy as the medium through which the enterprise realizes its potential as a fully dimensional personality.[7]

The trouble with Korobkin's argument is evident in the light of the preceding chapter: the enterprise does not possess a fully dimensional personality which can meaningfully be said to have a moral entitlement to exist in its own right. Lack of autonomy is the inherent flaw which excludes the corporation from the moral protection enjoyed by human beings and endorsed by discharge.

In the absence of a corporate equivalent of human rights there is no single, universally applicable ethical solution as to the details of company law or bankruptcy law. The numbers of directors, minimum level of capitalization, and powers given to different groups of stakeholders in the corporate reorganization are matters to be decided by a democratic process, hopefully after widely publicized academic studies have ensured that an enlightened debate precedes any decision. Whatever solution, within the public constraints specified above,[8] is then found to be the most expedient, its ethical status will be impeccable. This means that people deciding on the acceptable forms of incorporation have to be assured of the instrumental value of reorganization. That value cannot be extracted from corporate personhood, which does not exist.

Most probably, reorganization has instrumental value. It seems to better serve the complexities of the contractual web constituting the corporation, including the moral connotations we ascribe to it. Stakeholders may have interests in an insolvent company which are not included among the liabilities listed in the balance sheet. These interests may have a contractual basis in spite of not being immediately enforceable, and a straight liquidation is more prone to overlook them.

As an alternative, Katherine Daigle has presented an ingenious economic theory in favour of reorganization.[9] Her evidence shows that stockholders are usually aware of the impending financial problems well before the creditors, and that they use this advantage to milk personal gains before the imminent bankruptcy. Daigle aims at improved efficiency in the timing of bankruptcies, and proposes that in a reorganization stockholders could be granted benefits equal to the amount they would drain if the proceedings are delayed. She even formulates a quantitative model for the estimation of that amount. Her theory is a good example of the exact methods we have available for the approximation of the instrumental value of various institutional arrangements which, *prima facie*, have an equal ethical standing.

The moral justification for bringing corporations into existence stems from the good consequences of their inception, and from the autonomy of their constituents which is the basis of the freedom of contract. Freedom of contract is a human right. However, the exercise of this particular right requires voluntary participation from other contracting parties. In the case of limited liability incorporation, this means that our freedom of contract is only a necessary condition for projecting moral responsibility for our actions to legal artefacts. Sufficient conditions for the projection are satisfied once other contractors' approval of incorporation supplements the freedom of contract. We have a moral right to incorporate away our liability only if a democratic process has explicitly recognized the institution. Freedom of enterprise gives us freedom to agree with others, not the power to enforce our views upon them.

The morality of corporate death cannot have a basis much different from that of corporate birth and life. Hence, agreement and expediency should dictate the ethical verdict regarding whether businesses are allowed to reorganize and what forms the reorganization should take. Expediency is best estimated by the parties who have a stake in a corporation wanting rehabilitation. Ethical problems may arise if shareholders and managers are allowed to protect their own interests at the creditors' expense.[10] If the corporation has been created as a legal institution to limit liability, bankruptcy proceedings should not turn limited liability into no liability.[11]

Let us draw together the discussion on a corporation's liability for its debt. Once other parties agree, freedom of contract gives us a right to project moral and legal responsibility to the contractual nexus through incorporation. This veils us from personal moral liability for debt and insolvency when we act on behalf of a corporate borrower. As for the borrower itself, the lack of autonomous agency makes it unable to generate moral obligations.

It also appeared that our autonomy as natural persons does not directly put us under an obligation to project moral properties to a borrowing corporation – although emotional, social and utilitarian reasons may encourage us to agree to do so. These conclusions hint that a corporation's moral responsibility for its debt stands on a more speculative ethical platform than a natural person's debt obligations. In order to solidify the moral status of corporate debt we ought to show that an individual acting for a corporation is ethically bound to participate in the ascriptions of responsibility. Is the projection of moral liability for corporate debt really a matter of opinion and convenience, or are there stronger ethical bonds involved?

CORPORATE GOVERNANCE: DIRECTORS', MANAGERS' AND SHAREHOLDERS' MORAL RESPONSIBILITY

We have, above, repeatedly emphasized that there are limits to limiting our liability: it would be wrong to do away with the human rights protecting autonomy. This does not stop us from contractually organizing our lives as we find reasonable in respect to material values. If we are happy to trade between nexus of contracts rather than between our natural extensions, then that is more an exercise of our autonomy than a threat to it. Contracts imply voluntariness, and the absence of coercion means that human rights cannot provide ethical reasons for interventions that shred our contractual webs. The corporate veil does not hide individual moral responsibility altogether, but easily diminishes it in corporate finance.

In the 1990s some countries have found it fashionable to increase personal liability for corporate undertakings, in particular the liability of directors of insolvent corporations.[12] In regard to shareholders, the corporate veil has worn out less, although an occasional call to expose them in cases of tortious liability has been heard.[13]

We have concluded that the particular details of corporate and bankruptcy laws are a matter of expediency. Common sense and empirical studies rather than philosophical ethics should guide the democratic contrivance of commercial institutions. Prudish moralism is a particularly bad guide in economic matters. Crucifixion of a few corporate raiders might please the moralist who believes that the increasing conceptualization and intangibilization of business is a result of an evil conspiracy rendering honest work worthless. The moralist's remedy is a decrease in risk-taking, achieved through the tearing of the corporate veil.

Typical raiders are the often despised paper-shufflers: financial intermediaries and listed corporations. They have already been subjected to wide disclosure in their dealings, and there is nothing ethically wrong with this. On the contrary, disclosure is a major means to guarantee a fair and effective market. However, we ought to bear in mind that the same truth applies to a democratic process. Disclosure of facts leads to conscientious choices, which means that the process better serves the interests of those who participate in it. The moralist who preaches against modern corporate evils ignores this. She ignores the negative economic effect of the reduced level of risk-taking, and she ignores the innovations which are elevating business to ever more effective and sophisticated levels.

Empirical evidence has shown that social progress takes a toll in the form of insolvencies. As for ethical evidence, our inquiry has indicated that there is no inherent moral fault in bankruptcy. Some insolvents may be wrongdoers, but this is no reason to punish all of them or to reduce the overall level of risk through legal deterrence. As Michael Korotkin concludes from the comparison of the US and British bankruptcy laws, the key concern should not be the limitation of risk but the best way to control strong-headed debtors from taking unwarranted risks.[14]

There is no ethical obstacle to making the legal duties of corporate directors and managers more stringent in order to expose them to personal liability. We are free to decide the quality of the veil, and it does not have to be a chador blocking all access to the real faces behind corporate logos. However, we should remember that the purpose is to separate the identities of corporations from those of natural persons. If the veil is reduced to nothing but a transparent gauze between the two, then it loses the properties for which it was originally designed. A corporate gauze would diminish corporate agency and the economic benefits resulting from it.

Hence, instrumental reasons speak in favour of a relatively thick corporate veil. Does this mean that individuals acting for corporations are bound only by public constraints – human rights and laws – and that in contingent corporate undertakings moral ascriptions are an optional luxury? We may start the answer by recalling Milton Friedman's point which stated that the social responsibility of business is to serve its owners' interests by making profit. Our analysis has revealed that the corporation has a more varied constituency, each part of which counts in the determination of corporate responsibilities. Nevertheless, it has also appeared that directors and managers do not necessarily have any obligation to project moral responsibility to the corporation for which they act.

This suggests that Friedman may be right after all: in entering their company the directors[15] and managers enter a personal contract which, most likely, underlines the profit motive. This contract contains their personal promise which morally obliges them to improve the bottom line. If it is simultaneously true that they have no obligation to participate in wider moral projections, their ethical signposts would clearly put the emphasis on profit.

And Friedman is right. In a commercial enterprise the employees' personal contractual promises morally bind them to make money for their employer. But this is not the only consequence of these promises. A Friedmanite perspective is too narrow. An employment contract connects an executive to a nexus of contracts, and so does the board nomination to a non-executive director. Their personal contract or consent cannot make the rest of the contractual web constituting the employer ethically irrelevant. The web is a whole that imposes obligations upon the managers and directors which they cannot afford to ignore: it has to work to maximize profit, it may call for ascription of moral properties, and it does not work if the obligations it generates are ignored. This is the instrumental reason why all the web's obligations will be observed, and managers and directors will share in the moral ascriptions.

An even more fundamental moral reason affects any manager or director who is in a contractual or consensual relation to a corporation. It too flows out of the fact that the corporate party of the relation is a nexus of contracts. For the sake of argument, let us suppose that an employment contract says only that the manager entering the company has to maximize profits. Now, the employing party is a nexus of contracts each of which has, again, another party with its particular interests. It would be irrational to claim that the manager had only the responsibility to pursue profits regardless of the legal and moral obligations present in the rest of the contractual body making up the employer. The corporation as an employer cannot be indifferent to its obligations to other parties of the web because those obligations are the material constituting it as a corporation! A corporation denies its own existence if natural persons acting on its behalf refuse to participate in the projection of obligations that the web of contracts they are serving demands.

This somewhat Hegelian language is not as mystifying as it may first appear. The corporation is a legal fiat, the content of its obligations is embodied in a set of contracts, and some of the obligations require moral ascriptions. The material we use to read the corporate essence is much more concrete than the material available to explain the moral essence of human beings. This means that the Hegelian expressions lack the metaphysical ambiguity that normally bothers them, and can thus explain how a Friedmanite quest for profits is compatible with wider corporate moral responsibilities. They explain why directors and managers who are not personally liable for corporate debts are under a moral obligation to ascribe moral liability to a corporation for its debt.

What can be said in favour of preserving shareholders' limited liability? Many practical arguments speak for its usefulness, but the case can be braced up by the fact that the causal links between shareholder actions and corporate actions are usually not proximate. Shareholders seldom decide on corporate operations, nor do they execute them.

It is a necessary condition for moral responsibility that the agent who is said to be responsible for an action has caused that action. For a person to cause an action requires the involvement of her mind in that action. But a shareholder holds an asset in the corporation, and an asset is mindless. Only in the shareholders' meetings is a shareholder's mind involved, and that meeting does not constitute the corporation's mind,[16] but brings it into existence when directors are nominated. A shareholder is like a parent who cannot be held liable for the actions of her offspring after leaving home.

We have now found that a corporation has no inherent moral duties as a debtor or as a creditor, but that natural persons act for corporations as a result of contractual arrangements which impose moral duties upon them. Their contractual promises bind them to be loyal to the corporation they control or work for, which entails that in their corporate roles they have to honour the contracts which form the nexus called the corporation. Hence, their promise obliges them to project moral responsibilities to the corporation, a practice which is further supported by its Humean usefulness.

Executives' and directors' personal promises to the nexus of contracts they represent fill up the space of corporate actions, initially constrained by human rights, with more moral categories. What first appeared as an ethical vacuum turns out to be infused with both human rights and promissory obligations.

OUR MORAL DUTY TO PAY THE CORPORATE CREDITORS

The outcome of the discussion in Part II was that the moral obligation to pay back a debt emanates from within us, from our capacity to narrow our future options by determining that a deliberate default is a reprehensible act. This reasoning also gives the answer to the question of whether natural persons owe their corporate creditors a moral duty of payment. We do owe it because the source of our promissory moral obligations is our autonomy.

The fact that the corporation is not a person does not have an effect on this principle. Of course, the nature of the promisee is not totally irrelevant. A promise made to a cane toad to kiss it is different because a toad has no capacity to have intentions with regard to the promise. More generally, it is not capable of moral agency. Therefore, we may renege the promise to a toad at our will since we are free to assume that it agrees with our withdrawal.

A corporation has secondary moral agency. We have no such freedom to assume that it automatically agrees with our unilateral change of mind, and thus we are under the duty to honour our promises to corporations unless they explicitly tell us otherwise. Theoretically, a toad could gain secondary moral agency through projection, through autonomous persons agreeing to treat toads as agents and creating a decision structure that represents a toad's intentions. If this happened, our promises to toads would be morally binding, like our promises to corporations. However, the toad's agency would first have to gain public recognition through a democratic process, in the same way that the corporation has gained recognition through legislation setting out conditions for incorporation.

In summary, Part VI is compatible with the other sections of the ethics of bankruptcy in that autonomy remains the source of the moral duty to keep promises, while it also authorizes us to agree that we can limit our liability by extending promises via corporations. A promise is the moral essence of a contract, and the corporation is a set of contracts. Therefore, the moral essence of the corporation is a set of promises.

Natural persons borrowing from, or lending to, a corporation have the moral duty to honour their promises, and natural persons acting in the name of corporate borrowers and lenders have, in their corporate roles, the moral duty to account for the corporation's commitments. This is the ethical foundation which dictates why debts to corporations as well as corporate debts should be paid, and explains why the vast majority will be paid even when the corporate veil protects the individuals behind insolvent companies from personal moral and legal liability.

Epilogue

Business is business, yet business ethics is no oxymoron. Economic activity is made of intentional actions by human beings. Its peculiarity is that the actors have declared it a reserve free from some ethical constraints that apply elsewhere. The declaration is within their authority as long as it does not assault the universal moral values, that is, human rights which protect autonomy.

As a result, intentions which in everyday social intercourse would raise moral blame do not have that effect in a business context. A successful entrepreneur gets acclaim because she is more astute or lucky than the rest of us, yet her success may build on others' losses. If she had made less, someone might have had more! Good deals are often to the mutual benefit of the participants. But even when benefits are reaped from others' detriment, the beneficiary does not have to be ashamed for her fortune if it is achieved through voluntary contracting. It would be unethical if I hypnotized my neighbour to mow my lawn, but there is nothing wrong in hiring her to do it.

From our ethical space, which is filled with constraints, we carve out business as a less fettered area because it is a technical activity carried out for the production of the necessities of life. Through our experience we have learned that, in the long run, voluntary contracting delivers the best bounty. It means that those who are more cunning can get a licence to persuade the less shrewd to participate in unrewarding deals, but in return we have superior means to live by our will, commitments and duties.

We are not only allowed to seek profit from personal and corporate business. It is a necessity that we do so, even for a 'non-profit' venture. I understand 'profit' here in a weak sense: it stands for income at least equal to expenditure. A trade which defies the necessity of profit is doomed, and will go broke sooner or later. Of course, a business may decide to impose charitable and altruistic duties upon itself, but only after its profitability affords the benevolence. Virtue ethicists aim at the impossible when they try to subdue the necessity of profit to altruistic moral considerations. Their efforts can only lead to virtual ethics, window-dressing from the sphere of business and lip-service from the sphere of philosophers.

Nevertheless, business ethics is no oxymoron: it participates in the determination of the borders of the reserve where concessional ethics for productive trades apply, and in the determination of the concessions specific to that reserve. The most important tools of any trade are money and credit, and they become obsolete without trust and ethical behaviour.

This book has drafted rules for credit business, which is no different from any other commerce in that voluntary contracting between autonomous agents secures the best outcome. The idea that insolvencies could be prevented if governments allocated and priced credit is an illusion.

Governments may have a role in implementing distributive justice. Powerful ethical theories stress that those who are in want ought to be transferred wealth from those who live in superfluousness. But it is worth noting that these transfers redistribute existing wealth: they do not create any new prosperity! On the other hand, production brings about new wealth, and credit is its major engine.

A decision to grant or accept credit should be a matter of discretion between the contracting parties because only their discretion can effect an increment of wealth, and thus realize the productive potential credit carries. Extension of voluntary credit involves expansion of confidence and trust, which is crystallized in the promise of future repayment and interest, and which kicks off the creation of new wealth. It adds value for three reasons. First, it makes the debtor produce more to repay the debt. Second, it makes the debtor produce more to pay the interest. Third, it transfers capital to those who are most willing to consume and invest, thus driving demand and supply to a higher level of equilibrium.

These beneficial effects are largely lost if government orders creditors to give credit, and debtors to accept it, at a predetermined price. We have three alternatives. In the first, the regulated interest is set lower than the market would decide. As a consequence, the creditor would have less incentive to produce excess wealth available for credit, while the debtor would willingly accept a loan but would toil less to cover the interest. There would be a diminution of credit available and interest paid, translating to a decrease in the value added to economy.

In the second alternative, government would fix the rates higher than the market. Now the debtors would not be enticed to borrow although the supply of loans would grow. They would either have to be forced to take loans, or there would be few transactions. Neither situation is conducive to affluence.

The third, and happiest, situation would be if the government were to strike exactly the same price as the market would. Credit would now appeal equally to lenders and borrowers, and their efforts would yield maximal benefits. In addition, if the government were enlightened enough to fund only those debtors who never go broke, an optimal output would result.

Unfortunately, governments do not have any better crystal-balls than market participants do. Most probably bureaucrats are in a worse position to assess the price and chances of default than the creditors who expose something of their own. Hence, why ask the government to struggle towards a settlement which would be the processual outcome of the markets anyway? The contracting parties are the right judges to allocate and price credit.

Credit is a corollary to savings, and as such is a medium for the allocation of productive resources. A philosophical explanation of the dismal performance of command economies is that central planning violates human autonomy by extending a community's redistributive values to the sphere of individuals' productive interests and intentions. As the above example of regulated credit shows, these interventions can never improve gross output.[1]

Redistribution and production may co-exist if each is confined to its own quarters. When redistribution tampers with the productive process, the value adding effect of voluntary contracting is compelled to give way to enforced transfers of stagnant wealth. Voluntary contracting nurtures progress because human beings strive most for what they want, and only they themselves can decide what they want. In this spirit, credit markets generate mutual trust and confidence which no forced financial transactions can surpass.

There is no free lunch in credit, but it encourages and enables more individuals to have something cooking in their pots. Instead of the creditor alone having an asset, and the ensuing confidence that there will be a lunch tomorrow, extending a loan gives the confidence of a future meal, and the means to prepare it, to both the creditor and the debtor. The moral elements of the lending have a concrete impact in the world: one pot on the stove turns into two!

Ethics is an ingredient of the social cohesion conducive to trust and confidence in a market economy. Sound moral principles make sense to rational autonomous agents. Insolvency poses a threat to credence, and the aim of this inquiry has been to alleviate the threat. The ethics of bankruptcy points out that an honest insolvent, who has sincerely sought to satisfy her creditors, is not at moral fault. Her failure does not undermine the morally obligatory nature of promises.

On the contrary, she deserves a discharge. In this conclusion the ethics of bankruptcy pays tribute to autonomy, thus also respecting the moral agency behind the duty to pay debts. The shared foundation of ethics both protects the debtor, and cements the trust and confidence which protects the creditor and enhances everybody's well-being.

A society is best equipped to guard contractually based moral obligations against the menace of financial ruin when its institutions recognize the ultimate source of morality in us. Such a society employs discharge as an effective and economical safety net, whose esteem of autonomy infuses the community with esteem of all obligations springing from that valuable source. This explains why liberal discharge provisions do not encourage abuse of credit.

Human autonomy has been the thread running through the ethics of bankruptcy. Modern philosophy often takes autonomy and freedom as underivable. This is not a position adopted in this study: the metaethical affair was my effort to extract substantive normative ingredients from Kantian ideas without violating the rigours of rational reasoning. It is an effort to expand the justificatory potential of moral philosophy.

The metaethical route we have covered is not chimerical. The fact that we may observe some moral law points to freedom of will and autonomy. These human properties allow us to choose, and this includes the making of moral choices. One class of moral choices are promises, whereby we introduce permanence to our undertakings. That permanence may be interrupted if it threatens the most fundamental moral categories, which spring not from any particular choices, but from our autonomy alone. Insolvency has proved to be an instance in which the fundamentals take over the moral control of our lives by removing disastrous obligations our particular undertakings have induced.

The holistic approach of this applied study has guided us, stage by stage, from the depths of timeless philosophy, deep-frozen for much of the twentieth century, to the hotbed of topical political debate. In investigating the ethics of bankruptcy the excursion has uncovered an interpretation of Kant, a theory of promissory autonomy and a new philosophy of the corporation. These steps in the journey lead us towards the principal normative destination, but also offer scenery which has some philosophical interest of its own.

The thread of autonomy sews the fabric of the ethics of bankruptcy, but a diversity of other materials seam it to a winning social attire. The broad spectrum of philosophical support to insolvent liberation is the strongest indication that we have succeeded in identifying the hallmarks of good and right bankruptcy laws.

Notes

PROLOGUE

1 Quoted from Young (1969).

CHAPTER 1

1 Hawtrey (1950, p. 2); Homer and Sylla (1991, pp. 17–24); Wray (1990, pp. 8–9).
2 For the early history of laws regulating credit and insolvency, see e.g. Hayek (1967), Homer and Sylla (1991); Levinthal (1918); Sutherland (1988); Tamari (1990).
3 Hayek (1967, p. 4); Nelson (1981, p. 17); Sullivan (1968, p. 20); Treiman (1938, p. 189).
4 The development of modern bankruptcy laws is covered in Hoppit (1987); Jones (1979); *Insolvency Law and Practice*, Report of the Review Committee (1982); Warren (1972).
5 Differences between English, American and continental bankruptcy laws are illustrated in Fletcher (1990); Jackson (1985); Ross (1974); Sullivan *et al.* (1989). Korotkin (1993) is a recent comparison between the US and UK legislation.
6 Hallituksen esitys Eduskunnalle laiksi yksityishenkilön velkajär-jestelystä (1992).
7 Finnis (1986, p. 190).
8 Rawls (1971).
9 Jackson (1986, pp. 30–1).
10 *Ibid.*, p. 32.

PART II: INTRODUCTORY TEXT

1 The legal bindingness of contracts may, in some jurisdictions, depend on the consideration provided for the promise. However, we are here after the source of moral obligations in promising. Legally binding contracts are a subspecies of promises and as such may have extra conditions attached to them, like the requirement of consideration.

Besides, I do not think that it is evident, even in common law countries, that consideration has to be involved in all legally enforceable
promises.

An example of a contract which is enforceable but where there is no
consideration is a personal guarantee given for another person's loan
for reasons of affection. There is no tangible consideration to the
guarantor, yet the guarantee is legally binding. The example cannot be
countered by claiming that the guarantor receives mutual love because
of her deed, or that the borrower receives the consideration as a surro-
gate of the guarantor. These explanations would only distort the
nature of the transaction wherein a guarantor's promise induces a
liability without her getting any contractual consideration.

Treitel (1989, pp. 26–7) has a more detailed discussion on gratu-
itous promises.

CHAPTER 2

1   Gordley (1991, p. 112).
2   Hume (1960, p. 523).
3   *Ibid.*, p. 516.
4   *Ibid.*, p. 517.
5   Scanlon (1990, p. 199).
6   Baier (1985, p. 174).
7   *Ibid.*, p. 198.
8   *Ibid.*, p. 199.
9   Scanlon (1990, p. 200).
10 *Ibid.*, p. 208.
11 *Ibid.*, p. 220.
12 Rawls (1971, p. 347).
13 Scanlon (1990, pp. 208–9).
14 Rawls (1971, p. 587).
15 *Ibid.*, p. 587.
16 Yack (1993, pp. 227–9) deals with some aspects of Rawls' reliance on
    Kantian metaphysical assumptions.

CHAPTER 3

1   Locke, *An Essay Concerning Human Understanding* (1961, pp. 138–9).
2   v. Wright (1963).
3   See Rawls (1993, pp. 303–4).
4   v. Wright (1963, p. 171).
5   *Ibid.*, p. 175.
6   *Ibid.*, p. 111.
7   Rawls (1993, p. 307).
8   Smith (1994, p. 202).
9   Ebertz (1993, p. 194). The quotation marks within the extract refer to
    text from Rawls (1971, p. 20). I have, in this chapter, relied largely on

Ebertz's paper because it points out well reflective equilibrium's weaknesses which warrant further justificatory inquiry.

10 Ebertz (1993, p. 195).
11 *Ibid.*, p. 200, n. 14. DePaul's original article is 'Reflective equilibrium and foundationalism', *American Philosophical Quarterly* (1986) 23, 59–69.
12 *Ibid.*, p. 201.
13 *Ibid.*, p. 201.
14 *Ibid.*, p. 200.
15 *Ibid.*, p. 207.
16 *Ibid.*, p. 210–11.
17 *Ibid.*, p. 211.
18 *Ibid.*, p. 212.
19 *Ibid.*, p. 213.

CHAPTER 4

1 Kant, *Critique of Practical Reason* (1959, p. 260).
2 For Kant's view that phenomena stand for the real and objective world meaningful for our everyday life see, for instance, his Preface to the *Critique of Judgement* (1974, p. 3), where he describes nature as the complex of phenomena, and *Prolegomena* Sect. 19 Remark II (1883, p. 35), where he emphasizes that 'All that is given us as object, must be given us in intuition.'

   Although Kant's statements about this matter are not always without ambiguity I have adopted the interpretation that empirical substances are to him the true ultimate subjects because it is what he repeatedly underlines, and also because it makes his system a more fertile ground for further philosophical pursuits. For Kant's equivocality see, for instance, Ameriks (1992).
3 'The conception of a noumenon is therefore not the conception of an object, but merely a problematical conception inseparably connected with the limitation of our sensibility' Kant, *Critique of Pure Reason* (1974, p. 205); or 'The object in itself always remains unknown' Kant, *Prolegomena*, Sect. 19 (1883, p. 46).
4 Kant, *Critique of Practical Reason* (1959, p. 88).
5 For Kant's way of conciliating freedom of will and causality of nature, see Kant, *Critique of Practical Reason* (1959, pp. 131–2); *Critique of Pure Reason*, (1974, pp. 325–6); *Groundwork*, (1964, p. 114); *Prolegomena*, Sect. 53 (1883, pp. 91–6).
6 Kant, *Groundwork* (1964, p. 121).
7 *Ibid.*, p. 110.
8 *Ibid.*, pp. 57, 80.
9 *Ibid.*, pp. 81, 92–3, 129–30.
10 For the narrowness of Kant's conception of autonomy, see Young (1986, p. 2).
11 This reading of Kant is suggested in Buchdal (1969, pp. 538–9).

12 For the necessity of some basic moral principles or 'primary rules' for the existence of any human community, see Hart (1961, p. 89).
13 See above, p. 45.
14 Kant, *Critique of Pure Reason* (1974, p. 220).
15 Kant, *The Metaphysics of Morals* (1991, p. 63).
16 Kant, *Groundwork* (1964, p. 70).
17 Werhane (1985, p. 7).
18 Rawls (1993, p. 313).
19 Dworkin (1977).

CHAPTER 5

1 Kant, *The Metaphysics of Morals* (1991, p. 91).
2 *Ibid.*, pp. 92–3.
3 *Groundwork* (1964, p. 90).
4 *Ibid.*, p. 97.
5 Wolff (1973, p. 167).
6 *Ibid.*, p. 168.
7 Fried (1981, pp. 16–17).
8 *Ibid.*, p. 17.
9 *Ibid.*, p. 57.
10 Gordley (1991, p. 233).
11 See above, pp. 25 and 53.
12 Subject to the qualifications detailed in subsequent chapters.
13 This conclusion applies in the current context investigating obligations we voluntarily impose upon ourselves. Theories of punishment may well, in the context of wrongs calling for restitution, justify violations of autonomy.
14 For the critical points that follow I am indebted to J. Goldsworthy, H. Häyry, M. Häyry, J. Lamont, and participants at the Philosophy Postgraduate Conference at the University of Queensland in 1994.
15 This solves the problem for my theory without taking a stand on the debate on the interests of the dead; see e.g. Callahan (1987) and Pitcher (1984).
16 Gordley (1991, p. 232).
17 Rawls (1993, p. 304).

CHAPTER 6

1 *The Holy Bible*, Deuteronomy 15:1–2.
2 Sutherland (1988, p. 923).
3 'The Economics of Bankruptcy Reform. Discussion' (1977, p. 160).
4 *Ibid.*, p. 160.
5 Fried (1981, pp. 64–76).
6 Warren (1987).
7 Shuchman (1973).
8 *Hallituksen esitys Eduskunnalle laiksi yksityishenkilön velkajär-*

jestelystä (1992, p. 22); *Insolvency Law and Practice* (1982, p. 13); *General Insolvency Inquiry* (1988, p. 228).

9 That an insolvent who is denied discharge would substitute other activities for work is supported by economic theory. See Jackson (1986, p. 244).

10 Research done in several countries has, consistently, confirmed the frugality of bankrupts. See Ryan (1989, pp. 29, 54–5, 451); Stanley and Girth (1971, pp. 3–4); Sullivan *et al.* (1989, pp. 208–12). Although some of the empirical methods used by Sullivan *et al.* (1989) have been disputed, I have taken their findings as accurate enough for the purposes of reference in this philosophical inquiry, especially because the criticism acknowledges that they, by and large, replicate and confirm the results of the earlier studies. See Shuchman (1990).

   The overwhelming nature of the debt burden has also been recognized in committee reports reviewing bankruptcy laws: for Australia see *Insolvency: The Regular Payment of Debts* (1978, p. 65); and for Finland *Hallituksen esitys Eduskunnalle laiksi yksityishenkilön velkajärjestelystä* (1992, p. 20).

11 Meckling (1977, pp. 19–21).

12 Shuchman (1973, p. 440).

CHAPTER 7

1 Rawls (1971, pp. 15–20).
2 Rawls (1971, pp. 111–12).
3 *Ibid.*, pp. 302–3.
4 Scanlon (1990).
5 Shuchman (1973, p. 473).
6 Fried (1981, pp. 72–3).
7 See, for instance, Tenkku (1967).
8 See above, p. 14.
9 Convention quoted from Ste Croix (1988, p. 22).
10 See *Beckham v. Drake* (1849) 2HLC579, 9 ER 1213; and *Bailey v. Thurston & Co. Ltd* (1903) I KB 137.
11 Fry in *DeFransesco v Barnum* (1890) 45 ChD 430 at 438. Quoted from Jones and Goodhart (1986, p. 34).
12 Jackson (1986, pp. 225–56).
13 See also Jackson (1985).
14 Jackson (1986, pp. 255–6).
15 *Ibid.*, p. 272.
16 Schneewind (1992).
17 Kant, *The Metaphysics of Morals* (1991, p. 101).

CHAPTER 8

1 This division of rights and duties is closely analogous to the distinction Ronald Dworkin (1977, pp. 93–4) draws between universal and special background rights.

2 Parfit (1973, p. 146).
3 Christine Korsgaard (1989) gives another, more subtle Kantian
   defence for the unity of personhood. She points out that Parfit's metaphysical assumptions are untenable as they reduce a person to a mere
   locus of experiences, thus disregarding the agency in ourselves.
4 Parfit (1973, p. 146).
5 Schneewind (1992, p. 311).
6 Shuchman (1973, p. 428); Sullivan *et al.* (1989, p. 299).
7 Similar reasoning would apply to loss of autonomy that is not related
   to insolvency. For instance, a prisoner has, in an important sense, lost
   her freedom of choice, but this does not entail that she should automatically get rid of her debts.
       Her autonomy is constrained as a punishment. Theories of punish-
   ment can justify institutional violations of autonomy. Therefore, the
   enforcement of an inmate's pecuniary commitments is not ethically
   suspicious. On the other hand, after an inmate has expiated her crime
   she should have the same recourse to bankruptcy as anyone else, if she
   is insolvent.
8 Dworkin (1977, p. 182).

CHAPTER 9

1 Fried (1981, pp. 28, 64); Gordley (1991, pp. 230, 232).
2 See e.g. Treitel (1989, pp. 25–49, 98–198, 298–311).
3 Baird (1987, p. 821).
4 *Insolvency Law and Practice* (1982, p. 414).
5 This is a widely shared view; see Becker (1992, p. 197).
6 Aristotle, *Nicomachean Ethics* (1987, p. 216).
7 Miller (1977, p. 40).
8 See Chapter 8, n. 6.
9 Stanley and Girth (1971, p. 3); Sullivan *et al.* (1989, p. 289).
10 Smith A., *The Wealth of Nations* (1950, Vol. I, Bk. II, Ch. I, p. 301).
11 Smith A., *The Wealth of Nations* (1950, Vol. I, pp. 13–17, 318, and
   Vol. II, p. 179). The more or less hidden assumption behind many
   prejudices associated with insolvency is the idea that credit in general
   is suspicious, and that credit default is particularly pernicuous. As our
   inquiry proceeds, the refutation of this fallacy will become a recurring
   theme. Accordingly, pp. 117, 114 and 155 will contain further arguments to the effect that credit is conducive to growth and prosperity,
   and p. 145 will link the occurrence of insolvency to this cybernetics.
12 Blundell-Wignall and Gizycki (1992, pp. 30–2).
13 The Law Commission (1992).
14 *Ibid.*, p. 28.
15 *Ibid.*, pp. 29–30.
16 *Ibid.*, pp. 30.
17 Heuston and Buckley (1992 pp. 14–15).
18 *Ibid.*
19 Brazier (1993, pp. 249–50).

20 *Ibid.*, p. 573.
21 *Ibid.*, pp. 10–11.

CHAPTER 10

1 For the identification of bankruptcy with crime, and the ensuing stigmatizing effect, see Fletcher (1990, p. 6); Hoppit (1987, p. 25); Rubin (1984, p. 273).
2 Ten (1987, p. 5).
3 *Ibid.*, pp. 3–4.
4 *Ibid.*, p. 84.
5 That fraudulent conduct involves an intention to damage is recognized, for instance, by the *General Insolvency Inquiry* (1988, pp. 143–144).
6 Ten (1987, p. 101).
7 For past unsuccessful attempts to draw the distinction, see Haagen (1985, pp. 230–1).
8 Corden (1991, p. 6).
9 Each jurisdiction has, of course, its own idiosyncrasies. What is said here applies to common law countries which recognize the offence of insolvent trading.
10 Rubin (1984, esp. p. 273) gives an historical account of how the idea of faulty character was used to justify the imprisonment for debt.
11 Hawtrey (1950, pp. 92, 172); Hoppit (1987, pp. 176–81); Nelson (1981, p.17); Sullivan *et al.* (1989, p. 332).
12 Ryan (1989, p. 69).
13 Sullivan *et al.* (1989, p. 241).
14 Shuchman (1973, p. 433).
15 See above, p. 71.
16 Sutherland (1988, p. 924).
17 Altman (1971, p. 24); Stanley *et al.* (1971, pp. 111–12).
18 Ryan (1989, p. 69); Sullivan *et al.* (1989, p. 329).
19 Smith, *The Wealth of Nations* (1950, Vol. I, p. 363).
20 Hakman (1993).

CHAPTER 11

1 Quoted from *Insolvency Law and Practice* (1982, p. 28).
2 *Insolvency: The Regular Payment of Debts* (1978, p. 66).
3 *Insolvency Law and Practice* (1982, p. 13).
4 *General Insolvency Inquiry* (1988, pp. 16–17).
5 *Ibid.*, p. 17.
6 *Ibid.*, p. 232.
7 *Insolvency Law and Practice* (1982, p. 53).
8 *General Insolvency Inquiry* (1988, p. 18).
9 *Insolvency Law and Practice* (1982, p. 426).
10 *General Insolvency Inquiry* (1988, pp. 18–19).
11 Bankruptcy Act (Australia) (s 271).

12 *The Sunday Age*, 19 July 1992.
13 *Insolvency Law and Practice* (1982, p. 422).
14 *General Insolvency Inquiry* (1988, p. 18).
15 *Insolvency Law and Practice* (1982, p. 39).
16 *General Insolvency Inquiry* (1988, p. 239ff.); *Insolvency Law and Practice* (1982, p. 419–20).
17 *Insolvency Law and Practice* (1982, p. 13).
18 *General Insolvency Inquiry* (1988, p. 232).
19 Ryan (1989, p. 351).
20 As early as the 1950s Galbraith (1976, pp. 147–8) paid attention to the discrepancy between conservative attitudes towards credit and the central role it plays in any modern economy.
21 Haagen (1985, p. 230).
22 Kercher (1984); Rubin (1984).
23 Fletcher (1990, pp. 617–19).
24 *Insolvency Law and Practice* (1982, p. 429).
25 *General Insolvency Inquiry* (1988, p. 17).
26 House of Lords (1980, p. v).
27 Smart (1991, pp. 264–6) has a discussion of the EC Draft Bankruptcy Convention and the Istanbul Convention. The complete text of the latter treaty can be found in *Cross-Border Insolvency: Comparative Dimensions* (1990, pp. 297–308).
28 Council of Europe, European Convention on Certain International Aspects of Bankruptcy, Article 13.
29 Livadas (1983, pp. 351–52) gives an account of the liabilities which the directors of French companies may have in excess to those of their Anglo-Saxon colleagues. Although the company laws within the European Union are undergoing a process of homogenization, the problem of discrepancies will remain acute on the global scale.
30 Fletcher (1990, p. 622).

CHAPTER 12

1 Aris (1986, p. 133).
2 Barry (1991, p. 61).
3 Jackson (1986, p. 32).
4 As a general thesis, this view was refuted in Chapter 10. Now it is revisited in a narrower context where only a few 'tall poppies' are targeted as warning examples.
5 For instance, in the economic summit organized by President Clinton after his election it was widely agreed that increased access to credit for businesses and entrepreneurs is one of the keys to a sustainable recovery (*The New York Times*, 16 December 1992). See also pp. 96 and 155.
6 Barry (1991, p. 123).
7 In economic theory Schumpeter (1959) is a recognized account of the constructive role of failures. Hoppit (1987) gives support to the same idea from the perspective of the history of economy.

8   Freiermuth (1988, p. 124) says that 80 per cent of new business forma-
    tions fail, Sullivan *et al.* (1989, p. 109) put the figure at 50 per cent.
9   *The Age*, 20 September 1992.
10 Smith, *The Wealth of Nations* (1950, Vol. II, p. 179).
11 *General Insolvency Inquiry* (1988, p. 337).
12 Rawls (1971).
13 Nozick (1974, pp. 153–5).
14 Rawls (1971, pp. 302–3).
15 In *Two Treatises of Government* (1961, Book II, para. 27) Locke states
    the theory in a compact form:

> Though the earth and all inferior creatures be common to all men,
> yet every man has a property in his own person; this nobody has
> any right to but himself. The labour of his body and the work of his
> hands, we may say, are properly his. Whatsoever he then removes
> out of the state that nature hath provided, and left it in, he hath
> mixed his labour with, and joined to it something that is his own,
> and thereby makes it his property.

> Nozick criticizes Locke's account but has, as Scanlon (1982) points
> out, to derive property rights from something like Locke's original
> acquisition.

16 Schumpeter (1959, p. 107).
17 Galbraith (1976, pp. 147–8). A contemporary work by Wray (1990)
    argues against both Keynesians and monetarists that money was not
    introduced to facilitate trade but is created naturally in debtor–
    creditor relationships. This would make debt the most fundamental
    mover of economic forces, not only an essential part of modern
    production, as Galbraith says, but of all production.
18 Smith, *The Wealth of Nations*, (1950, Vol. I, pp. 312, 359–60).
19 *Ibid.*, p. 15.
20 Hoppit (1987, p. 164).
21 Warren (1972, pp. 121–2).

PART VI: INTRODUCTORY TEXT

1   For an example of descriptive business ethics, see Henderson (1992).
2   Solomon and Hanson (1985, p. 181).
3   Des Jardins (1984, p. 141).
4   See the criticism of full-fledged corporate moral personhood below.

CHAPTER 13

1   The original article was published in *New York Times Magazine*, 13
    September 1970. References here are to Friedman (1993).
2   'Agency' is here understood in the sense of being entrusted with the
    concerns of another. This is a meaning different from the Kantian
    'agency' which stands for an originator of judgements and choices.
3   Friedman (1993, p. 162).

4 This claim is made in DesJardins and McCall (1990, p. 1).
5 Millon (1990, pp. 220–9).
6 Fama (1980, pp. 288–9).
7 French (1993, p. 228).
8 *Ibid.*, pp. 228–30; French *et al.* (1992, pp. 14–15, 43).
9 French (1985, p. 74).
10 Ladd (1993); Pfeiffer (1990); Velasquez (1990); Werhane (1985, pp. 34–40).
11 French (1993, p. 235).
12 Versions of this impact argument can be found in Davis (1990, p. 166); Solomon and Hanson (1985, p. 186 ff.); and Werhane (1985, p. 4).
13 DesJardins and McCall (1990, p. 98).
14 Donaldson (1993, pp. 183–184).
15 Hodapp (1990, p. 130).
16 Rawls (1971).
17 Stoljar (1973, p. 177).
18 Goodpaster and Matthews (1990); Goodpaster (1993).
19 Goodpaster and Matthews (1990, p. 105).
20 Werhane (1985, p. 59).
21 *Ibid.*, p. 36.
22 *Ibid.*, p. 46.
23 *Ibid.*, p. 50.
24 *Ibid.*, p. 50.
25 *Ibid.*, p. 57.
26 *Ibid.*, p. 60.
27 *Ibid.*, p. 61.
28 *Ibid.*, p. 61.
29 *Ibid.*, p. 61.
30 *Ibid.*, p. 62.
31 Fama (1980, p. 289).
32 Millon (1990, p. 229).
33 Dworkin (1977).
34 Bratton (1989, p. 1526).
35 Above, p. 172.

CHAPTER 14

1 Mill (1956).
2 Daigle (1989, p. 47).
3 *Ibid.*, p. 49.
4 Korobkin (1991).
5 *Ibid.*, p. 745.
6 *Ibid.*, p. 762 ff.
7 *Ibid.*, p. 772.
8 Above, p. 179.
9 Daigle (1989).
10 Salem and Martin (1994).
11 Salem and Martin suggest practical measures against misuse of reor-

ganization, including the requirement of a petitioner's insolvency and better evidence for a plan's viability.

12 See Korotkin (1993).

13 Leebron (1991).

14 Korotkin (1993).

15 A company's non-executive directors are not employees, nevertheless their consent to become board members establishes a promise of loyalty to the company and allegiance to the law even in the absence of an explicit contract. If the company is a commercial venture, their promise implies loyalty to the company's aspiration for profit.

16 Shareholders do not normally run the daily operations of companies, but have the power to elect the body in charge of those operations. As the following law quotation shows, shareholders' intentions are not corporate intentions:

> Where . . . it is necessary to establish the state of mind of the body corporate, it is sufficient to show that a director, servant or agent of the body corporate, being a director, servant or agent by whom the conduct was engaged in within the scope of the person's actual or apparent authority, had that state of mind.
>
> Trade Practices Act (Australia), 1974 Part VI s. 84(1)

EPILOGUE

1 This is assuming that the political process is one based on voluntary contracting too, i.e. a democratic system, and that the prevalent shares of productive assets are recognized by that process. This qualification explains why, for instance, a land reform which intervenes in individuals' productive interests and intentions may spur output: it abolishes a social anomaly hampering the voluntary contracting in economy, deriving from the fact that the feudal concentrations of land were enforced by authoritarian rule.

The links between voluntary contracting in economy and in political society are ample, but do not fall in the scope of the present study.

Bibliography

Age, The (1992) 'Tycoons leave a $30 billion legacy', September 20, p. 15.

Altman, E.I. (1971) *Corporate Bankruptcy in America*, London, DC Heath.

Ameriks, K. (1992) 'The critique of metaphysics: Kant and traditional ontology', pp. 249–79 in Guyer, P. (ed.) *The Cambridge Companion to Kant*, Cambridge, Cambridge University Press.

Aris, S. (1986) *Going Bust: Inside the Bankruptcy Business*, Sevenoaks, Coronet.

Aristotle (1987) *The Nicomachean Ethics*, trans. by Ross, D., rev. by Ackrill, J.L. and Urmson, J.O., Oxford, Oxford University Press.

Baier, A. (1985) 'Promises, promises, promises', pp. 174–206 in *Postures of the Mind. Essays on Mind and Morals*, Minneapolis, University of Minnesota Press.

Baird, D.G. (1987) 'Loss distribution, forum shopping and bankruptcy: a reply to Warren', *The University of Chicago Law Review*, 54, 815–34.

Barry, P. (1991) *The Rise and Fall of Alan Bond*, 3rd edn, Sydney, Bantam Books.

Becker, L.C. (1992) 'Too much property', *Philosophy & Public Affairs*, 21(2), 196–206.

Blundell-Wignall, A. and Gizycki, M. (1992) *Credit Supply and Demand and the Australian Economy*, Research Discussion Paper 9208, Reserve Bank of Australia, Economic Research Department.

Bratton, W.W. (1989) 'The new economic theory of the firm: critical perspectives from history', *Stanford Law Review*, 41, 1471–527.

Brazier, M. (1993) *Street on Torts. The Law of Torts*, 9th edn, London, Butterworths.

Buchdal, G. (1969) *Metaphysics and the Philosophy of Science*, Oxford, Basil Blackwell.

Callahan, J.C. (1987) 'On harming the dead', *Ethics*, 97, 341–52.

Corden, M. (1991) 'Does the current account matter? The old view and the new', *Economic Papers*, 10(3), September.

Cross-Border Insolvency: Comparative Dimensions (1990) The Aberystwyth Insolvency Papers, United Kingdom National Committee of Comparative Law, Vol. 12, ed. by Fletcher, I., London, UKNCCL.

Daigle, K.H. (1989) *Positive Shares in Bankruptcy: An Agency Theory*

Explanation, a dissertation presented to the Graduate School of Clemson University (unpubl.).

Davis, K. (1990) 'Five propositions for social responsibility', excerpted in pp. 165–70 in Hoffman, W.M. and Moore, J.M. (eds) *Business Ethics*, 2nd edn, New York, McGraw-Hill.

Des Jardins, J. (1984) 'Virtues and Corporate Responsibility', pp. 135–42 in Hoffman *et al.* (ed.) *Corporate Governance and Institutionalizing Ethics*, Lexington MA, Lexington Books.

DesJardins, J.R. and McCall, J.J. (eds) (1990) *Contemporary Issues in Business Ethics*, 2nd edn, Belmont, CA, Wadsworth.

Donaldson, T. (1993) 'Constructing a Social Contract for Business', reprinted in pp. 167–87 in White, T.I. (ed.) *Business Ethics. A Philosophical Reader*, New York, Macmillan.

Dworkin, R. (1977) *Taking Rights Seriously*, London, Duckworth.

Ebertz, R. (1993) 'Is Reflective Equilibrium a Coherentist Model?', *Canadian Journal of Philosophy*, 23(2), 193–214.

'Economics of bankruptcy reform, The Discussion' (1977) *Law and Contemporary Problems*, 41(4), 123–77.

Fama, E.F. (1980) 'Agency problems and the theory of the firm', *Journal of Political Economy*, 88(2), 288–307.

Finnis, J. (1986) *Natural Law and Natural Rights*, Oxford, Clarendon Press.

Fletcher, I. (1990) *The Law of Insolvency*, London, Sweet and Maxwell.

Freiermuth, E.P. (1988) *Life after Debt*, Homewood IL., Dow Jones-Irwin.

French, P.A. (1985) 'Fishing the red herrings out of the sea of moral responsibility', pp. 73–87 in Le Pore, E. and McLaughlin, B.P. (eds) *Actions and Events*, Oxford, Basil Blackwell.

—— (1993) 'The corporation as a moral person', reprinted in pp. 228–35 in White, T.I. (ed.) *Business Ethics. A Philosophical Reader*, New York, Macmillan.

French, P.A., Nesteruk, J., Risser, D.T. and Abbarno, J. (1992) *Corporations in the Moral Community*, Fort Worth FL, Harcourt Brace Jovanovich.

Fried, C. (1981) *Contract as Promise*, Cambridge MA, Harvard University Press.

Friedman, M. (1993) 'The social responsibility of business is to increase its profits', reprinted in pp. 162–7 in White, T.I. (ed.) *Business Ethics. A Philosophical Reader*, New York, Macmillan.

Galbraith, J.K. (1976) *The Affluent Society*, 3rd revised edn, Boston, Houghton Mifflin.

General Insolvency Inquiry (1988) Commonwealth of Australia Law Reform Commission, Rep. No. 45, Canberra, Australian Government Publication Service.

Goodpaster, K.E. (1993) 'Business ethics and stakeholder analysis', reprinted in pp. 205–23 in White, T.I. (ed.) *Business Ethics. A Philosophical Reader*, New York, Macmillan.

Goodpaster, K.E. and Matthews, J.B. Jr, 'Can a corporation have a conscience?', reprinted in pp. 104–13 in DesJardins, J.R. and McCall, J.J. (eds) (1990) *Contemporary Issues in Business Ethics*, 2nd edn, Belmont CA, Wadsworth.

Gordley, J. (1991) *The Philosophical Origins of Modern Contract*, New York, Oxford University Press.

Haagen, P.H. (1985) 'English society and the debt law', pp. 222–47 in Cohen, S. and Scull, A. (eds) *Social Control and the State*, Worcester, Basil Blackwell.

Hakman, M. (1993) *Sata konkurssia. Verotarkastuksiin ja asiantuntijahaastatteluihin perustuva tutkimus konkursseihin liittyvistä rikoksista*, Helsinki, Oikeuspoliittisen tutkimuslaitoksen julkaisuja 121.

Hallituksen esitys Eduskunnalle laiksi yksityishenkilön velkajärjestelystä (1992) HE 183, Helsinki, Valtion Painatuskeskus.

Hart, H.L.A. (1961) *The Concept of Law*, Oxford, Clarendon Press.

Hawtrey, R.G. (1950) *Currency and Credit*, London, Longmans Green.

Hayek, E.J. (1967) *Principles of Bankruptcy in Australia*, St Lucia, Brisbane, University of Queensland Press.

Henderson, V.E. (1992) *What's Ethical in Business*, New York, McGraw-Hill.

Heuston, R. and Buckley, R. (1992) *Salmond and Heuston on the Law of Torts*, 20th edn, London, Sweet and Maxwell.

Hodapp, P.F. (1990) 'Can there be a social contract with business?', *Journal of Business Ethics*, 9, 127–31.

Holy Bible, The (1978) Authorized version, Cambridge, Cambridge University Press.

Homer, S. and Sylla, R. (1991) *A History of Interest Rates*, 3rd edn, New Brunswick, Rutgers University Press.

Hoppit, J. (1987) *Risk and Failure in English Business 1700–1800*, Cambridge NY, Cambridge University Press.

House of Lords (1980–1) *Select Committee on the European Communities, Session 1980–81*, 26th report, 9004/80, Draft Convention on Bankruptcy, Winding-up, Arrangements, Compositions and Similar Proceedings.

Hume, D. (1960) *A Treatise of Human Nature*, ed. by Selby-Bigge, L.A., repr., Oxford, Clarendon Press.

Insolvency Law and Practice (1982) Report of the Review Committee, Chairman Sir K. Cork, London, Her Majesty's Stationery Office.

Insolvency: The Regular Payment of Debts (1978) Commonwealth of Australia Law Reform Commission, Rep. No 6, Canberra, The Commonwealth Government Printer.

Jackson, T. (1985) 'The fresh start policy in bankruptcy law', *Harvard Law Review*, 98(7), 1393–448.

—— (1986) *The Logic and Limits of Bankruptcy Law*, Cambridge MA and London, Harvard University Press.

Jones, B. (1979) *The Foundations of English Bankruptcy*, Philadelphia, American Philosophical Society.

Jones, G. and Goodhart, W. (1986) *Specific Performance*, London, Butterworths.

Kant, I. (1883) <u>*Prolegomena*</u> *and Metaphysical Foundations of Natural Science*, trans. by Bax, E.B., London, George Bell and Sons.

—— (1959) *Critique of Practical Reason*, trans. by Abbott, T.K., 6th edn, repr., London, Lowe and Brydone.

—— (1964) *The Moral Law. Kant's <u>Groundwork</u> of the Metaphysics of Morals*, trans. by Paton, H.J., 3rd edn, London, Hutchinson University Library.

—— (1974) *Critique of Judgement*, trans. by Bernard, J.H., repr., New York, Hafner Press, London, Collier Macmillan.

—— (1974) *Critique of Pure Reason*, trans. by Meiklejohn, J.M.D., repr., London, Dent, New York, Dutton, Everyman's Library.

—— (1991) *The Metaphysics of Morals*, trans. by Gregor, M., Cambridge, Cambridge University Press.

Kercher, B. (1984) 'The transformation of imprisonment for debt in England, 1828 to 1838', *Australian Journal of Law and Society*, 2(1), 60–109.

Korobkin, D.R. (1991) 'Rehabilitating values: a jurisprudence of bankruptcy', *Columbia Law Review*, 9(4), 715–89.

Korotkin, M. (1993) 'Comparing methods of rehabilitation: Which works best?', *Secured Lender*, 49(4), 22–8.

Korsgaard, C.M. (1989) 'Personal identity and the unity of agency: a Kantian response to Parfit', *Philosophy & Public Affairs*, 18(2), 101–32.

Ladd, J. (1993) 'Corporate mythology and individual responsibility', reprinted in pp. 236–51 in White, T.I. (ed.) *Business Ethics. A Philosophical Reader*, New York, Macmillan.

Law Commission (1992) *Fiduciary Duties and Regulatory Rules. A Consultation Paper*, Consultation Paper No. 124, London, Her Majesty's Stationery Office.

Leebron, D.W. (1991) 'Limited liability, tort victims, and creditors', *Columbia Law Review*, 91(7), 1565–650.

Levinthal, L.E. (1918) 'Early history of bankruptcy law', *University of Pennsylvania Law Review*, 66, 223–50.

Livadas, C. (1983) *The Winding-up of Insolvent Companies in England and France*, Dewenton, Netherlands, Kluwer.

Locke, J. (1961) *An Essay Concerning Human Understanding*, Vol. Two, ed. by Yolton, J.W., rev. edn, London, Dent, Everyman's Library.

—— (1961) *Two Treatises of Government*, ed. by Cook, T.I., New York, Hafner.

Meckling, W.H. (1977) 'Financial markets, default, and bankruptcy: the role of the state', *Law and Contemporary Problems*, 41(4), 13–38.

Mill, J.S. (1956) *On Liberty*, New York, Liberal Arts Press.

Miller, M. (1977) 'The wealth transfers of bankruptcy: the spherical chicken', *Law and Contemporary Problems*, 41(4), 39–46.

Millon, D. (1990) 'Theories of the corporation', *Duke Law Journal*, 201–62.

Nelson, P.B. (1981) *Corporations in Crisis: Behavioural Observations for Bankruptcy Policy*, New York, Praeger.

New York Times, The (1992) 'Economic talks sharpen goals, if not solutions', December 16, p. A27.

Nozick, R. (1974) *Anarchy, State, and Utopia*, Oxford, Basil Blackwell.

Parfit, D. (1973) 'Later selves and moral principles', in Montefiori, A. (ed.), *Philosophy and Personal Relations*, London, Routledge and Kegan Paul.

Pfeiffer, R.S. (1990) 'The central distinction in the theory of corporate moral personhood', *Journal of Business Ethics*, 9, 473–80.

Pitcher, G. (1984) 'The misfortunes of the dead', *American Philosophical Quarterly*, 21(2), 183–8.

Rawls, J. (1971) *A Theory of Justice*, Cambridge MA, Harvard University Press.

—— (1993) 'Themes in Kant's moral philosophy', pp. 291–319 in Beiner, R. and Booth, W. J. (eds) *Kant & Political Philosophy. The Contemporary Legacy*, New Haven and London,Yale University Press.

Ross, I.A. (ed.) (1974) *European Bankruptcy Laws*, American Bar Association.

Rubin, G.R. (1984) 'Law, poverty and imprisonment for debt, 1869–1914', in Rubin, G.R. and Sugardman, D. (eds) *Law, Economy and Society 1750–1914: Essays in the History of English Law*, Abingdon, Professional Books.

Ryan, M. (1989) *The Last Resort: An Empirical Study of Non-business, Voluntary, Undischarged Bankrupts in Melbourne, Australia*, thesis for the degree of Doctor of Philosophy (unpubl.), Bundoora, Victoria, La Trobe University.

Salem, M. and Martin, O-D. (1994) 'The Ethics of Using Chapter XI as a Management Strategy', *Journal of Business Ethics*, 13, 95–104.

Scanlon, T. (1982) 'Nozick on Rights, Liberty and Property', in Paul, J. (ed.) *Reading Nozick. Essays on Anarchy, State and Utopia*, Oxford, Basil Blackwell.

—— (1990) 'Promises and practices', *Philosophy and Public Affairs*, 19(3), 199–226.

Schneewind, J.B. (1992) 'Autonomy, obligation, and virtue: an overview of Kant's moral philosophy', in Guyer, P. (ed.) *The Cambridge Companion to Kant*, Cambridge, Cambridge University Press.

Schumpeter. J. (1959) *The Theory of Economic Development*, trans. by Opie, R., Cambridge MA, Harvard University Press.

Shuchman, P. (1973) 'An attempt at a "philosophy" of bankrutpcy', *UCLA Law Review*, 21, 403–76.

—— (1990) 'Social science research on bankruptcy', *Rutgers Law Review*, 43, 185–244.

Smart, P. (1991) *Cross-Border Insolvency*, London, Butterworths.

Smith, A. (1950) *The Wealth of Nations*, Vol. I–II, ed. by Cannan, E., 6th edn, London, Methuen.

Smith, M. (1994) *The Moral Problem*, Oxford UK and Cambridge USA, Blackwell.

Solomon, R.C. and Hanson, K.R. (1985) *It's Good Business*, New York, Atheneum.

Stanley, D.T. and Girth, M. (1971) *Bankruptcy: Problem, Process, Reform*, Washington, Brookings Institution.

Ste Croix GEM de (1988) 'Slavery and other forms of unfree labour', in

Archer, L.J. (ed.) *Slavery and Other Forms of Unfree Labour*, London and New York, Routledge.

Stoljar, S.J. (1973) *Groups and Entities. An Inquiry into Corporate Theory*, Canberra, ANU Press.

Sullivan, G. (1968) *The Boom in Going Bust*, New York, Macmillan.

Sullivan, T.A., Warren, E. and Westbrooke, J.L. (1989) *As We Forgive Our Debtors: Bankruptcy and Consumer Credit in America*, New York, Oxford University Press.

Sutherland, J.R. (1988) 'The ethics of bankruptcy: a biblical perspective', *Journal of Business Ethics*, 7, 917–27.

Tamari, M. (1990) 'Ethical issues in bankruptcy', *Journal of Business Ethics*, 9, 785–9.

Ten, C.L. (1987) *Crime, Guilt, and Punishment: A Philosophical Introduction*, Oxford, Clarendon Press, New York, OUP.

Tenkku, J. (1967) *Are Single Moral Rules Absolute in Kant's Ethics*, Jyväskylä Studies in Education, Psychology and Social Research, 14, Pieksämäki, University of Jyvaskyla.

Treiman, I. (1938) 'Acts of bankruptcy: a medieval code in modern bankruptcy law', *Harvard Law Review*, 52(2), 189–215.

Treitel, G.H. (1989) *An outline of The Law of Contract*, London, Butterworths.

Velasquez, M.G. (1990) 'Why corporations are not morally responsible for anything they do', reprinted on pp. 114–26 in DesJardins J.R. and McCall, J.J. (eds), *Contemporary Issues in Business Ethics*, 2nd edn, Belmont, CA, Wadsworth.

Warren, C. (1972) *Bankruptcy in United States History*, Da Capo Press.

Warren, E. (1987) 'Bankruptcy policy', *University of Chicago Law Review*, 54, 775–814.

Werhane, P. (1985) *Persons, Rights, and Corporations*, Englewood Cliffs NJ, Prentice-Hall.

Wolff, R.P. (1973) *The Autonomy of Reason. A Commentary on Kant's Groundwork of the Metaphysics of Morals*, New York, Harper Torchbooks, Harper and Row.

Wray, L.R. (1990) *Money and Credit in Capitalist Economies*, Aldershot, UK, Brookfield VT, USA, E. Elgar.

v. Wright, G.H. (1963) *The Varieties of Goodness*, London, Routledge and Kegan Paul, London.

Yack, B. (1993) 'The problem with Kantian liberalism', pp. 224–44 in Beiner, R. and Booth, W.J. *Kant & Political Philosophy. The Contemporary Legacy*, New Haven and London, Yale University Press.

Young, N.S. (1969) *Young's Bankruptcy Practice in Australia*, 3rd edn, by Brooker, R.P., Sydney, Butterworths.

Young, R. (1986) *Personal Autonomy: Beyond Negative and Positive Liberty*, London and Sydney, Croom Helm.

Index